DATA SCIENCE USING PYTHON AND R

WILEY SERIES ON METHODS AND APPLICATIONS IN DATA MINING

Series Editor: **Daniel T. Larose**

Practical Text Mining with Perl • Roger Bilisoly

Knowledge Discovery Support Vector Machines • Lutz Hamel

Data Mining for Genomics and Proteomics: Analysis of Gene and Protein Expression Data • Darius M. Dziuda

Discovering Knowledge in Data: An Introduction to Data Mining, Second Edition • Daniel T. Larose and Chantal D. Larose

Data Mining and Predictive Analytics • Daniel T. Larose and Chantal D. Larose

Data Mining and Learning Analytics: Applications in Educational Research • Samira ElAtia, Donald Ipperciel, and Osmar R. Zaïane

Pattern Recognition: A Quality of Data Perspective • Władysław Homenda and Witold Pedrycz

DATA SCIENCE USING PYTHON AND R

CHANTAL D. LAROSE

Eastern Connecticut State University
Windham, CT, USA

DANIEL T. LAROSE

Central Connecticut State University
New Britain, CT, USA

Registered Office
John Wiley & Sons, Inc., 111 River Street, Hoboken, NJ 07030, USA

Editorial Office
111 River Street, Hoboken, NJ 07030, USA

For details of our global editorial offices, customer services, and more information about Wiley products visit us at www.wiley.com.

Wiley also publishes its books in a variety of electronic formats and by print-on-demand. Some content that appears in standard print versions of this book may not be available in other formats.

Library of Congress Cataloging-in-Publication Data

Names: Larose, Chantal D., author. | Larose, Daniel T., author.
Title: Data science using Python and R / Chantal D. Larose, Eastern Connecticut
    State University, Connecticut, USA, Daniel T. Larose, Central Connecticut
    State University, Conntecticut, USA.
Description: Hoboken, NJ : John Wiley & Sons, Inc, 2019. | Includes index. |
Identifiers: LCCN 2019007280 (print) | LCCN 2019009632 (ebook) | ISBN 9781119526834
    (Adobe PDF) | ISBN 9781119526841 (ePub) | ISBN 9781119526810 (hardback)
Subjects: LCSH: Data mining. | Python (Computer program language) |
    R (Computer program language) | Big data. | Data structures (Computer science)
Classification: LCC QA76.9.D343 (ebook) | LCC QA76.9.D343 L376 2019 (print) |
    DDC 006.3/12–dc23
LC record available at https://lccn.loc.gov/2019007280

Cover Design: Wiley
Cover Image: © LumenGraphics/Shutterstock

Set in 10/12pt Times by SPi Global, Pondicherry, India

10 9 8 7 6 5 4 3 2 1

CONTENTS

CHAPTER 13 *GENERALIZED LINEAR MODELS* *187*

CHAPTER 14 *ASSOCIATION RULES* *199*

APPENDIX *DATA SUMMARIZATION AND VISUALIZATION* *215*

PREFACE

DATA SCIENCE USING PYTHON AND R

Why this Book is Needed

Reason 1. Data Science is Hot. Really hot. *Bloomberg* called data scientist "the hottest job in America."[1] *Business Insider* called it "The best job in America right now."[2] *Glassdoor.com* rated it the best job in the world in 2018 for the third year in a row.[3] The *Harvard Business Review* called data scientist "The sexiest job in the 21st century."[4]

Reason 2: Top Two Open-source Tools. Python and R are the top two open-source data science tools in the world.[5] Analysts and coders from around the world work hard to build analytic packages that Python and R users can then apply, free of charge.

Data Science Using Python and R will awaken your expertise in this cutting-edge field using the most widespread open-source analytics tools in the world. In *Data Science Using Python and R*, you will find step-by-step hands-on solutions of real-world business problems, using state-of-the-art techniques. In short, *you will learn data science by doing data science*.

Written for Beginners and Non-Beginners Alike

Data Science Using Python and R is written for the general reader, with no previous analytics or programming experience. We know that the information-age economy is making many English majors and History majors retool to take advantage of the great demand for data scientists.[6] This is why we provide the following materials to help those who are new to the field hit the ground running.

---

[1] https://www.bloomberg.com/news/articles/2018-05-18/-sexiest-job-ignites-talent-wars-as-demand-for-data-geeks-soars.

[2] https://www.businessinsider.com/what-its-like-to-be-a-data-scientist-best-job-in-america-2017-9.

[3] https://www.forbes.com/sites/louiscolumbus/2018/01/29/data-scientist-is-the-best-job-in-america-according-glassdoors-2018-rankings/#dd3f65055357.

[4] https://www.hbs.edu/faculty/Pages/item.aspx?num=43110.

[5] See, for example, https://www.kdnuggets.com/2017/08/python-overtakes-r-leader-analytics-data-science.html.

[6] For example, in May 2017, IBM projected that yearly demand for "data scientist, data developers, and data engineers will reach nearly 700,000 openings by 2020." Forbes, https://www.forbes.com/sites/louiscolumbus/2017/05/13/ibm-predicts-demand-for-data-scientists-will-soar-28-by-2020/#6b6fde277e3b

- An entire chapter dedicated to learning the basics of using Python and R, for beginners. Which platform to use. Which packages to download. Everything you need to get started.
- An appendix dedicated to filling in any holes you might have in your introductory data analysis knowledge, called *Data Summarization and Visualization*.
- Step-by-step instructions throughout. Every instruction for every action.
- Every chapter has Exercises, where you may check your understanding and progress.

Those with analytics or programming experience will enjoy having a one-stop-shop for learning how to do data science using both Python and R. Managers, CIOs, CEOs, and CFOs will enjoy being able to communicate better with their data analysts and database analysts. The emphasis in this book on accurately accounting for model costs will help everyone uncover the most profitable nuggets of knowledge from the data, while avoiding the potential pitfalls that may cost your company millions of dollars.

Data Science Using Python and R covers exciting new topics, such as the following:

- Random Forests,
- General Linear Models, and
- Data-driven error costs to enhance profitability.

All of the many data sets used in the book are freely available on the book series website: *DataMiningConsultant.com*.

Data Science Using Python and R as a Textbook

Data Science Using Python and R naturally fits the role of textbook for a one-semester course or two-semester sequence of courses in introductory and intermediate data science. Faculty instructors will appreciate the *exercises at the end of every chapter*, totaling over 500 exercises in the book. There are three categories of exercises, from testing basic understanding toward more hands-on analysis of new and challenging applications.

- **Clarifying the Concepts**. These exercises test the students' basic understanding of the material, to make sure the students have absorbed what they have read.
- **Working with the Data**. These applied exercises ask the student to work in Python and R, following the step-by-step instructions that were presented in the chapter.
- **Hands-on Analysis**. Here is the real meat of the learning process for the students, where they apply their newly found knowledge and skills to uncover patterns and trends in new data sets. Here is where the students' expertise is challenged, in near real-world conditions. More than half of the exercises in the book consist of *Hands-on Analysis*.

The following supporting materials are also available to faculty adopters of the book at no cost.

- **Full solutions manual**, providing not just the answers, but how to arrive at the answers.
- **Powerpoint presentations of each chapter**, so that you may help the students understand the material, rather than just assigning them to read it.

To obtain access to these materials, contact your local Wiley representation and ask them to email the authors confirming that you have adopted the book for your course.

Data Science Using Python and R is appropriate for advanced undergraduate or graduate-level courses. No previous statistics, computer programming, or database expertise is required. What is required is a desire to learn.

How the Book is Structured

Data Science Using Python and R is structured around the Data Science Methodology.

The Data Science Methodology is a phased, adaptive, iterative, approach to the analysis of data, within a scientific framework.

1. **Problem Understanding Phase.** First, clearly enunciate the project objectives. Then, translate these objectives into the formulation of a problem that can be solved using data science.
2. **Data Preparation Phase.** Data cleaning/preparation is probably the most labor-intensive phase of the entire data science process.
   - Covered in Chapter 3: *Data Preparation*.
3. **Exploratory Data Analysis Phase.** Gain insights into your data through graphical exploration.
   - Covered in Chapter 4: *Exploratory Data Analysis*.
4. **Setup Phase.** Establish baseline model performance. Partition the data. Balance the data, if needed.
   - Covered in Chapter 5: *Preparing to Model the Data*.
5. **Modeling Phase**. The core of the data science process. Apply state-of-the-art algorithms to uncover some seriously profitable relationships lying hidden in the data.
   - Covered in Chapters 6 and 8–14.
6. **Evaluation Phase.** Determine whether your models are any good. Select the best-performing model from a set of competing models.
   - Covered in Chapter 7: *Model Evaluation*.
7. **Deployment Phase.** Interface with management to adapt your models for real-world deployment.

ABOUT THE AUTHORS

Chantal D. Larose, PhD, and Daniel T. Larose, PhD, form a unique father–daughter pair of data scientists. This is their third book as coauthors. Previously, they wrote:

- *Data Mining and Predictive Analytics*, Second Edition, Wiley, 2015.
  - This 800-page tome would be a wonderful companion to this book, for those looking to dive deeper in to the field.
- *Discovering Knowledge in Data: An Introduction to Data Mining*, Second Edition, Wiley, 2014.

Chantal D. Larose completed her PhD in Statistics at the University of Connecticut in 2015, with dissertation *Model-Based Clustering of Incomplete Data*. As an Assistant Professor of Decision Science at SUNY, New Paltz, she helped develop the Bachelor of Science in Business Analytics. Now, as an Assistant Professor of Statistics and Data Science at Eastern Connecticut State University, she is helping to develop the Mathematical Science Department's data science curriculum.

Daniel T. Larose completed his PhD in Statistics at the University of Connecticut in 1996, with dissertation *Bayesian Approaches to Meta-Analysis*. He is a Professor of Statistics and Data Science at Central Connecticut State University. In 2001, he developed the world's first online Master of Science in Data Mining. This is the 12th textbook that he has authored or coauthored. He runs a small consulting business, *DataMiningConsultant.com*. He also directs the online Master of Data Science program at CCSU.

ACKNOWLEDGMENTS

CHANTAL'S ACKNOWLEDGMENTS

Deepest thanks to my father Daniel, for his corny quips when proofreading. His guidance and passion for the craft reflects and enhances my own, and makes working with him a joy. Many thanks to my little sister Ravel, for her boundless love and incredible musical and scientific gifts. My fellow-traveler, she is an inspiration. Thanks to my brother Tristan, for all his hard work in school and letting me beat him at Mario Kart exactly once. Thanks to my mother Debra, for food and hugs. Also, coffee. Many, many thanks to coffee.

CHANTAL D. LAROSE, PH. D.

Assistant Professor of Statistics & Data Science
Eastern Connecticut State University

DANIEL'S ACKNOWLEDGMENTS

It is all about family. I would like to thank my daughter Chantal, for her insightful mind, her gentle presence, and for the joy she brings to every day. Thanks to my daughter Ravel, for her uniqueness, and for having the courage to follow her dream and become a chemist. Thanks to my son Tristan, for his math and computer skills, and for his help moving rocks in the backyard. I would also like to acknowledge my stillborn daughter Ellyriane Soleil. How we miss what you would have become. Finally, thanks to my loving wife, Debra, for her deep love and care for all of us, all these years. I love you all very much.

DANIEL T. LAROSE, PH. D.

Professor of Statistics and Data Science
Central Connecticut State University
www.ccsu.edu/faculty/larose

CHAPTER 1

INTRODUCTION TO DATA SCIENCE

1.1 WHY DATA SCIENCE?

Data science is one of the fastest growing fields in the world, with 6.5 times as many job openings in 2017 as compared to 2012.[1] Demand for data scientists is expected to increase in the future. For example, in May 2017, IBM projected that yearly demand for "data scientist, data developers, and data engineers will reach nearly 700,000 openings by 2020."[2] http://InfoWorld.com reported that the #1 "reason why data scientist remains the top job in America"[3] is that "there is a shortage of talent." That is why we wrote this book, to help alleviate the shortage of qualified data scientists.

1.2 WHAT IS DATA SCIENCE?

Simply put, *data science* is the systematic analysis of data within a scientific framework. That is, data science is the

- adaptive, iterative, and phased approach to the analysis of data,
- performed within a systematic framework,
- that uncovers optimal models,
- by assessing and accounting for the true costs of prediction errors.

---

[1] Forbes, https://www.forbes.com/sites/louiscolumbus/2017/12/11/linkedins-fastest-growing-jobs-today-are-in-data-science-machine-learning/#5b3100f051bd

[2] Forbes, https://www.forbes.com/sites/louiscolumbus/2017/05/13/ibm-predicts-demand-for-data-scientists-will-soar-28-by-2020/#6b6fde277e3b

[3] http://Infoworld.com, https://www.infoworld.com/article/3190008/big-data/3-reasons-why-data-scientist-remains-the-top-job-in-america.html

---

Data Science Using Python and R, First Edition. Chantal D. Larose and Daniel T. Larose.
© 2019 John Wiley & Sons, Inc. Published 2019 by John Wiley & Sons, Inc.

Data science combines the

- data-driven approach of statistical data analysis,
- the computational power and programming acumen of computer science, and
- domain-specific business intelligence,

in order to uncover actionable and profitable nuggets of information from large databases.

In other words, data science allows us to extract actionable knowledge from under-utilized databases. Thus, data warehouses that have been gathering dust can now be leveraged to uncover hidden profit and enhance the bottom line. Data science lets people leverage large amounts of data and computing power to tackle complex questions. Patterns can arise out of data which could not have been uncovered otherwise. These discoveries can lead to powerful results, such as more effective treatment of medical patients or more profits for a company.

1.3 THE DATA SCIENCE METHODOLOGY

We follow the *Data Science Methodology* (DSM),[4] which helps the analyst keep track of which phase of the analysis he or she is performing. Figure 1.1 illustrates the adaptive and iterative nature of the DSM, using the following phases:

1. **Problem Understanding Phase.** How often have teams worked hard to solve a problem, only to find out later that they solved the wrong problem? Further, how often have the marketing team and the analytics team not been on the same page? This phase attempts to avoid these pitfalls.

   a. First, clearly enunciate the project objectives,

   b. Then, translate these objectives into the formulation of a problem that can be solved using data science.

2. **Data Preparation Phase.** Raw data from data repositories is seldom ready for the algorithms straight out of the box. Instead, it needs to be cleaned or "prepared for analysis." When analysts first examine the data, they uncover the inevitable problems with data quality that always seem to occur. It is in this phase that we fix these problems. Data cleaning/preparation is probably the most labor-intensive phase of the entire data science process. The following is a non-exhaustive list of the issues that await the data preparer.

   a. Identifying outliers and determining what to do about them.

   b. Transforming and standardizing the data.

   c. Reclassifying categorical variables.

   d. Binning numerical variables.

   e. Adding an index field.

---

[4]Adapted from the Cross-Industry Standard Practice for Data Mining (CRISP-DM). See, for example, *Data Mining and Predictive Analytics*, by Daniel T. Larose and Chantal D. Larose, John Wiley and Sons, Inc, 2015.

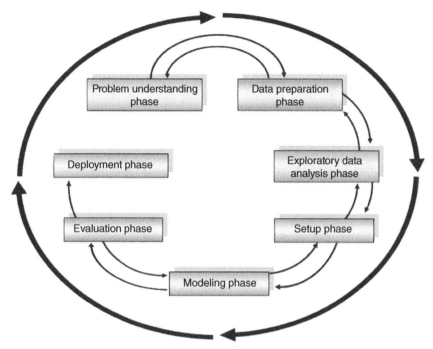

Figure 1.1   Data science methodology: the seven phases.

The data preparation phase is covered in Chapter 3.

3. **Exploratory Data Analysis Phase.** Now that your data are nice and clean, we can begin to explore the data, and learn some basic information. Graphical exploration is the focus here. Now is not the time for complex algorithms. Rather, we use simple exploratory methods to help us gain some preliminary insights. You might find that you can learn quite a bit just by using these simple methods. Here are some of the ways we can do this.

   a. Exploring the univariate relationships between predictors and the target variable.

   b. Exploring multivariate relationships among the variables.

   c. Binning based on predictive value to enhance our models.

   d. Deriving new variables based on a combination of existing variables.

   We cover the exploratory data analysis phase in Chapter 4.

4. **Setup Phase.** At this point we are nearly ready to begin modeling the data. We just need to take care of a few important chores first, such as the following:

   a. Cross-validation, either twofold or n-fold. This is necessary to avoid data dredging. In addition, your data partitions need to be evaluated to ensure that they are indeed random.

   b. Balancing the data. This enhances the ability of certain algorithms to uncover relationships in the data.

   c. Establishing baseline performance. Suppose we told you we had a model that could predict correctly whether a credit card transaction was fraudulent or not 99% of the time. Impressed? You should not be. The non-fraudulent transaction rate is 99.932%.[5] So, our model could simply predict that *every* transaction was non-fraudulent and be correct 99.932% of the time. This illustrates the importance of establishing baseline performance for your models, so that we can calibrate our models and determine whether they are any good.

The Setup Phase is covered in Chapter 5.

5. **Modeling Phase.** The modeling phase represents the opportunity to apply state-of-the-art algorithms to uncover some seriously profitable relationships lying hidden in the data. The modeling phase is the heart of your data scientific investigation and includes the following:

   a. Selecting and implementing the appropriate modeling algorithms. Applying inappropriate techniques will lead to inaccurate results that could cost your company big bucks.

   b. Making sure that our models outperform the baseline models.

   c. Fine-tuning your model algorithms to optimize the results. Should our decision tree be wide or deep? Should our neural network have one hidden layer or two? What should be our cutoff point to maximize profits? Analysts will need to spend some time fine-tuning their models before arriving at the optimal solution.

The modeling phase represents the core of your data science endeavor and is covered in Chapters 6 and 8–14.

6. **Evaluation Phase.** Your buddy at work may think he has a lock on his prediction for the Super Bowl. But is his prediction any good? That is the question. Anyone can make predictions. It is how the predictions perform against real data that is the real test. In the evaluation phase, we assess how our models are doing, whether they are making any money, or whether we need to go back and try to improve our prediction models.

   a. Your models need to be evaluated against the baseline performance measures from the Setup Phase. Are we beating the monkeys-with-darts model? If not, better try again.

   b. You need to determine whether your models are actually solving the problem at hand. Are your models actually achieving the objectives set for it back in the Problem Understanding Phase? Has some important aspect of the problem not been sufficiently accounted for?

[5] The Alaric Fraud Report, 2015, https://www.paymentscardsandmobile.com/wp-content/uploads/2015/03/PCM_Alaric_Fraud-Report_2015.pdf

    c. Apply error costs intrinsic to the data, because data-driven cost evaluation is the best way to model the actual costs involved. For instance, in a marketing campaign, a false positive is not as costly as a false negative. However, for a mortgage lender, a false positive is much more costly.

    d. You should tabulate a suite of models and determine which model performs the best. Choose either a single best model, or a small number of models, to move forward to the Deployment Phase.

The Evaluation Phase is covered in Chapter 7.

7. **Deployment Phase.** Finally, your models are ready for prime time! Report to management on your best models and work with management to adapt your models for real-world deployment.

    a. Writing a report of your results may be considered a simple example of deployment. In your report, concentrate on the results of interest to management. Show that you solved the problem and report on the estimated profit, if applicable.

    b. Stay involved with the project! Participate in the meetings and processes involved in model deployment, so that they stay focused on the problem at hand.

It should be emphasized that the DSM is iterative and adaptive. By *adaptive*, we mean that sometimes it is necessary to return to a previous phase for further work, based on some knowledge gained in the current phase. This is why there are arrows pointing both ways between most of the phases. For example, in the Evaluation Phase, we may find that the model we crafted does not actually address the original problem at hand, and that we need to return to the Modeling Phase to develop a model that will do so.

Also, the DSM is *iterative*, in that sometimes we may use our experience of building an effective model on a similar problem. That is, the model we created serves as an input to the investigation of a related problem. This is why the outer ring of arrows in Figure 1.1 shows a constant recycling of older models used as inputs to examining new solutions to new problems.

1.4 DATA SCIENCE TASKS

The most common data science tasks are the following:

- Description
- Estimation
- Classification
- Clustering
- Prediction
- Association

Next, we describe what each of these tasks represent and in which chapters these tasks are covered.

1.4.1 Description

Data scientists are often called upon to *describe* patterns and trends lying within the data. For example, a data scientist may describe a cluster of customers most likely to leave our company's service as those with high-usage minutes and a high number of customer service calls. After describing this cluster, the data scientist may explain that the high number of customer service calls indicates perhaps that the customer is unhappy. Working with the marketing team, the analyst can then suggest possible interventions to explore to retain such customers.

The description task is in widespread use around the world by specialists and nonspecialists alike. For example, when a sports announcer states that a baseball player has a lifetime batting average (hits/at-bats) of 0.350, he or she is describing this player's lifetime batting performance. This is an example of *descriptive statistics*,[6] further examples of which may be found in the Appendix: Data Summarization and Visualization. Nearly every chapter in the book contains examples of the description task, from the graphical EDA methods of Chapter 4, to the descriptions of data clusters in Chapter 10, to the bivariate relationships in Chapter 11.

1.4.2 Estimation

Estimation refers to the approximation of the value of a numeric target variable using a collection of predictor variables. Estimation models are built using records where the target values are known, so that the models can learn which target values are associated with which predictor values. Then, the estimation models can estimate the target values for new data, for which the target value is unknown. For example, the analyst can estimate the mortgage amount a potential customer can afford, based on a set of personal and demographic factors. This estimate is based on a model built by looking at past models of how much previous customers could afford. Estimation requires that the target variable be numeric. Estimation methods are covered in Chapters 9, 11, and 13.

1.4.3 Classification

Classification is similar to estimation, except that the target variable is categorical rather than continuous. Classification represents perhaps the most widespread task in data science, and the most profitable. For instance, a mortgage lender would be interested in determining which of their customers is likely to default on their

---

[6]For example, see *Discovering Statistics*, by Daniel T. Larose, W.H. Freeman, 2016.

mortgage loans. Similarly, for credit card companies. The classification models are shown lots of complete records containing the actual default status of past customers. The models then learn which attributes are associated with customers who default. Finally, these trained models are then deployed to new data, customers who have applied for a loan or a credit card, with the expectation that the models will help to classify which customers are most likely to default on their loans. Classification methods are covered in Chapters 6, 8, 9, and 13.

1.4.4 Clustering

The clustering task seeks to identify groups of records which are similar. For example, in a data set of credit card applicants, one cluster might represent younger, more educated customers, while another cluster might represent older, less educated customers. The idea is that the records in a cluster are similar to other records in the same cluster, but different from the records in other clusters. Finding workable clusters is useful in at least two respects: (i) your client may be interested in the cluster profiles, that is, detailed descriptions of the characteristics of each cluster, and (ii) the clusters may themselves be used as inputs to classification or estimation models downstream. Clustering methods are covered in Chapter 10.

1.4.5 Prediction

The prediction task is similar to estimation or classification, except that for prediction the forecasts relate to the future. For example, a financial analyst may be interested in predicting the price of Apple stock three months down the road. This would represent estimation, since price is a numeric variable, and prediction, since it relates to the future. Alternatively, a drug discovery chemist may be interested in whether a particular molecule will lead to a profitable new drug for a pharmaceutical company. This represents both prediction and classification, since the target variable is a yes/no variable, whether the drug will be profitable.

1.4.6 Association

The association task involves determining which attributes are associated with each other, that is, which attributes "go together." The data scientist using association seeks to uncover rules for quantifying the relationship between two or more attributes. These association rules take the form, "If *antecedent*, then *consequent*," together with measures of the support and confidence of the association rule. For example, marketers trying to avoid customer churn might uncover the following association rule: "If calls to customer service greater than three, then customer will churn." The support refers to the proportion of records the rule applies to; the confidence is the proportion of times the rule is correct. We cover the association task in Chapter 14.

EXERCISES

CLARIFYING THE CONCEPTS

1. What is data science?

2. Which areas of study does data science combine?

3. What is the goal of data science?

4. Name the seven phases of the DSM.

5. Why is it a good idea to have a Problem Understanding Phase?

6. Why do we need a Data Preparation Phase? Name three issues that are handled in this phase.

7. In which phase does the data analyst begin to explore the data to learn some simple information?

8. Explain in your own words why we need to establish baseline performance for our models. Which phase does this occur in?

9. Which phase represents the heart of your data scientific investigation? Why might we apply more than one algorithm to solve a problem?

10. How do we determine whether our predictions are any good? During which phase does this occur?

11. True or false: The data scientist's work is done with the Evaluation Phase. Explain.

12. Explain how the DSM is adaptive.

13. Describe how the DSM is iterative.

14. List the most common data science tasks.

15. Which of these tasks have many nonspecialists been doing all along?

16. What is estimation? In estimation, what must be true of the target variable?

17. What is the most widespread task in data science? For this task, what must be true of the target variable?

18. What are cluster profiles?

19. True or false: Prediction can only be used for categorical target variables. Explain.

20. For an association rule, what do we mean by support?

CHAPTER 2

THE BASICS OF PYTHON AND R

2.1 DOWNLOADING PYTHON

To run Python code, you need to use a Python compiler. In this text, we will be using the Spyder compiler, which is included in the Anaconda software package. By downloading and installing Anaconda, we will also download and install Python at the same time.

To download Anaconda, go to the Spyder installation page[1] and select the *Anaconda* link under either the Windows or MacOS X options. After the installation is complete, locate the Spyder program and open it.

When you open Spyder for the first time, you will see the screen shown in Figure 2.1. The left-hand box is where you will write Python code. That box is where we will spend most of our time. The top-right box lists data sets and other items that have been created by running Python code. The bottom-right box is where our output will appear, as well as any error messages or other information.

2.2 BASICS OF CODING IN PYTHON

In Python, as in most other programming languages, you run code which performs an action. Some actions also generate output. There are five kinds of actions we will focus on in this chapter: Using comments, Importing packages, Executing commands, Saving output, and Getting data into Python.

2.2.1 Using Comments in Python

Comments are pieces of code that are not executed by the compiler. Why are we starting our programming chapter with commands that would not be run? Because comments are a vital part of any programming project.

[1] http://pythonhosted.org/spyder/installation.html

Data Science Using Python and R, First Edition. Chantal D. Larose and Daniel T. Larose.
© 2019 John Wiley & Sons, Inc. Published 2019 by John Wiley & Sons, Inc.

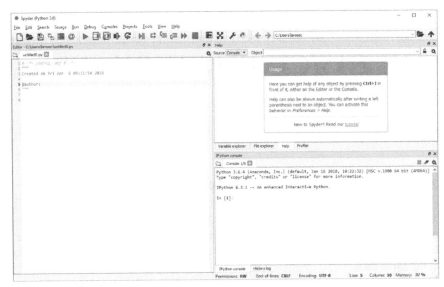

Figure 2.1   The Spyder window when you first open the program.

Comments are lines of code that the programmer puts there for others to understand the code better. For example, if you want to explain what a particular piece of code does, you may begin with a comment that explains what it does and what the result will be.

How do we write comments in Python? Comments are lines of code that start with a pound sign, #. The following is an example of a comment.

```
# This is a comment!
```

Notice that the typeface for any code, even comments, will be given in bold-face in this textbook. This applies to both Python and R code.

2.2.2   Executing Commands in Python

Any code you type needs to be run, or *executed*, before it will work. There are a few different ways to execute code.

Most often, your cursor will be on one line of code, and you will want to run that line. There is a button in Spyder to run a single line of code. There is also a keyboard shortcut, which is revealed if you hover over that button. Both the button and the hover text are shown in Figure 2.2.

You may want to run multiple lines of code at the same time. In that case, highlight the relevant lines and press the "Run selection or current line" button, or press the keyboard shortcut. All highlighted code will be run at the same time.

You can also try executing comments. As discussed previously, comments will not be compiled, and there will be no output. They will, however, appear in the

Figure 2.2   The button and hover text for running a selection or line of Python code in Spyder.

bottom-right window of Spyder. This tells you that the Spyder compiler has looked at the comment, even though there is nothing for Spyder to do after reading the comment.

2.2.3   Importing Packages in Python

While many things can be done in Python "out of the box," meaning directly after you download and install it, most of what we want to accomplish requires *importing packages*. Packages contain specially designed code that will enable us to perform complex data science tasks without writing the code ourselves. For example, in Chapter 6, we need to build a classification and regression tree (CART) model. Instead of figuring out how to build a CART model from scratch, we will import a package that contains that code. Once the package is imported, we can run the code to create a CART model.

Some commands are specialized, such as the **MultinomialNB()** command in the *sklearn.naive_bayes* package (see Chapter 10). On the other hand, there are some commands that will be used in every chapter. These are the *pandas* and *numpy* packages. To import these packages, you need to type and run the following two lines of code:

```
import pandas as pd
import numpy as np
```

Note that we import the packages using **import**. What about the **as pd** and **as np** code afterward? The **as** code renames the package using a name that we can specify. We rename packages to make working with them easier.

To use the commands contained in the *pandas* and *numpy* packages, we will need to state the package names before the command name. For example, in Section 2.2.4, we use the **read_csv()** command from *pandas*. To use that command, we would need to type **pandas.read_csv()**. If you are using a particular command multiple times or using code from a package with a long name, you will end up doing a lot of typing! To save some of that typing, we can give a nickname to the package. In the case above, we rename the *pandas* package as *pd* using **as pd** and rename the *numpy* package as *np* using **as np**. This is how, in Section 2.2.4, we can use the **read_csv()** command using the code **pd.read_csv()**. Renaming packages will save us a lot of typing in the long run!

We can also import specific pieces from a package, without importing the entire package. For example, in Chapter 6 we will be using the **DecisionTreeClassifier()** and export_graphviz commands from the *sklearn.tree* package. To do so, we will use the following code:

```
from sklearn.tree import DecisionTreeClassifier, export_
graphviz
```

Note that the syntax has changed from how we imported a package previously. Instead of saying *import sklearn.tree*, we now begin by saying **from sklearn. tree**. Using **from** tells Python where to look for the commands we want. After **from sklearn.tree**, we then specify what we want to import using **import**. If we were only importing the **DecisionTreeClassifier** command, we would end the line after that command name. However, since we want to import two commands, we add a comma and continue with the second command name, **export_graphviz**. Executing this line will import both commands.

2.2.4 Getting Data into Python

Now we will discuss how to get a data set into Python. In this text, we will use the **read_csv** command, using the following structure:

```
your_name_for_the_data_set = pd.read_csv("the_path_to_
the_file")
```

The command **read_csv** comes from the *pandas* package. Following the code in Section 2.2.3, we imported the *pandas* package as *pd*. After importing the *pandas* package, we can access the **read_csv** command by typing **pd**. To use the **read_csv()** command, type **pd** followed by a period, then the command **read_csv**.

The next part of the code is the *path to the data file*, contained in double quotes. For many Windows users, the path will start with **C:/**and end with the file-name. For example, in Chapter 4 you will need to import the **bank_marketing_training** data set. The code to import the data set is given below.

```
bank_train = pd.read_csv("C:/.../bank_marketing_
training")
```

The programmer will substitute their own file path for the "**C:/.../**" portion of the path given above. An example of importing a data file is given below.

```
bank_train = pd.read_csv("C:/Users/Data Science/Data/
bank_marketing_training")
```

The Python guide in Chapter 4 tells the reader to "read in the *bank_marketing_training* data set as *bank_train*." This specifies not only the data set to be imported but also the name to call the data set. To follow the instruction, you should specify the name for the data set as *bank_train*, as illustrated in the code above. It is important to remember what name you save the data set as and try to keep it relatively short. The name you save the data as will be the name you will type whenever you want to use that data in the rest of your code.

2.2.5 Saving Output in Python

Certain commands generate output that can be used in other lines of code. To use the output in later code, you need to save the output as a named object. To save the output, follow this structure:

```
your_name_for_the_output = the_command_that_generated_
the_output
```

You may notice the similarity of the above structure to the structure we used to import the *bank_marketing_training* data set. You may have inferred correctly that the command we used, **read_csv()**, generated an "output" of the *bank_marketing_training* data set, and that we named that output *bank*. Importing data sets uses the same coding syntax as saving output under a particular name. Now let us illustrate the difference between running a command and not saving the output versus running a command and saving the output, using a contingency table.

In Chapter 4, you need to make a contingency table and save it in order to make a bar chart using that table. The code to make a contingency table is one line of code, given below and shown in Figure 2.3.

```
pd.crosstab(bank_train['previous_outcome'], bank_
train['response'])
```

If you do not save the output generated by the **crosstab()** command, the resulting contingency table is displayed in Spyder as in Figure 2.3. In the figure, "In" denotes the code we have run, and "Out" denotes the resulting output.

If we only wanted to make a table, and not use it elsewhere in our code, this would be sufficient. However, we want to use this table to make a bar chart. Therefore, we have to save it. To save it, we add a name for the saved item and an equal sign to the left of the command that generated the output. The code is given below and shown in Figure 2.4.

```
In [9]: pd.crosstab(bank_train['previous_outcome'], bank_train['response'])
Out[9]:
response              no   yes
previous_outcome
failure             2390   385
nonexistent        21176  2034
success              320   569
```

Figure 2.3   Creating a contingency table in Python without saving the output.

```
In [10]: crosstab_01 = pd.crosstab(bank_train['previous_outcome'], bank_train['response'])

In [11]:
```

Figure 2.4 Creating a contingency table in Python and saving the output under the name crosstab_01.

```
In [11]: crosstab_01
Out[11]:
response             no    yes
previous_outcome
failure            2390    385
nonexistent       21176   2034
success             320    569
```

Figure 2.5 In Python we run the name of the saved output, crosstab_01, to view the output.

```
crosstab_01 = pd.crosstab(bank_train['previous_
outcome'], bank_train['response'])
```

The name can be anything, provided it starts with a letter (not a number or symbol) and does not contain periods or other special characters other than an underscore. In Figure 2.4, we named our table **crosstab_01**.

Notice how there is no output in Figure 2.4. The "In" statements jump from "In [10]" to "In [11]" without specifying an "Out [10]" in between. Python skips the "Out" statement because the output generated from the **crosstab()** command has been saved under the name **crosstab_01**.

To view the output, run the name we have given the output, in this case **crosstab_01**, by itself. The result is shown in Figure 2.5.

2.2.6 Accessing Records and Variables in Python

In your data science adventures, you may want to examine a particular record. For example, how do we access a record inside the *bank_train* data set? We use the **loc** attribute, which all *pandas* data frames have, and state what part of the data frame you want to see.

Python references its records starting at record zero, so if we want to view the first record we request record 0. Similarly, to view the second record, request record 1, and so on. For example, to see the first record of *bank_train*, use the following code:

```
bank_train.loc[0]
```

Using the **.loc** attribute as above to view the first record will return the values of all variables for that record. Figure 2.6 shows the first four variable values for the first record in the *bank_train* data set.

```
In [30]: bank_train.loc[0]
Out[30]:
age                           56
job                    housemaid
marital                  married
education                basic.4y
```

Figure 2.6   Python shows us the variable values of the first record in the *bank_train* data set (first four variables shown).

What if we want to access many records? We will use the **.loc** attribute and list the records we want to see. If you want the first, third, and fourth rows, use the following code:

```
bank_train.loc[[0, 2, 3]]
```

If, on the other hand, you want the first 10 rows, inclusive, you would use the following code:

```
bank_train[0:10]
```

While we reference the rows by numbers, our columns have names. This means that if we want to specify which variable we want to see, we give its name.

```
bank_train['age']
```

Using one set of brackets and putting the variable name in single quotes returns the entire variable. The code and first four age values are shown in Figure 2.7.

What if we want to see multiple variables? We will use the **.loc** attribute and list the variables we want to see. If we want to see the age and job variables, we put each of those variable names inside single quotes, inside double brackets, separated by commas.

```
bank_train[['age', 'job']]
```

The output of this command is shown in Figure 2.8.

2.2.7   Setting Up Graphics in Python

Before we leave the Python coding section, we need to address one more thing: how to obtain and tweak graphical output in Python.

By default, Spyder shows all graphics in the IPython console in the lower-right window. An example of this is shown in Figure 2.9, using a histogram. These small displays, with no edit options, may be acceptable for simple graphs. However, we are going to be making complex graphics, which will require further editing and a larger display. To enable us to view and manipulate the graphs in detail, we need to change Spyder's graphics settings.

```
In [48]: bank_train['age']
Out[48]:
0        56
1        57
2        41
3        25
```

Figure 2.7   Python shows the values of the age variable (first four values shown).


```
In [49]: bank_train[['age', 'job']]
Out[49]:
        age           job
0        56     housemaid
1        57      services
2        41   blue-collar
3        25      services
```

Figure 2.8   Python shows the values of the age and job variables (first four values shown).

The following steps, which only need to be done once, will set up the graphics options we need:

1. In Spyder, click on *Tools* in the menu bar, then select *Preferences*.
2. In the list on the left-hand side of the Preferences window, click *IPython console*.
3. Select the *Graphics* tab on the top of the right-hand-side window.
4. Under *Graphics backend*, click the *Backend* drop-down menu and select *Automatic*. An example of the window at this point in the process is shown in Figure 2.10.
5. Once *Automatic* is chosen, click the *Apply* and *OK* buttons.

Once the graphics options are changed by the steps above, close Spyder and reopen it for the new settings to take effect.

Changing the graphics backend will open graphical output in a new window. The window, with the graphic displayed, is shown in Figure 2.11. In addition to letting us view the graphics in more detail, the window offers several customization options that will come in handy throughout the rest of this book. For example, consider the Configure subplots button, third from the right, which is indicated in Figure 2.11 by the hover text. Selecting this button will let us change the margins of the plot. The Edit Axis button, second from the right, will allow us to edit the title and axis labels. The save button, first on the right, will let you save the graphic. Feel free to experiment with these settings as you obtain graphical output from the code in this text.

Now you have learned the core actions of programming in Python and are well on your way to becoming a Python programmer! We will cover more specific commands, packages, and output in the following chapters, with tips and explanations throughout.

```
In [5]: bank_train['age'].plot(kind='hist')
Out[5]: <matplotlib.axes._subplots.AxesSubplot at 0x1aff31e1518>
```

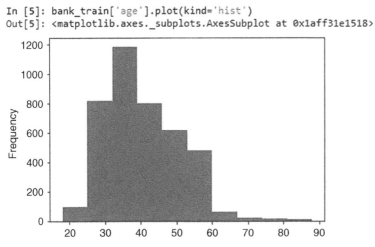

Figure 2.9   An example of a histogram displayed in the output section of Spyder.

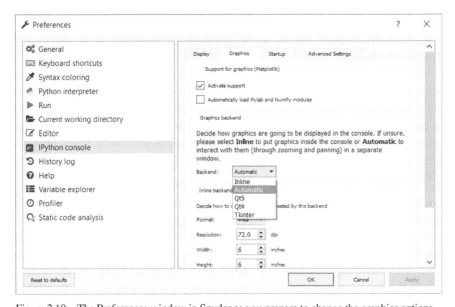

Figure 2.10   The Preferences window in Spyder as you prepare to change the graphics options.

2.3 DOWNLOADING R AND RSTUDIO

It is time to switch programming languages. In this section we cover the same fundamental skills for the statistical programming language R that we did in the previous section for Python. In this chapter and throughout this book, you will find a lot of similarities in the way Python and R do things, such as saving output, and a lot of differences, such as importing packages.

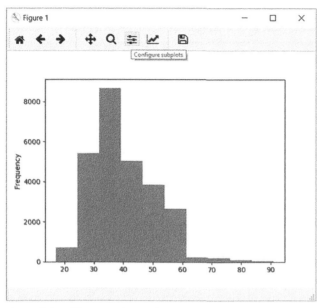

Figure 2.11   The new window from Spyder that holds our graphical output, with the *Configure subplots* button indicated.

To run R code, we need to download both R and RStudio. To download R, go to the R installation page,[2] choose a mirror, and follow the directions for downloading R for your operating system. To download RStudio, go to the RStudio installation page[3] and select the download link for your operating system. After installation, locate RStudio and open it.

Figure 2.12 shows the RStudio window when you first open it. If you open RStudio and there are only three panels, click on **File > New File > R Script** to get the four-panel display shown in Figure 2.12. The top-left box is where you will type your R code. The top-right box has the "Import Dataset" button, which we will use to read data into R. It also has the "Environment" tab, which will show all data sets and objects you import or create in R. The bottom-left box is where text-based output will appear, as well as any feedback or error messages. Finally, the bottom-right box has many tabs. We will spend most of our time in the "Plots" tab, where any graphical output will be displayed. The bottom-right box also has the "Help" tab, which is useful for quickly accessing the documentation on R commands.

[2] https://cran.r-project.org/mirrors.html

[3] http://rstudio.com/products/rstudio/download

Figure 2.12   The RStudio window when you first open the program.

2.4   BASICS OF CODING IN R

With R, as with Python, you execute a command which generates output. Much of the structure of R code will feel similar to Python code, with a few important differences. In this section we discuss the five kinds of programming actions we previously covered using Python, this time using R: Using comments, Importing packages, Executing commands, Saving output, and Getting data into Python.

2.4.1   Using Comments in R

The use of comments is just as important for coding in R as they are for coding in Python. Comments allow you to describe what the code does and other vital information.

Comments are lines of code which begin with a pound sign, #, such as the code below.

```
# This is a comment, and won't be compiled by R!
```

Remember that R code will be presented in boldface throughout this text. Do not be afraid of putting comments in your code, even when not prompted by the examples and exercises in this text. Use the tool to keep your code as clear and understandable for others as possible!

2.4.2   Executing Commands in R

The R code you write needs to be executed before it will do what it is supposed to do.

Most of the time, you will want to run a single line of code. There are two ways to accomplish this. First, you can click the Run button inside the top-left panel in RStudio, which is the same panel in which you will be typing the R code. You can also use the keyboard shortcut, which is revealed if you hover over the Run button. Both the button and the hover text (for a Windows OS) are shown in Figure 2.13.

2.4.3   Importing Packages in R

While the "base" or initial download of R includes many commands that are useful to data scientists, it does not include everything we will need in this textbook. Thus, throughout the book, we will need to download and open specially designed batches of R commands, called *packages*. There are two steps to making this extra code available for use: (i) Downloading the package that contains the code and (ii) Opening the package.

Let us demonstrate this process for a package called *ggplot2*. This package will be used in Chapter 4, so by importing this code we will prepare for that chapter now. The two lines of code for downloading and accessing the code are given below.

```
install.packages("ggplot2")
library(ggplot2)
```

First, let us look at the first line of code. The command to download a package is **install. packages()**. To download the *ggplot2* package, put the name of the package inside the **install. packages()** command in double quotes. Doing so gives us the first line of code above.

If you are downloading a package for the first time, you will have to pick a CRAN mirror before the installation can continue. While you may choose any, you may want to select one close to your geographic location.

It is important to note that you only need to download a package once. After the package is done installing, it is on your computer, ready to be opened and used

Figure 2.13   The button, and hover text, for running a selection or line of R code in RStudio.

in whatever code you wish. Before you use the commands in the *ggplot2* package, however, you need to open it. You will need to do this whenever you wish to use the functions in the package.

To do so, we use the second line of code above. The command to open a package is **library()**. To open the *ggplot2* package, put the name of the package inside the **library()** command, this time without quotes. Doing so gives us the second line of code above.

2.4.4   Getting Data into R

There are two ways to get a data set into R: using the "Import Dataset" button in the RStudio Environment tab (which we highly recommend!) or coding the file path into R.

The easiest method for getting a data set into R is the Import Dataset button, found at the top of the top-right window in RStudio. The top-right window is shown in Figure 2.14, with the Import Dataset button selected. Selecting the button will present you with different options. We will choose "From Text (base)…" as our option.

After selecting "From Text (base)…" you are presented with a file explorer window. Use the window to locate your data set. Navigate to your data set and select "Open."

Once you select your data set file and click on "Open," a new "Import Dataset" window appears. The window, shown in Figure 2.15, lists on the left-hand side many options for importing the data set. The "Heading" selection is of particular importance. All the data sets we will use in this text have column headers, so it is important to tell R that these headings exist. Make sure the "Yes" button for "Heading" is selected. If you move between the "Yes" and "No" options, you will see changes in the lower-right window, which is a preview of the data set as it will be imported into R. Make sure the column names ("age," "job," etc.) are in bold.

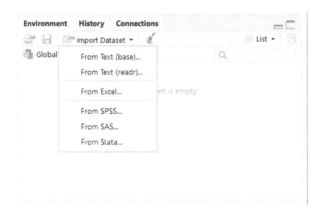

Figure 2.14   After clicking the "Import Dataset" button in RStudio, a drop-down menu is presented, from which we select "From Test (base).…"

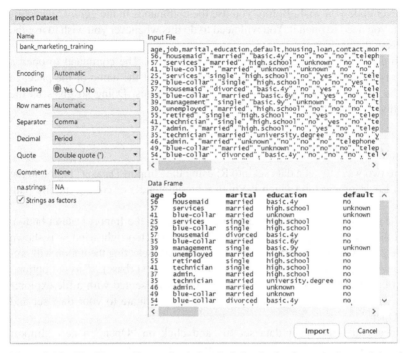

Figure 2.15   The "Import Dataset" window in R for the *bank_marketing_training* data set, with "Heading: Yes" selected.

The boldface indicates that they will be imported as the variable names, and not as an actual record in our data set. In this window, you can also change the delimiter, the missing value codes, and other options for importing the data set. Finally, to import the data set, click "Import." A new tab will open on the top-left window displaying the data set. Return to the tab that contains your code to continue working.

While you can change the name of the data set as it will be imported, using the "Name" field, we recommend leaving it as the default value. In the R code itself you can shorten the name by saving the data set as a shorter name. The instructions in Chapter 4 state "Read in the *bank_marketing_training* data set as *bank_train*." Once you import the data set, you can save the data set using a shortened name using the left-pointing arrow, as shown below.

```
bank_train <- bank_marketing_training
```

Notice that the less-than and minus signs shown below form a left-pointing arrow, **<-**. This arrow points from the object being renamed, on the right, toward its new name, on the left. There cannot be a space between the less-than and minus signs, although there can be spaces on either side of the left-pointed arrow they form. The general form to rename a data set is:

```
object_name <- object_to_be_saved
```

If you are very familiar with coding and accessing the properties of your files, you can open a data set by coding the file path into R via the following structure:

```
your_name_for_the_data <- read.csv(file = "the path to
the file")
```

Using this method, we will use the command **read.csv()** to input the data. The **file = input** in the **read.csv()** command states the path to the file inside double quotes.

An example of what the code to open the *bank_marketing_training* data set would look like is given below.

```
bank_train <- read.csv(file = "C:/Users/Data Science/
Data/bank_marketing_training")
```

2.4.5 Saving Output in R

As in Python, you will often want to save the output of code under a particular name to use later in the program. To save your output under a particular name, use the same structure that we used to rename a data set:

```
object_name <- object_to_be_saved
```

For example, to create a contingency table, you would use the code given below. The code and its output are shown in Figure 2.16.

```
table(bank_train$response, bank_train$previous_outcome)
```

If you want to create row and column totals, or to calculate proportions of this table, you should save the table under its own name first. For simplicity, let us save the table as **t1** for "Table #1."

The code is given below and shown in Figure 2.17. Notice how the contingency table is not shown if we save it under the name **t1**. To view the table, run the **t1** code by itself. The result of running only **t1** is shown in Figure 2.18.

```
> table(bank_train$response, bank_train$previous_outcome)

      failure nonexistent success
  no     2390       21176     320
  yes     385        2034     569
```

Figure 2.16 Creating a contingency table in R without saving the output.

```
> t1 <- table(bank_train$response, bank_train$previous_outcome)
>
```

Figure 2.17 Creating a contingency table in R and saving the output under the name t1.

```
> t1
```

```
       failure nonexistent success
   no     2390       21176     320
   yes     385        2034     569
```

Figure 2.18 The output of the saved table t1 in R.

2.4.6 Accessing Records and Variables in R

As with Python, there will be times when you want R to give you a particular record or variable. For example, how do we access the first record in the *bank_train* data set? Or the *age* variable in that data set?

R references its records starting at one, so if we want to view the first record we request record 1. For example, to access the first record in the *bank_train* data set, use the following code:

```
bank_train[1, ]
```

Note that there is no separate command to use to isolate a particular record. Instead, bracket notation is used. The structure of the bracket notation is:

```
data_set_name[ rows of interest , columns of interest ]
```

Note that there should be no space between the data set name and the open bracket.

Let us take a look at some examples. The data set we will work with is named **bank_train**. Since we are interested in the first row, we put a **1** in the rows of interest area. Currently, there are no columns of interest, so we leave that input blank.

```
bank_train[ 1, ]
```

If you want the first, third, and fourth record, use the following code:

```
bank_train[c(1,3,4), ]
```

We specify the rows of interest using the **1, 3, 4** input. Enclosing those numbers within a **c()** command tells R that all those numbers belong together, so they are all considered rows of interest. Since columns of interest are not specified, all columns will be returned. The output (showing only the first four columns) is shown in Figure 2.19.

```
> bank_train[c(1,3,4), ]
  age         job marital   education
1  56   housemaid married    basic.4y
3  41 blue-collar married     unknown
4  25    services  single high.school
```

Figure 2.19   R shows us the contents of the first, third, and fourth records in the *bank_train* data set (first four variables shown).

```
> bank_train[, c(1, 3)]
      age  marital
1      56  married
2      57  married
3      41  married
4      25   single
5      29   single
```

Figure 2.20   R shows us the contents of the first and third variables (first five records shown).

What about variables? We can identify variables of interest in the same way as records of interest: by using the bracket notation and putting the numbers of the columns we want in the *columns of interest* section. For example, variables age and marital are the first and third variables in the data set. To access these variables, put a **1** and a **3** in the appropriate location within the brackets, as shown below.

```
bank_train[, c(1, 3)]
```

The results are shown in Figure 2.20.

Of course, you can combine the rows of interest and columns of interest to specify particular rows and columns you are interested in. For example, you can ask for the first three records of the *age* and *marital* variables. We leave the results of this as an exercise.

When we import data sets, they are imported as data frames. These data frames have a very nice property: we can identify variables of interest using a dollar sign, $. For example, say we want the *age* variable from the *bank_train* data set. We write the name of the data set and the name of the variable, connected with a dollar sign, as shown below.

```
bank_train$age
```

Congratulations, you have now learned the core actions of programming in R! You are well on your way to becoming an R programmer. Just like with Python, the remainder of this book will cover more specific commands, packages, and output, which will be accompanied by programming tips and explanations.

Now that you have the basics of our two programming languages, you are ready to do Data Science using Python and R!

REFERENCES

K. Jarrod Millman and Michael Aivazis, Python for scientists and engineers, *Computing in Science & Engineering*, 13, 9–12, 2011, doi:https://doi.org/10.1109/MCSE.2011.36.

Wes McKinney, Data Structures for Statistical Computing in Python. In Proceedings of the 9th Python in Science Conference, pp. 51–56, 2010.

Travis E. Oliphant, *A Guide to NumPy*, Trelgol Publishing, Spanish Fork, 2006.

Travis E. Oliphant, Python for scientific computing, *Computing in Science & Engineering*, 9, 10–20, 2007, doi:https://doi.org/10.1109/MCSE.2007.58.

R Core Team, *R: A Language and Environment for Statistical Computing*, R Foundation for Statistical Computing, Vienna, Austria, 2018.

EXERCISES

CLARIFYING THE CONCEPTS

1. What are the five actions of Python and R code we discuss in this chapter?

2. What are comments used for? What output is generated by a comment? What special character begins a comment?

3. Why do we want to import packages?

4. What is the use of the "**as**" code when importing Python packages?

5. How do we save output generated by Python code?

6. How do we save output generated by R code?

7. Why would we want to save output?

8. How do we get a data set into Python?

9. Why is it important to specify if our data set has column headings or not?

10. What are the two ways we can get a data set into R?

WORKING WITH THE DATA

For the following exercises, work with the *bank_marketing_training* data set. Use either Python or R to solve each problem.

11. Download the program and open the compiler. What is contained in the bottom-right window? The left (for Python) or top-left (for R)?

12. Type a comment stating that you are working on Chapter 2 exercises.

13. Locate the "Run" button and note whether there is a keyboard shortcut.

14. Execute the comment from the previous exercise. What is the output? Explain your answer.

15. Import the following packages:

    a. For Python, import the *pandas* and *numpy* packages. Rename the *pandas* package "pd" and rename the *numpy* package "np."

    b. For R, import the *ggplot2* package. Make sure you both install and open the package.

16. Import the *bank_marketing_training* data set and name it *bank_train*.

17. Create a contingency table of the variables *response* and *previous_outcome* from the *bank_train* data set. Do not save the output from the code.

18. Rerun the code from the previous exercise, this time saving the output as *crosstab_01* (for Python code) or *t1* (for R code).

19. After saving the output in the previous exercise, display the output using the name of the saved output.

20. Save the contingency table under a different name. This time, use your last name and favorite number as the name; for example, *larose42*.

21. Save the first nine records of the *bank_train* data set as their own data frame.

22. Save the age and marital records of the *bank_train* data set as their own data frame.

23. Save the first three records of the *age* and *marital* variables as their own data frame.

HANDS-ON ANALYSIS

24. Import the *adult_ch3_training* data set using the "Heading: Yes" setting. Rename the data set *adult* once it is imported.

25. Write a comment explaining the change in the data set name.

26. Import the following packages:

    a. For Python, import the *DecisionTreeClassifier* command from the *sklearn.tree* package.

    b. For R, import the *rpart* package. Make sure you both install and open the package.

27. Create a contingency table of *workclass* and *sex*. Save the output as *table01*.

28. Create a contingency table of *sex* and *marital status*. Save the output as *table02*.

29. Display the *sex* and *workclass* values of the person in the first record. What cell of *table01* do they belong to? How many other records in the data set have the same *sex* and *workclass* values?

30. Display the *sex* and *marital status* values of the people in records 6–10. Which cells of *table02* do they belong to? How many other records in the data set have the same combinations of *sex* and *marital status* values?

31. Create a new data set that has only records whose *marital status* is "Married-civ-spouse" and name the data set *adultMarried*.

32. Recreate the contingency table of *sex* and *workclass* using the *adultMarried* data set. What differences do you notice between the sexes?

33. Create a new data set that has only records whose *age* value is greater than 40. Name the new data set *adultOver40*.

34. Recreate the contingency table of *sex* and *marital status* using the *adultOver40* data set. What differences do you notice?

CHAPTER 3

DATA PREPARATION

3.1 THE BANK MARKETING DATA SET

We will illustrate how to perform the first two phases of the Data Science Methodology using the *bank_marketing_training* and *bank_marketing_test* data sets. Readers may download these data sets from the book series web site: www. dataminingconsultant.com. These data sets are adapted from the *bank-additional-full.txt* data set[1] from the UCI Machine Learning Repository.[2] We use only four predictors (*age, educations, previous_outcome,* and *days_since_previous*), plus the target, *response.* The data relate to a phone-based direct marketing campaign conducted by a bank in Portugal. The bank was interested in whether or not the contacts would subscribe to a term deposit account with the bank. The *bank_marketing_training* data set contains 26,874 records, while *bank_marketing_test* contains 10,255 records.

3.2 THE PROBLEM UNDERSTANDING PHASE

We begin with the Problem Understanding Phase, in order to make sure that the ladder we are working so hard to climb is not leaning against the wrong wall.

3.2.1 Clearly Enunciate the Project Objectives

The objectives of this analysis are as follows:

1. Learn about our potential customers. That is, learn the characteristics of those who choose to bank with us, as well as those who do not.

---

[1] Sérgio Moro, Paulo Cortez, and Paulo Rita, A data-driven approach to predict the success of Bank Telemarketing, *Decision Support Systems*, Elsevier, 62,: 22–31, June 2014.

[2] The University of California at Irvine Machine Learning Repository, https://archive.ics.uci.edu/ml/index.php.

Data Science Using Python and R, First Edition. Chantal D. Larose and Daniel T. Larose.

2. Develop a profitable method of identifying likely positive responders, so that we may save time and money. That is, develop a model or models that will identify likely positive responders. Quantify the expected profit from using these models.

3.2.2 Translate These Objectives into a Data Science Problem

How shall we use data science to accomplish the project objectives?

1. There are many ways to learn about our potential customers.

   a. Use Exploratory Data Analysis to express some simple graphic relationships among the variables. For example, use a histogram of *age* overlain with information about the response *yes/no* to visualize whether age has a bearing on customer response.

   b. Use Clustering to determine whether there are natural groupings within our potential customers, for example, younger/more-educated vs older/less-educated. Then, see if these clusters differ with respect to their response to the marketing.

   c. Use Association Rules to see whether there are useful relationships among subsets of the records. For example, suppose the rule, "If cell phone, then response = yes" has good support and high confidence. This would allow our marketing people to develop a targeted campaign to cellphone users, independent of the results of our overall modeling.

2. We can develop a powerful suite of data science models to identify likely positive responders. Note that, since the response (yes/no) is categorical, we can use classification models but not estimation models.

   a. Develop the best classification model we can, using the following algorithms:

      i. Decision Trees

      ii. Random Forests

      iii. Naïve Bayes Classification

      iv. Neural Networks

      v. Logistic Regression

   b. Evaluate each model based on predetermined model evaluation criteria, such as misclassification costs. Construct a table of the best models and their costs.

   c. Consult with management regarding the best model or models with which to move forward to the deployment phase.

Thus, we have (i) clearly enunciated our objectives and (ii) translated these objectives into a set of data science tasks to be implemented. Thus, Phase One: Problem Understanding Phase is complete.

3.3   DATA PREPARATION PHASE

Next, we turn to the Data Preparation Phase, where the data are cleaned and prepped for analysis. A complete guide to data preparation would require much more space than we have here. (The reader is encouraged to see *Data Mining and Predictive Analytics*[3] for much more on data preparation.) Every data set has its own requisite data prep tasks. In this chapter we will focus on the following data preparation tasks:

- Adding an index field
- Changing misleading field values
- Reexpressing categorical data as numeric data
- Standardizing the numeric fields
- Identifying outliers.

3.4   ADDING AN INDEX FIELD

The data scientist may want to augment the data set with new variables that can enhance understanding. For example, not all data sets, including the *bank_marketing* data sets, come equipped with an ID field. Thus, we can add an index field to the data, which will serve two purposes: (i) it acts as an ID field for data sets without such a field and (ii) it tracks the sort order of the records in the database. In data science, we often repartition and re-sort the data; it is therefore helpful to have an index field, in order to recover the original sort order when desired. How to add an index field using Python and R follows.

3.4.1   How to Add an Index Field Using Python

First, we need to open the required package, using the code discussed in the previous chapter.

```
import pandas as pd
```

Next, import the data set under the name **bank_train** by using the **read_csv()** command and specifying the file's location.

```
bank_train = pd.read_csv("C:/.../bank_marketing_training")
```

As discussed in the previous chapter, since the **read_csv** command is in the *pandas* package, we need to give the name of the package before the command. As we opened the *pandas* package as **pd**, the full command is **pd.read_csv()**.

---

[3] By Daniel T. Larose and Chantal D. Larose, John Wiley and Sons, Inc., 2015.

To create the index, we first need to find the number of records and columns in the data set.

```
bank_train.shape
```

Using **.shape** after the name of the data set will give us the number of rows and columns in the data set. The first number in the output is the number of records, 26,874. The second is the number of variables.

Once we know the number of records, we create a new variable that assigns every record a unique integer.

```
bank_train['index'] = pd.Series(range(0,26874))
```

The nested commands **Series()** and **range()** create a string of numbers whose lower bound is zero and upper bound is the number of records. Since the **Series()** command is contained in the *pandas* package, and we renamed the *pandas* package *pd*, we preface the **Series()** command with **pd** and a period. The result is the code **pd.Series()**. Note that the lower bound of the **range()** command is zero and not one, as Python begins counting locations at zero. We save the series of numbers as a new variable in the data set, **index**, by assigning the output of **pd.Series(range())** to the **index** variable of the **bank_train** data set using **bank_train['index']**.

To view the data set with its new variable, we can look at the head of the data set.

```
bank_train.head
```

Using **.head** after the name of the data set will generate output containing the first and last 30 records for every variable in the data set.

3.4.2 How to Add an Index Field Using R

Import the data set under the name *bank_train*, using the *Import Dataset* button in RStudio. To create an index field, we first need to know how many records are in the data set.

```
n <- dim(bank_train)[1]
```

The **dim()** command gives the number of records and the number of variables for the data set whose name is used as the input value; in this case, the **bank_train** data set. Adding **[1]** at the end of **dim(bank_train)** will result in only the first number, the number of records, being given as the output. We save the output as a lowercase letter "**n**," which is the commonly used notation for sample size. If you execute **n** by itself, the output will be the number 26,874, which is the number of records in the data set.

Once we have the number of records, we create a new variable that gives every record a unique integer which specifies its order in the data set.

```
bank_train$Index <- c(1:n)
```

The function **c()** will combine its input values into a single object. The input in our case is **1:n**, which stands for "the integers 1 through n, inclusive." The command **c(1:n)** will give us a series of numbers from 1 to the number of records in the *bank* data set. We save this series of numbers as a new variable in the data set, named **Index**, by saving **c(1:n)** as **bank_train$Index**.

To see the data set with its new index variable, run the **head()** command with the **bank_train** data set as the sole input.

```
head(bank_train)
```

The resulting output is the first six records across all variables, including the **Index** variable.

3.5 CHANGING MISLEADING FIELD VALUES

The field *days_since_previous* is a count of the number of days since the client was last contacted from a previous campaign. This field is clearly numeric, so we can look at a histogram[4] of *days_since_previous* provided by R in Figure 3.1. Note that

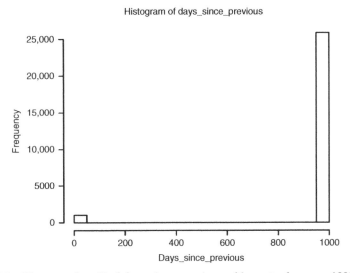

Figure 3.1   Histogram from R of *days_since_previous*, with most values near 1000.

---

[4] See the Appendix, *Data Summarization and Visualization.*

most of the data values are near 1000, with a minority of values near zero. It turns out that the database administrator used the code *999* to represent customers who had not been contacted previously. Thus, we need to change the field value *999* to *missing*, which is done as follows in Python and R.

3.5.1 How to Change Misleading Field Values Using Python

If you did not open the *pandas* package or read in the data set, as described in the previous Python section, do so now. We also need to import the *numpy* package for this section.

```
import numpy as np
```

We need to identify all records with *days_since_previous* value of 999 and replace them with the Python code for missing numbers, **NaN**. Once the replacement is made, we will save the variable under the *days_since_previous* variable name, effectively overriding the previous variable's values.

```
bank_train['days_since_previous'] =
    bank_train['days_since_previous'].replace({999: np.NaN})
```

The code **bank_train['days_since_previous']** accesses the variable *days_since_previous*. The command **replace({999: np.NaN })** finds each instance of 999 in the *days_since_previous* variable and replaces it with the value **NaN**. To save the newly edited variable under its original name, we set the right-hand side equal to the original *days_since_previous* variable on the left by reusing the variable name **bank_train['days_since_previous']**.

To create a histogram of the variable, use the **hist**() command.

```
bank_train['days_since_previous'].plot(kind = 'hist',
    title = 'Histogram of Days Since Previous')
```

Using **.plot**() after the variable name will make a plot of the variable. We use **kind = 'hist'** to specify that a histogram should be made. The **title** input, contained in single quotes, creates the title of the histogram. The output is shown in Figure 3.2. In Chapter 4, we will look at more complex histograms.

3.5.2 How to Change Misleading Field Values Using R

If you did not read in the data set, as described in the previous R section, do so now.

We need to identify each instance of 999 in the *days_since_previous* variable, and replace it with the R code value for a missing value, NA.

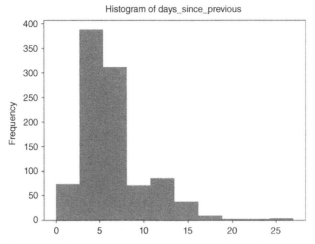

Figure 3.2   Histogram of *days_since_previous* in Python with missing values properly coded.

```
bank_train$days_since_previous <- ifelse(test = bank_
train$days_since_previous == 999,
    yes = NA, no = bank_train$days_since_previous)
```

The **ifelse()** command checks the condition specified under **test =**, then assigns the *days_since_previous* variable the value given after **yes =** if the test condition is true, and assigns the *days_since_previous* variable the value given after **no =** if the test condition is false.

In our case, each record is checked to see if it contains the value 999 in the *days_since_previous* variable. If it does, the value **NA** is returned. If it does not, the original value in the *days_since_previous* variable is returned. To save the string of returned values as the variable *days_since_previous*, save the output as the variable using **bank_train$days_since_previous**.

To create a histogram of the variable, use the **hist()** command.

```
hist(bank_train$days_since_previous, xlab = "days_since_
previous",
    main = "Histogram of days_since_previous - Missing
Values replaced by NA")
```

The **hist()** command has one required input, the variable of interest. We use **bank_train$days_since_previous** as our variable of interest. The optional input values **main** and **xlab** specify the title and X-axis label of the histogram, respectively. Note that the labels must be contained in quotes.

Figure 3.3 shows the histogram of *days_since_previous* with the missing values excluded.

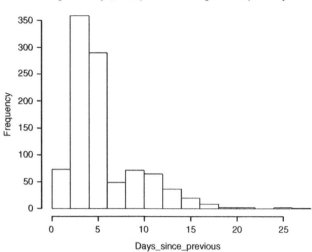

Figure 3.3   Histogram in R of *days_since_previous*, with the missing values excluded.

3.6   REEXPRESSION OF CATEGORICAL DATA AS NUMERIC

Figure 3.4 shows a bar graph[5] of the *education* field. Note that the field is categorical, meaning that there is no ordering of the field values. In other words, if we left the field as it is, then our data science algorithms would not know that *university_ degree* represents more education than *basic.4yr*. To provide this information to our algorithms, we transform the data values into numeric values, where it is clear that one value is larger than another. One needs to proceed with care when doing this, so that the relative differences among the various categories are preserved.

Table 3.1 shows how we plan to accomplish this transformation. The value of *12* for *professional course* was obtained from the publication shown in the footnote, as representing an alternative to the usual high-school course of study. Of course, the *unknown* values will also need to be reexpressed as *missing*.

3.6.1   How to Reexpress Categorical Field Values Using Python

We will replicate the *education* variable, and name it *education_numeric*, in preparation for replacing its categorical values with numeric ones.

```
bank_train['education_numeric'] = bank_
train['education']
```

[5] See the Appendix, *Data Summarization and Visualization*.

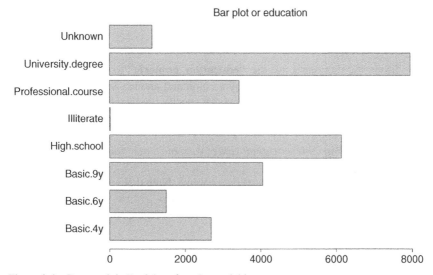

Figure 3.4   Bar graph in R of the *education* variable.

TABLE 3.1   Reexpressing the values of *education* as numeric

Categorical Value	Numeric Value
illiterate	0
basic.4y	4
basic.6y	6
basic.9y	9
high.school	12
professional.course	12[a]
university.degree	16
unknown	Missing

[a] This value based on *In-Vet, Preventing initial dropout and fostering initial inclusion*, http://invet-project.eu/wp-content/uploads/2014/06/National-Report_ Portugal_Final.pdf. The two groups, *professional course* and *high school*, will be combined with the same numeric value, *12*. The proportion of positive responders among these two groups is similar (11.1 vs. 10.7%), so we can probably live with their being combined.

The right-hand side of the equal sign specifies the *education* variable, and the equal sign assigns those values to the left-hand side. There is currently no variable named *education_numeric*, so one will be created and given the values of the variable *education*.

We need to set up a dictionary specifically for converting the categorical values in the *education_numeric* variable to numeric values. The dictionary is contained in curly brackets, **{ }**, to set up our dictionary, as follows:

```
dict_edu = {"education_numeric": {"illiterate": 0,
"basic.4y": 4, "basic.6y": 6,
```

```
"basic.9y": 9, "high.school":12, "professional.
course": 12, "university.degree":16,
    "unknown": np.NaN}}
```

Inside the dictionary, we use **"education_numeric"** to specify the variable which we want to recode, followed by a colon and another set of curly brackets. Within this second set of curly brackets, we specify the recoding in the following order:

Variable's original value : *Variable's new value*

Each specification is separated by a comma. Note that we use Python's value for missing numeric values, **NaN**, where necessary.

Finally, we tell Python to use the dictionary to replace the variable's values.

```
bank_train.replace(dict_edu, inplace=True)
```

The command **replace()** will replace the values according to the rules in the dictionary **dict_edu**.

3.6.2   How to Reexpress Categorical Field Values Using R

First, we need to install and load the *plyr* package.

```
install.packages("plyr"); library(plyr)
```

We need to specify which values of education go with which numeric values, following the rules specified in Table 3.1.

```
edu.num <- revalue(x = bank_train$education, replace =
c("illiterate" = 0, "basic.4y" = 4,
    "basic.6y" = 6, "basic.9y" = 9, "high.school" = 12,
"professional.course" = 12,
    "university.degree" = 16, "unknown" = NA))
```

The **revalue()** function replaces values in the variable given in the **x** input, according to the rules given in the **replace** input. Within the **replace =** input, we use **c()** to string together each piece of recoding, using the structure

Variable's original value = Variable's new value

Each specification is separated by a comma. Note that we are using R's value for missing values, **NA**, where necessary. We save the output as **edu.num**.

Currently, the values of **edu.num** are not numeric (e.g. you cannot make a histogram using them), so we need to convert the levels of the variable to the

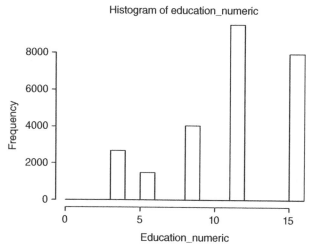

Figure 3.5   Histogram in R of *education_numeric*.

numeric type. The object **edu.num** is a factor, and we convert its values to numbers using the following code:

```
bank_train$education_numeric <- as.numeric(levels
(edu.num))[edu.num]
```

The **levels()** command obtains the factor levels of the **edu.num** variable, which are strings. The **as.numeric()** command converts them to numbers. These new values are applied to the **edu.num** variable, and the result saved as our new variable, **education_numeric**. Figure 3.5 shows a histogram of the reexpressed education field *education_numeric*.

3.7   STANDARDIZING THE NUMERIC FIELDS

Certain algorithms perform better when the numeric fields are standardized so that the field mean equals 0 and the field standard deviation equals 1,[6] as follows:

$$z = Standardized\ Value = \frac{x - \bar{x}}{s} = \frac{Data\ value - mean}{Standard\ deviation}$$

Positive *z*-values may be interpreted as representing the number of standard deviations above the mean the data value lies, while negative *z*-values represent the number of standard deviations below the mean. Some analysts standardize all their

---

[6]For mean and standard deviation, see the Appendix, *Data Summarization and Visualization*. For more on standardization, see *Discovering Statistics*, Third Edition, by Daniel T. Larose, W.H. Freeman, 2016.

numeric fields as a matter of course. Next, we show how to standardize numeric fields in Python and R.

3.7.1 How to Standardize Numeric Fields Using Python

Import the required package.

```
from scipy import stats
```

We will standardize the *age* variable and save it as a new variable, *age_z*.

```
bank_train['age_z'] = stats.zscore(bank_train['age'])
```

The **zscore** function calculates the *z*-value of the given variable, in this case *age*, written in the code as **bank_train['age']**. As the **zscore()** command is part of the *stats* package, we write the command as **stats.zscore()**. We save it as a new variable in the data set, **age_z**.

3.7.2 How to Standardize Numeric Fields Using R

We do not have to install or load a package for this code. The command we will use, **scale()**, is included in the initial download of R.

```
bank_train$age_z <- scale(x = bank_train$age)
```

The **scale()** function can center a variable by subtracting its mean, scale it by dividing by the standard deviation, or both. By default, it does both, as needed to calculate the *z*-score. Thus, using the default settings of the **scale()** function on the **bank_train$age** variable will return the *z*-scores of the variable. We can save the *z*-values as a new variable in the data set using **bank_train$age_z**.

3.8 IDENTIFYING OUTLIERS

Once the numeric fields are standardized, one may use the *z*-values to identify outliers, which are records with extreme values along a particular dimension or dimensions. For example, consider the field *number_of_contacts*, which represents the number of customer contacts made over the course of the marketing campaign. The mean number of contacts per customer is 2.6, with a standard deviation of 2.7 (allowing for rounding). So, we obtain the standardized field as follows:

$$number\_of\_contacts\_z = \frac{number\_of\_contacts - 2.6}{2.7}$$

A rough rule of thumb is that a data value is an outlier if its *z*-value is either greater than 3, or less than −3. For instance, a customer who had been contacted 10 times (which seems like a lot) would have standardized value,

$$number\_of\_contacts\_z = \frac{10-2.6}{2.7} = 2.7$$

Thus, 10 contacts, while a lot, is not identified as an outlier using this method, since 2.7 < 3.

The data scientist should consult with the client regarding what he or she would like to do with any outliers. Outliers should not be automatically removed! Nor should they be automatically changed. Their unusual values may bring to light important aspects of the data that should be discussed with the client or with the database administrator.

3.8.1   How to Identify Outliers Using Python

For this example, we will continue using the **age_z** variable that we created in the previous section. We will find outliers by using the **query()** function, which identifies rows that meet a particular condition.

```
bank_train.query('age_z > 3 | age_z < -3')
```

The condition we want all returned records to meet is given as **'age_z > 3 | age_z < -3'**. In words, this condition requires each record to either have an **age_z** value greater than 3, or an **age_z** value less than −3. The "or" is specified by the character | between the two conditions.

All records which meet the specified condition are returned. In our example, there are 228 records that have **age_z** values greater than 3 or less than −3. We can use these records to create a new data set, which is made up only of these values.

```
bank_train_outliers = bank_train.query('age_z > 3 |
age_z < -3')
```

By giving the output of the **query()** command a name, we create a new data set of only outliers, which we have called **bank_train_outliers**.

Let us sort the data set **bank_train_outliers** by its **age_z** variable.

```
bank_train_sort = bank_train.sort_values(['age_z'],
ascending = False)
```

The **sort_values()** command will sort the records in the data set based on a specified variable. The sort can be ascending or descending. In this example, we want the largest **age_z** values at the top, so we sort in descending order by specifying **ascending = False**. We can save this sorted data set under its own name, say **bank_train_sort**.

Finally, let us say we want to report the age and marital status of the 15 people who have the largest **age_z** values. This condition specifies both the number of rows to report (15) and the columns to report (the variables named *age* and *marital*).

```
bank_train_sort[['age', 'marital']].head(n=15)
```

The double-bracket notation given after the data set name lets us specify which columns to include. The **head()** command will give the top records, stopping after **n** records if **n** is given, or after five records if no **n** value is given. In our case, we specify **n = 15**. The results are the age and marital status of the people with the 15 largest **age_z** values.

3.8.2 How to Identify Outliers Using R

For this example, we will continue using the **age_z** variable that we created in the previous section. We can isolate individual records using bracket notation detailed in the previous chapter. The structure of our code will begin as follows:

```
bank_train[ rows of interest, ]
```

Note that the right-hand side of the comma is left blank. As we have not specified any columns of interest, all columns will be returned in the output of this command.

We now need to fill in which rows we are interested in. The **which()** command will identify the records that meet specified conditions.

```
bank_outliers <- bank_train[ which(bank_train$age_z < -3
| bank_train$age_z > 3), ]
```

The condition given as the input to the **which()** command states that we want all records whose **age_z** values are less than −3 or greater than 3. The **which()** command returns the row indices of all such records. The bracket notation will return a subset of the **bank_train** data set that holds only those records. We can save those records as a new data set, **bank_outliers**.

To sort a data set by a variable, we use the **order()** command.

```
bank_train_sort <- bank_train[ order(- bank_
train$age_z), ]
```

The **order()** command takes as input a variable to be sorted. It returns the row indices of the variable after it has been sorted. By default, the values are sorted in ascending order. To sort instead by descending order, we add a minus sign in front of the variable, as shown.

Placing the **order()** command inside bracket notation, specifically where the rows of interest are located, will reorder the records in the data set based on the ordering returned by the **order()** command. We save this new, sorted data set as **bank_train_sort**.

To view the first 10 records of the new data set, which are the 10 records with the largest **age_z** values, use bracket notation and specify rows 1 through 10.

```
bank_train_sort[ 1:10, ]
```

Once again, leaving the columns blank will return all the columns (variables) of the data set.

To return only a few columns, we need to take note of which variable is in what column. We can do this using **head()**.

```
head(bank_train_sort)
```

The variable **age** is in column 1 and the variable marital is in column 3. To return the first 10 records of columns 1 and 3, specify both the rows and columns of interest in bracket notation.

```
bank_train_sort[1:10, c(1,3)]
```

The output contains the age and marital status of the 10 customers with the largest **age_z** values.

The topics addressed in this chapter are intended to provide a flavor of the types of challenges awaiting you in the Data Preparation Phase. In the **Hands-On Analysis** exercises, we explore how to derive new variables that are functions of the original variables, in order to extract more information from the data set. For more on data preparation, see *Data Mining and Predictive Analytics*,[7] which provides more data preparation topics, along with how to do them using R.

REFERENCES

The *scipy* package in Python handles many different mathematics and computing tasks. For more details, have a look at the website: E. Jones, E. Oliphant, and P. Peterson, et al., *SciPy: Open Source Scientific Tools for Python*, 2001–, www.scipy.org

The *plyr* package in R has a similar goal of handling and organizing data. For more details, see the original publication: Hadley Wickham, The split-apply-combine strategy for data analysis, *Journal of Statistical Software*, 40(1), 1–29, 2011.

---

[7]*Data Mining and Predictive Analytics*, by Daniel T. Larose and Chantal D. Larose, Second Edition, John Wiley and Sons, Inc., 2015.

EXERCISES

CLARIFYING THE CONCEPTS

1. What are the two main objectives of the *bank_marketing* analysis, as stated in the Problem Understanding Phase?

2. What are the three ways we plan to accomplish the objective of learning about our potential customers.

3. Explain how we plan to accomplish the objective of developing profitable models for identifying likely positive responders.

4. Describe two reasons why it might be a good idea to add an index field to the data set.

5. Explain why the field *days_since_previous* is essentially useless until we handle the *999* code.

6. Why was it important to reexpress *education* as a numeric field?

7. Suppose a data value has a *z*-value of 1. How may we interpret this value?

8. What is the rough rule of thumb for identifying outliers using *z*-values?

9. Should outliers be automatically removed or changed? Why or why not?

10. What should we do with outliers we have identified?

WORKING WITH THE DATA

For the following exercises, work with the *bank_marketing_training* data set. Use either Python or R to solve each problem.

11. Derive an index field and add it to the data set.

12. For the *days_since_previous* field, change the field value *999* to the appropriate code for missing values.

13. For the *education* field, reexpress the field values as the numeric values shown in Table 3.1.

14. Standardize the field *age*. Print out a list of the first 10 records, including the variables *age* and *age_z*.

15. Obtain a listing of all records that are outliers according to the field *age_z*. Print out a listing of the 10 largest *age_z* values.

16. For the *job* field, combine the jobs with less than 5% of the records into a field called *other*.

17. Rename the *default* predictor to *credit_default*.

18. For the variable *month*, change the field values to 1–12, but keep the variable as categorical.

19. Do the following for the *duration* field.

    a. Standardize the variable.

    b. Identify how many outliers there are and identify the most extreme outlier.

20. Do the following for the *campaign* field.

    a. Standardize the variable.

    b. Identify how many outliers there are and identify the most extreme outlier.

HANDS-ON ANALYSIS

For Exercises 21–25, work with the *Nutrition_subset* data set. The data set contains the weight in grams along with the amount of saturated fat and the amount of cholesterol for a set of 961 foods. Use either Python or R to solve each problem.

21. The elements in the data set are food items of various sizes, ranging from a teaspoon of cinnamon to an entire carrot cake.

    a. Sort the data set by the saturated fat (*saturated_fat*) and produce a listing of the five food items highest in saturated fat.

    b. Comment on the validity of comparing food items of different sizes.

22. Derive a new variable, *saturated_fat_per_gram*, by dividing the amount of saturated fat by the weight in grams.

    a. Sort the data set by *saturated_fat_per_gram* and produce a listing of the five food items highest in saturated fat per gram.

    b. Which food has the most saturated fat per gram?

23. Derive a new variable, *cholesterol_per_gram*.

    a. Sort the data set by *cholesterol_per_gram* and produce a listing of the five food items highest in cholesterol fat per gram.

    b. Which food has the most cholesterol fat per gram?

24. Standardize the field *saturated_fat_per_gram*. Produce a listing of all the food items that are outliers at the high end of the scale. How many food items are outliers at the low end of the scale?

25. Standardize the field *cholesterol_per_gram*. Produce a listing of all the food items that are outliers at the high end of the scale.

    For Exercises 26–30, work with the *adult_ch3_training* data set. The response is whether *income* exceeds $50,000.

26. Add a record index field to the data set.

27. Determine whether any outliers exist for the *education* field.

28. Do the following for the *age* field.

    a. Standardize the variable.

    b. Identify how many outliers there are and identify the most extreme outlier.

29. Derive a flag for *capital-gain*, called capital-gain-flag, which equals 0 for capital gain equals zero, and 1 otherwise.

30. Age anomaly? Select only records with age at least 80. Construct a histogram of age. Explain what you see in one sentence and why it is like that in another sentence.

CHAPTER 4

EXPLORATORY DATA ANALYSIS

4.1 EDA VERSUS HT

Clients or analysts often have a priori hypotheses that they would like the data to test. An example of such a hypothesis is: Do cellphone users have a higher rate of positive responses than landline users? The resulting *hypothesis test* (HT) could be carried out using either classical statistical methods or using the cross-validation methods of data science (Chapter 5).

On the other hand, the client or the analyst may not have any salient a priori notions about what the data might uncover. In such cases, they would prefer to use *exploratory data analysis* (EDA) or *graphical data analysis*. EDA allows the user to:

- Use graphics to explore the relationship between the predictor variables and the target variable.
- Use graphics and tables to derive new variables that will increase predictive value.
- Use binning productively, to increase predictive value.

In this chapter, we will continue to explore the *bank_marketing_training* data set from Chapter 3. We begin by using graphics to investigate the relationship between the target *response* and a categorical predictor.

4.2 BAR GRAPHS WITH RESPONSE OVERLAY

We can use bar graphs with a response overlay for exploring the relationship between a categorical predictor and the target variable. Figure 4.1 shows a bar graph of *previous_outcome* with an overlay of the target *response*. *Previous_outcome* refers to the result of a previous marketing campaign with this same customer, with most customers not having had such a previous experience.

Clearly, most customers did not have any previous marketing experience with the company (variable value *nonexistent*). In general, (non-normalized) bar graphs

Data Science Using Python and R, First Edition. Chantal D. Larose and Daniel T. Larose.

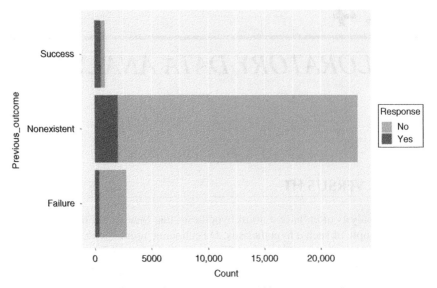

Figure 4.1   Bar graph from R of *previous_outcome* with *response* overlay.

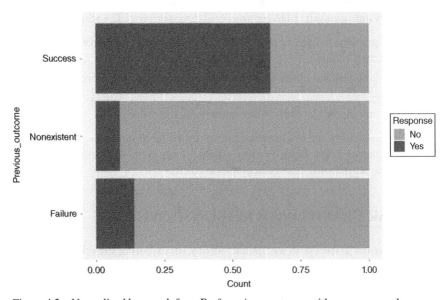

Figure 4.2   Normalized bar graph from R of *previous_outcome* with *response* overlay.

are useful for showing the distribution of the values of the categorical variable. However, it is not clear which category has the greater proportion of responders. *Nonexistent* has the most responders but it also has the most nonresponders.

To clarify situations like these, we may obtain a *normalized bar graph*, which equalizes the length of each bar, so that we may more easily compare the response proportions. Figure 4.2 represents such a normalized bar graph of *previous_outcome*, with a *response* overlay. From Figure 4.2, it is clear that the group with the highest proportion of positive responders is *success*, those customers who had responded positively to the company's previous campaign. Interestingly, those who responded negatively last time (*failure*) also had a slightly better success rate this time than those with no previous contacts.

This exercise demonstrates two best practices when working with bar graphs.

Best Practices: Bar Graphs

- When a bar graph with overlay is unclear regarding the response proportion, supplement it with a normalized bar graph.
- However, never provide a normalized bar graph without its non-normalized version, because the normalized version gives no indication of the original distribution (how many records in each category).

4.2.1 How to Construct a Bar Graph with Overlay Using Python

Load the required package and read in the *bank_marketing_training* data set as *bank_train*.

```
import pandas as pd
bank_train = pd.read_csv("C:/.../bank_marketing_
training")
```

The first step in creating a bar graph is to create a contingency table of the values in the predictor and target variables. We create the table using the **crosstab()** command.

```
crosstab_01 = pd.crosstab(bank_train['previous_
outcome'], bank_train['response'])
```

This code will be examined in detail a bit later. For now, we save the table as **crosstab_01.**

Now, we can create the bar graph based on the table.

```
crosstab_01.plot(kind='bar', stacked = True)
```

To create the bar graph, append **.plot()** to the end of the **crosstab_01** object. The **plot()** command takes various optional input values. We specify the input **kind = 'bar'** to plot a bar graph and **stacked = True** to specify a stacked bar graph.

To create a normalized version, we need to change the table so that the values in each cell are the proportions of "no" and "yes" *response* values within each value of the predictor *previous_outcome*, as follows:

```
crosstab_norm = crosstab_01.div(crosstab_01.sum(1),
axis = 0)
```

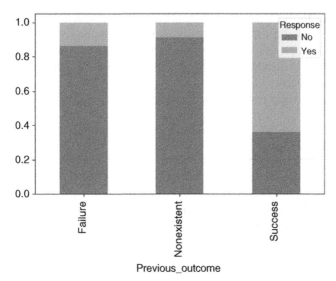

Figure 4.3 Normalized bar graph from Python of *previous_outcome* with *response* overlay.

The **div()** command will divide the values of the table by another object, within each specified axis. In our example, we want to divide the cells in row 1 of the table by the sum of the cells in row 1, and so on for row 2 and row 3. To accomplish this, we first set the value we want to divide by to be **crosstab_01.sum(1)**, which is the sum of each row in the table. We then set **axis = 0** to specify that we want to divide the rows of the table by these values. The result is a table whose cells are the proportion of data in that row that falls in that column. We save the resulting table as **crosstab_norm**.

Once the table is saved, visualize it using the code for a stacked bar chart, as above.

```
crosstab_norm.plot(kind='bar', stacked = True)
```

The resulting graph is shown in Figure 4.3.

4.2.2 How to Construct a Bar Graph with Overlay Using R

Read in the *bank_marketing_training* data set as *bank_train*. We will be using the **ggplot2** package to create our graphs. You need to install the package once using **install.packages()**, then open it each time you write new code using **library()**.

```
install.packages("ggplot2"); library(ggplot2)
```

The *ggplot* code uses different commands chained together using plus signs (+), as shown in the following example. Note that the plus signs must immediately follow the preceding command, with no line break in between, but may be followed by a line break.

To create a bar graph of the *previous_outcome* variable, we use the **ggplot()** and **geom_bar()** commands.

```
ggplot(bank_train, aes(previous_outcome)) + geom_bar() +
coord_flip()
```

The **ggplot()** command begins the graph. The **bank_train** input specifies the data set being used, and the variable of interest is listed under **aes()** ("aes" for "aesthetics"). The second piece of code is **geom_bar()**, which specifies that a bar chart should be made. The code knows what variable to use because of the previous **ggplot()** command. An optional third piece of code is **coord_flip()**, which will make the bars run horizontally.

To create a bar chart with an overlay of *response*, we add a **fill** input.

```
ggplot(bank_train, aes(previous_outcome)) + geom_
bar(aes(fill = response)) + coord_flip()
```

Note that the only change is the addition of **aes(fill = response)** inside **geom_bar()**. The result is the graph shown in Figure 4.1.

To normalize the bar chart, add **position = "fill"** inside **geom_bar()**, as shown below.

```
ggplot(bank_train, aes(previous_outcome)) + geom_
bar(aes(fill = response),
        position = "fill") + coord_flip()
```

The input **position = "fill"** is added inside the **geom_bar()** command, but outside of **aes()**. The result is the graph shown in Figure 4.2.

4.3   CONTINGENCY TABLES

To help quantify the relationship between a categorical predictor and the target, we can construct a *contingency table*, which is a cross-tabulation of the two variables, and contains a cell for every combination of variable values (that is, for every contingency). Figure 4.4 contains a contingency table of *previous_outcome* with *response*. Note that the usual practice is to have the target variable representing the rows, with the predictor representing the columns. For EDA, it is also helpful to include the column percentages. Figure 4.5 contains the table with column percentages. Most customers had no previous marketing campaign (*nonexistent*), so note that 21,176 of these responded *no* while 2034 responded *yes*. Overall, note that the proportion of *yes* response is only 13.9% for *failure* and only 8.8% for *nonexistent*, but a very high 64% when the customer's previous marketing campaign was a success.

The best practices for contingency tables follow.

Best Practices: Contingency Tables

- Let the response variable represent the rows.
- Then, obtain the column percentages to directly compare the response proportions for each category of the predictor.

```
       failure nonexistent success total
no        2390       21176     320 23886
yes        385        2034     569  2988
total     2775       23210     889 26874
```

Figure 4.4   Contingency table from R of *previous_outcome* with *response*.

```
       failure nonexistent success
no        86.1        91.2    36.0
yes       13.9         8.8    64.0
```

Figure 4.5   Contingency table from R of *previous_outcome* with *response* table with column percentages instead of counts.

4.3.1 How to Construct Contingency Tables Using Python

We had to create a contingency table in order to make a bar chart, but did not investigate the code in detail. Let us examine the code for the table more closely.

```
crosstab_01 = pd.crosstab(bank_train['previous_
outcome'], bank_train['outcome'])
```

Note the order of the variables. The table as built by this code will have *previous_outcome* as the rows. This table created the bar chart we needed in the previous section, but to abide by best practice and have the target variable represent the rows, we need to change the code to:

```
crosstab_02 = pd.crosstab(bank_train['response'], bank_
train['previous_outcome'])
```

Make sure to save the table. We save the output as **crosstab_02**. The result will be a table equivalent to Figure 4.4.

To calculate the column proportions of the table, we need to divide each column by the column sum. We utilize the **sum()** and **div()** commands, in a similar way to the previous section. However, this time we are obtaining column, and not row, percentages.

```
round(crosstab_02.div(crosstab_02.sum(0), axis = 1)*100, 1)
```

Note that we multiply the resulting table by 100 to obtain percentages instead of proportions. In addition to the **sum**() and **div**() commands, we put the code for the table inside a **round**() command. The **round**() command will round the numbers in the table to the specified number of significant digits; here, we specify one digit. The result is a table equivalent to Figure 4.5.

4.3.2 How to Construct Contingency Tables Using R

The command to create a table is **table**(), with the variables of interest inside the parentheses.

```
t.v1 <- table(bank_train$response, bank_train$previous_
outcome)
```

The first variable, **bank_train$response**, makes up the rows, while the second variable, **bank_train$previous_outcome**, makes up the columns. We will save our table as **t.v1**, so we can edit it.

To add row and column totals to the table, use the **addmargins**() command.

```
t.v2 <- addmargins(A = t.v1, FUN = list(total = sum),
quiet = TRUE)
```

The input **A = t.v1** specifies the table to be edited, in our case **t.v1**. The **FUN = list(total = sum)** input specifies a list of functions to be performed to create the marginal row and column. In our case, we want to create a row and column named **total** which contains the **sum** of the rows and columns. We save the edited table as **t.v2**. To see the finished table, run **t.v2** by itself. The result is shown in Figure 4.4. Now we want to edit table **t.v1** so it gives us the column percentages.

```
round(prop.table(t.v1, margin = 2)*100, 1)
```

To calculate the proportion of entries in the cells of the table, use **prop.table**(). The input **t.v1** tells **prop.table**() for what table to calculate proportions. The **margin = 2** input tells R to calculate column percentages. Multiplying the result by 100 using ***100** will give us percentages instead of proportions. Finally, putting the **prop.table**() command inside a **round**() command will round the entries to a certain number of decimal points; in our case, one (**1**) decimal point. The result is shown in Figure 4.5.

4.4 HISTOGRAMS WITH RESPONSE OVERLAY

A *histogram* is a graphical representation of a frequency distribution for a numerical variable. Figure 4.6 shows a histogram of the *age* variable with an overlay of *response*. Most customers range from, say, mid-20s to about 60 years of age. So

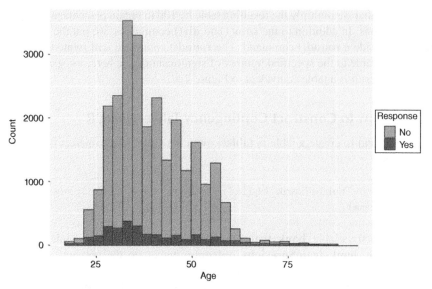

Figure 4.6   Histogram from R of *age* with *response* overlay.

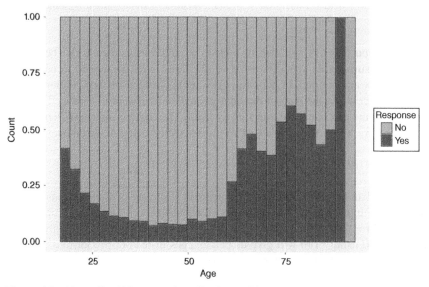

Figure 4.7   Normalized histogram from R of *age* with *response* overlay.

(non-normalized) histograms are useful for seeing the distribution of the values of a numeric variable.

Again, however, it is somewhat difficult to ascertain any pattern in the *response* proportions. To better clarify these response proportions, we turn to a *normalized histogram* with response overlay, shown in Figure 4.7. Suddenly the response pattern becomes crystal clear. Customer response starts off high for

20-year olds, gradually decreases, flattening out low for 30–60-year olds, and rising sharply again for those over 60. So, the normalized histogram allows us to better distinguish these response patterns, but unfortunately the normalized histogram does not tell us about the original distribution of *age* in our customer population.

This leads us to our two best practices for histograms.

Best Practices: Histograms

- Use a non-normalized histogram to obtain the original distribution of the data values.
- If needed, use a normalized histogram to help better distinguish the response patterns.

4.4.1   How to Construct Histograms with Overlay Using Python

Load the required packages.

```
import numpy as np
import matplotlib.pyplot as plt
```

Separate the variable you want to graph by the overlay you want to use. Since we are creating a histogram of *age* using an overlay of *response*, we separate the variable *age*, **bank_train['age']**, by the two values of the variable *response*. Save each piece as its own variable.

```
bt_age_y = bank_train[bank_train.response == "yes"]
['age']
bt_age_n = bank_train[bank_train.response == "no"]
['age']
```

The result is two variables, **bt_age_y** and **bt_age_n**, which have age values from only those records which have **response = "yes"** and **response = "no,"** respectively.

Once the variables are created, create a stacked histogram of the two variables.

```
plt.hist([bt_age_y, bt_age_n], bins = 10, stacked = True)
plt.legend(['Response = Yes', 'Response = No'])
plt.title('Histogram of Age with Response Overlay')
plt.xlabel('Age'); plt.ylabel('Frequency'); plt.show()
```

For the **hist()** command, the input **stacked = True** will stack the two variables, while **bins = 10** specifies the number of bins in the histogram. The **legend()**, **title()**, **xlabel()**, and **ylabel()** commands specify the values of the legend, title, *x*-axis label, and *y*-axis label. Finally, **show()** displays the figure. The result is shown in Figure 4.8.

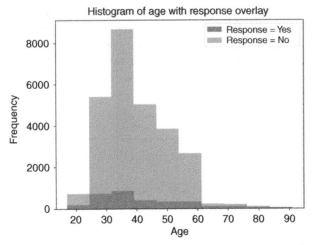

Figure 4.8   Histogram from Python of *age* with *response* overlay.

We will now create a normalized histogram. First, create a stacked histogram, but this time save the information generated by the histogram.

```
(n, bins, patches) = plt.hist([bt_age_y, bt_age_n], bins =
10, stacked = True)
```

The left-hand side of the code saves several pieces of information from the histogram. Specifically, **n** is the height of the histogram bars and **bins** are the boundaries of each bin in the histogram. Note that, since two variables are being plotted in the histogram, **n** has two series of numbers. The first series is for the first variable and the second one is for the second variable. The first number in each series is the height of the first bar for each variable.

To create our normalized histogram, we need to know what proportion of each bin each variable represents. To accomplish this, we need to put the information contained in **n** into a matrix and obtain the column proportions.

To begin construction of the matrix, combine the heights of the two variables' bars into one array using the **column_stack()** command.

```
n_table = np.column_stack((n[0], n[1]))
```

The result, **n_table**, is a two-column matrix where each column's entries hold the heights of each bar.

To calculate what proportion of the bar is accounted for by each variable, we need to divide each row by the sum across that row.

```
n_norm = n_table / n_table.sum(axis=1)[:, None]
```

Now, each row in **n_norm** sums to one and the columns within each row give the proportion of that variable that makes up the row.

In our final preparatory step, we create an array whose rows are the exact cuts of each bin.

```
ourbins = np.column_stack((bins[0:10], bins[1:11]))
```

Each row in **ourbins** gives the upper and lower bounds of each bin. Now, we are ready to create our normalized histogram.

```
p1 = plt.bar(x = ourbins[:,0], height = n_norm[:,0],
width = ourbins[:, 1] - ourbins[:, 0])
p2 = plt.bar(x = ourbins[:,0], height = n_norm[:,1],
width = ourbins[:, 1] - ourbins[:, 0],
        bottom = n_norm[:,0])
plt.legend(['Response = Yes', 'Response = No'])
plt.title('Normalized Histogram of Age with Response
Overlay')
plt.xlabel('Age'); plt.ylabel('Proportion'); plt.show()
```

In the **bar()** commands, the **x** input specifies the upper and lower bounds of the bins, the **height** input uses the normalized count values we created previously to specify the height of each of the two sections of each bar, and the **width** input reuses the bar widths from the original bar chart. The **bottom = n_norm[:,0]** input in the second **bar()** command specifies the second of the two bar sections to start on top of the first. The remaining commands are the same customization options we used in the stacked bar chart previously. The result is shown in Figure 4.9.

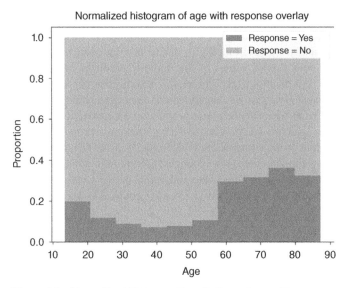

Figure 4.9   Normalized histogram from Python of *age* with *response* overlay.

4.4.2   How to Construct Histograms with Overlay Using R

We begin with the **ggplot()** command, with the data set **bank_train** specified, and the variable **age** specified in the **aes()** command. To make a histogram, we add the **geom_histogram()** command.

```
ggplot(bank_train, aes(age)) + geom_
histogram(color="black")
```

The optional **color = "black"** input creates black lines around each bar of the histogram. The result is a histogram with no overlay.

To add an overlay to the histogram using the target variable, the **aes(fill = response)** input is added to **geom_histogram()**.

```
ggplot(bank_train, aes(age)) + geom_histogram(aes(fill =
response), color="black")
```

The resulting histogram with overlay is shown in Figure 4.6.

To normalize the histogram, the **position = "fill"** input is added to **geom_histogram()**.

```
ggplot(bank_train, aes(age)) +
geom_histogram(aes(fill = response), color="black",
position = "fill")
```

The resulting normalized histogram with overlay is shown in Figure 4.7.

4.5   BINNING BASED ON PREDICTIVE VALUE

Some algorithms work better with categorical rather than numeric variables, so it may be useful for the analyst to use binning to derive new categorical variables based on how the different sets of values of the numeric predictor behave with respect to the response. For example, take Figure 4.7. To optimize our signal from the data, we ask ourselves: *How can we categorize the numerical values of age so that the categories had widely varying response proportions?* Clearly, one category would be the customers aged 60 and up, who have a high response proportion. This is in contrast to the middle group (somewhere in the mid-20s up to 60) which has a low response probability. Finally, there is the youngest group (up to mid-20s) which also has a high response proportion. Thus, we could define our new variable somewhat as follows (the 27 cutoff is a bit arbitrary; 25 or 26 would also work):

$$age\_binned = \begin{cases} 1 : Under\,27 \\ 2 : 27\,to\,60 \\ 3 : 60\,and\,up \end{cases}$$

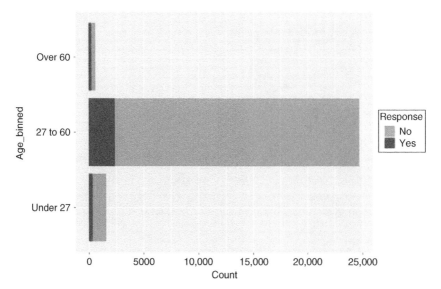

Figure 4.10   Bar graph from R of *age_binned* with *response* overlay.

Figure 4.10 shows the bar graph with overlay for *age_binned*. Figure 4.11 shows the normalized version of the bar graph. Then, Figure 4.12 shows the contingency table of *age_binned* with *response* and Figure 4.13 gives the column percentages of the contingency table. Clearly, both the older and the younger groups have a much higher response rate than the middle group. Unfortunately, over 90% of our customers belong to this middle group.

Here is an important best practice to remember regarding binning.

Best Practice: Binning

- Many software packages provide "automatic" binning methods, such as equal-category-width binning or equal-number-of-records-per-category binning. Though these may have their uses, if you are interested in enhancing the predictive power of your analysis, you should always try to use the binning based on predictive value that we have demonstrated here.

4.5.1 How to Perform Binning Based on Predictive Value Using Python

Load the required package.

```
import pandas as pd
```

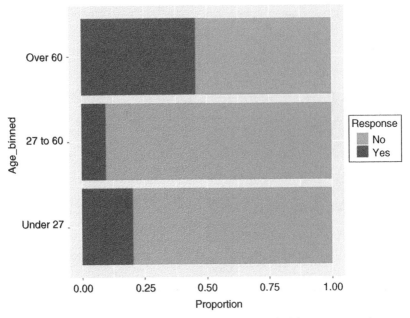

Figure 4.11   Normalized bar graph from R of *age_binned* with *response* overlay.

	Under 27	27 to 60	Over 60	total
no	1255	22315	316	23886
yes	322	2399	267	2988
total	1577	24714	583	26874

Figure 4.12   Contingency table from R of *age_binned* and *response*.

	Under 27	27 to 60	Over 60
no	79.6	90.3	54.2
yes	20.4	9.7	45.8

Figure 4.13   Contingency table from R of *age_binned* and *response* with column percentages.

Bin the values using **cut()** from the **pandas** package.

```
bank_train['age_binned'] = pd.cut(x = bank_train['age'],
bins = [0, 27, 60.01, 100],
     labels=["Under 27", "27 to 60", "Over 60"], right =
False)
```

The **x =** input specifies the variable that you want to divide into categories. The **bins =** input specifies the edges of each bin. The **labels =** input specifies the bin label. The **right = False** input specifies that we want our bins to exclude the right-hand cutpoint. For example, the first bin will include all ages from 0 up to (but

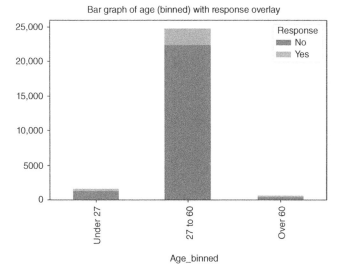

Figure 4.14   Bar graph from Python of *age_binned* with an overlay of *response*.

excluding) 27 years old. We save the new categorical variable in the data set under the name **age_binned** by using **bank_train['age_binned']**.

Note that, while we have mostly intuitive cutpoints for the bins, such as zero for the lower bound of the first bin and 100 for the upper bound of the last bin, we also have a cutpoint of 60.01. Specifying a cutpoint of 60.01 (or any number between but excluding 60 and 61), combined with the input **right = False**, will ensure that our middle category includes all ages from 27 to 60 inclusive. Specifically, we tell Python to make a bin from 27 up to but excluding 60.01. Since ages are integers in this data set, this effectively makes the bin include ages 27–60, inclusive.

To graph the binning with an overlay of response, create the necessary contingency table and plot it, using code similar to code we used earlier. The result-ing graph is shown in Figure 4.14.

```
crosstab_02 = pd.crosstab(bank_train['age_binned'],
bank_train['response'])
crosstab_02.plot(kind='bar', stacked = True,
        title = 'Bar Graph of Age (Binned) with Response
        Overlay')
```

To create a normalized bar graph, follow the same guidelines as discussed previously. The resulting graph is shown in Figure 4.15.

To obtain a contingency table of the response variable and our new categorical variable, use the **crosstab()** command. Remember to use the target variable *response* as the rows of the table. To obtain the table of column proportions, use the **div()** and **sum()** commands on the resulting table. We discussed this code earlier when creating histograms using Python.

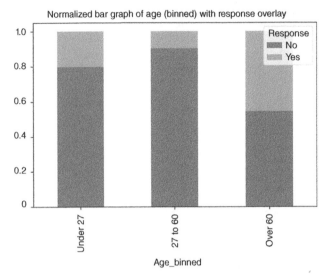

Figure 4.15   Normalized bar graph from Python of *age_binned* with an overlay of *response.*

4.5.2   How to Perform Binning Based on Predictive Value Using R

To create our categorical variable, we will use the **cut()** command on the age variable.

```
bank_train$age_binned <- cut(x = bank_train$age, breaks =
c(0, 27, 60.01, 100),
      right = FALSE, labels = c("Under 27", "27 to 60",
      "Over 60"))
```

The **x** input specifies the variable to be binned. The **breaks** input specifies the cutpoints of each bin. The **right = FALSE** input states that the right-hand cutpoint of each bin should be excluded from the category. The optional **labels** input overrides the default labels of each bin with user-specified labels, which will apply to each bin in order (e.g. "Under 27" for the 0–27 bin). We use the bin value 60.01, instead of 60, and the **right = FALSE** input for the same reasons discussed in the Python section above. We save the result in the **bank_train** data set as **age_binned**.

Once we have our categorical variable, we can plot it with an overlay of **response** using the **ggplot** commands covered previously.

```
ggplot(bank_train, aes(age_binned)) + geom_bar(aes(fill =
response)) + coord_flip()
```

The resulting bar graph with overlay is shown in Figure 4.10. To create a normalized bar graph for these variables, follow the same guidelines as discussed for the previous normalized bar chart. The resulting normalized bar graph is shown in Figure 4.11.

We can construct a contingency table of our categorical variable and the response variable using the **table()** command, and a table of column proportions using the **prop.table()** command. The details of both commands have been discussed previously. The code is given below.

```
t2 <- table(bank_train$response, bank_train$age_bin); t2
round(prop.table(t2, margin = 2)*100, 1)
```

Note how the use of the semicolon in the first line allows both the construction and saving of the table, and the printing of the table, to happen in one line. The resulting tables are shown in Figures 4.12 and 4.13.

Further methods in EDA may be found in *Data Mining and Predictive Analytics.*[1]

REFERENCES

Python's matplotlib package has a wide range of graphical options. To start investigating further, see the publication: John D. Hunter, Matplotlib: a 2D graphics environment, *Computing in Science & Engineering*, 9, 90–95, 2007, doi:https://doi.org/10.1109/MCSE.2007.55

We have just brushed the surface of the *ggplot2* package! For more information, see the following publication: H. Wickham, *ggplot2: Elegant Graphics for Data Analysis*, Springer-Verlag, New York, 2009.

EXERCISES

CLARIFYING THE CONCEPTS

1. When should analysts use exploratory data analysis (EDA) rather than hypothesis testing?

2. What are some examples of what EDA allows the user to do?

3. Which graph do we use to explore the relationship between a categorical predictor and the target variable?

4. What are (non-normalized) bar graphs useful for?

5. State one advantage and one disadvantage of using a normalized bar graph.

6. State the two best practices when working with bar graphs for EDA?

7. What does a contingency table help us to do?

8. Explain the two best practices when working with contingency tables in EDA?

---

[1]By Daniel T. Larose and Chantal D. Larose, John Wiley and Sons, Inc., 2015.

9. What is a histogram?

10. Describe one advantage and one disadvantage of using a normalized histogram.

11. What are the best practices for working with histograms in EDA?

12. Why might it be useful for the analyst to bin a numeric variable?

13. Why do we use the binning method shown in this chapter rather than automatic binning methods?

14. Extrapolate from your answer to the previous question and explain why data scientists should use automatic methods of data analysis very carefully.

WORKING WITH THE DATA

For the following exercises, work with the *bank_marketing_training* data set. Use either Python or R to solve each problem.

15. Create a bar graph of the *previous_outcome* variable, with *response* overlay.

16. Create a normalized bar graph of *previous_outcome* variable with *response* overlay. Describe the relationship between *previous_outcome* and *response*.

17. Create a contingency table of *previous_outcome* and *response*. Compare the contingency table with the non-normalized bar graph and the normalized bar graph.

18. Create a histogram of *age* with *response* overlay.

19. Create a normalized histogram of *age* with *response* overlay. Describe the relationship between *age* and *response*.

20. Bin the *age* variable using the bins specified in this chapter and create a bar chart of the binned age variable with *response* overlay.

HANDS-ON ANALYSIS

For Exercises 21–30, continue working with the *bank_marketing_training* data set. Use either Python or R to solve each problem.

21. Produce the following graphs. What is the strength of each graph? Weakness?

    a. Bar graph of *marital.*

    b. Bar graph of *marital*, with overlay of *response*.

    c. Normalized bar graph of *marital*, with overlay of *response*.

22. Using the graph from Exercise 21c, describe the relationship between *marital* and *response*.

23. Do the following with the variables *marital* and *response*.

    a. Build a contingency table, being careful to have the correct variables representing the rows and columns. Report the counts and the column percentages.

    b. Describe what the contingency table is telling you.

24. Repeat the previous exercise, this time reporting the row percentages. Explain the difference between the interpretation of this table and the previous contingency table.

25. Produce the following graphs. What is the strength of each graph? Weakness?

    a. Histogram of *duration*.

    b. Histogram of *duration*, with overlay of *response*.

    c. Normalized histogram of *duration*, with overlay of *response*.

26. Using the graph from Exercise 25c, describe the relationship between *duration* and *response*.

27. Examine the non-normalized and normalized histograms of *duration*, with overlay of *response*. Identify cutoff point(s) for *duration*, which separate low values of *response* from high values. Define a new categorical variable, *duration_binned*, using the cutoff points you identified.

28. Provide the following. Describe each of the results.

    a. Contingency table of *duration_binned* with *response*, with counts and column percentages.

    b. Non-normalized bar graph of *duration_binned*, with *response* overlay.

    c. Normalized bar graph of *duration_binned*, with *response* overlay.

29. Construct a contingency table of *job* with *response*, with counts and column percentages.

30. Referring to the previous exercise, do the following:

    a. Combine the *job* categories according to the following *response* percentages: $0 < 10$, $10 < 25$, $25 < 33$. Name the new variable *job2*.

    b. Provide a contingency table of *job2* with *response*, with counts and column percentages. Describe what you see.

    c. Provide a normalized histogram of *job2* with *response*. Describe the relationship.

For Exercises 31–36, work with the *cereals* data set. Use either Python or R to solve each problem.

31. Create a bar graph of the *Manuf* variable with *Type* overlay.

32. Create a normalized bar graph of the *Manuf* variable with *Type* overlay.

33. Create a contingency table of *Manuf* and *Type*.

34. Create a histogram of *Calories* with *Manuf* overlay.

35. Create a normalized histogram of *Calories* with *Manuf* overlay.

36. Bin the *Calories* variable using bins for 0–90, 90–110, and over 110 calories. Create a bar chart of the binned calories variable with *Manuf* overlay.

For Exercises 37–60, use the *adult_ch3_training* data set.

For Exercises 37–40 we demonstrate an example of why it is not recommended to delete outliers at the EDA stage, because it results in changing the character of the data set.

37. Consider *capital-loss*. Identify the outliers in *capital-loss* using the Z-score method. How many outliers are there?

38. Construct a bar graph of Income for these outlier records.

39. Construct a bar graph of Income for the *adult_ch3_training* data set as a whole, without omitting the outliers.

40. Compare your bar graphs from the previous two exercises. Describe the difference between the two bar graphs. Describe the change to the character of the data set that will result if we delete these outlier records. State your conclusion regarding deleting outliers at the EDA stage.

41. Derive a flag for *capital-loss*, called *capital-loss-flag*, which equals 0 when *capital-loss* equals 0, and 1 otherwise. Provide a bar graph of *capital-loss-flag*.

42. Repeat the previous exercise for *capital-gain-flag*.

43. Construct a contingency table of *capital-loss-flag* vs *Income*. Include counts and column percentages. Clearly describe the effect of having any capital losses on *Income*.

44. Construct a contingency table of *capital-gain-flag* vs *Income*. Include counts and column percentages. Clearly describe the effect of having any capital gains on *Income*.

45. To prepare for further work, rename *workclass* as *workclass-old*, *marital-status* as *marital-status-old*, and *occupation* as *occupation-old*.

46. Construct a contingency table with *income* for the rows and *workclass-old* for the columns, asking for counts and column percentages.

47. Referring to the contingency table from the previous exercise, do the following:

    a. Provide a one-sentence rationale for why we should combine *never-worked* and *without-pay* into *no-pay*.

    b. Provide a one-sentence rationale for why we may combine *local-gov* and *state-gov* into *state-local-gov*.

48. Perform the changes mentioned in the previous exercise, along with changing "*?*" to "*unknown*." Call the new variable *workclass*. Construct a contingency table with *income* for the rows and *workclass* for the columns, with counts and column percentages. Describe your table using a couple of sentences.

49. Construct a contingency table with *income* for the rows and *marital-status-old* for the columns, asking for counts and column percentages.

50. Referring to the contingency table from the previous sentence, provide two sentences of rationale for why we should combine *Married-AF-spouse* and *Married-civ-spouse* into the new category *Married*, and combine the other statuses into the new category *Other*.

51. Perform the changes mentioned in the previous exercise. Construct a contingency table with *income* for the rows and *marital-status* for the columns, with counts and column percentages. Describe your table using a couple of sentences.

52. Construct a contingency table with *income* for the rows and *occupation-old* for the columns, asking for counts and column percentages.

53. Provide one sentence each for why we should do the following combinations:

a. *Exec-managerial* and *Prof-specialty* into the new category *Exec/prof.*

b. The occupations with income percentages >50k into the new category *Mid-level.*

c. The remaining occupations into the new category *Low-Level.*

d. Fold the *unknown* category into the *Low-Level* category.

54. Perform the changes referred to in the previous exercise. Call the new variable *occupation.* Construct a contingency table with *income* for the rows and *occupation* for the columns, with counts and column percentages. Describe your table using a couple of sentences.

55. Do the following for the *education* variable.

a. Provide a non-normalized and normalized histogram of *education*, with an *income* overlay.

b. Provide a one-sentence description of the relationship and another sentence on your expectation regarding the usefulness of *education* in predicting *income.*

56. Do the following for the *age* variable.

a. Provide a non-normalized and normalized histogram of *age*, with an *income* overlay.

b. Provide a one-sentence description of the relationship.

c. Provide another sentence rationale for the following binning: *age < 30, age 30–60, age > 60.*

57. Execute the binning mentioned in the previous exercise, by deriving a new variable, *age_binned.*

a. Provide a normalized bar graph of *age_binned* with an *income* overlay.

b. Interpret the bar graph using a sentence.

58. Provide the following analysis of the *sex* predictor.

a. A non-normalized bar graph of *sex*, with an overlay of *income.*

b. A normalized bar graph of *sex*, with an overlay of *income.*

c. Interpret the normalized bar graph using a sentence.

59. Construct the following:

a. A non-normalized bar graph of *occupation* with a *sex* overlay.

b. A normalized bar graph of *occupation* with a *sex* overlay. Describe the relationship.

60. Construct a contingency table with *sex* for the rows and *occupation* for the columns, with counts and column percentages. Compare the contingency table with the normalized bar graph.

CHAPTER 5

PREPARING TO MODEL THE DATA

5.1 THE STORY SO FAR

To recapitulate our progress thus far, we are working our way through the Data Science Methodology.

1. In Chapter 3, we discussed the importance of the Problem Understanding Phase.

2. Also in Chapter 3, we dealt with several issues regarding the Data Preparation Phase.

3. In Chapter 4, we covered some important topics in the Exploratory Data Analysis Phase.

4. Now, here in Chapter 5, we are ready to tackle the Setup Phase.

The Setup Phase consists of a number of very important tasks that must be completed before we can begin our data modeling. These include:

- Partitioning the data
- Validating the data partition
- Balancing the data
- Establishing baseline model performance

We cover each of these topics in turn in this chapter.

5.2 PARTITIONING THE DATA

The Data Science Methodology does not use the statistical inference paradigm where generalization is made from a sample to a population. There are two reasons for this.

Data Science Using Python and R, First Edition. Chantal D. Larose and Daniel T. Larose.
© 2019 John Wiley & Sons, Inc. Published 2019 by John Wiley & Sons, Inc.

1. Applying statistical inference to the huge sample sizes encountered in data science tends to result in statistical significance, even when the results are not of practical significance.

2. In the statistical paradigm, the statistician has an a priori hypothesis in mind, whereas the Data Science Methodology requires no such a priori hypothesis, instead freely searching through the data for actionable results.

Because of the lack of a priori hypotheses, data scientists need to beware of *data dredging*, whereby phantom spurious results are uncovered, due merely to random variation rather than real effects. Data science avoids data dredging through the process of *cross-validation*, a technique for ensuring that results are generalizable to an independent, unseen, data set. The most common methods are *twofold cross-validation* and *k-fold cross-validation*. In twofold cross-validation, the data are partitioned, using random assignment, into a *training data set* and a *test data set* (also called the *holdout data set*).

The training set records are complete, but the test set records should have the target variable (temporarily) omitted. So, the data science models learn about the patterns and trends in the data using the training data set. These models are applied to the test set, where they make predictions for the temporarily unknown values of the target variable. These predictions are then evaluated against the (now restored) true target values, using evaluation measures such as overall error rate or mean-squared error. In this way, cross-validation guards against spurious results, since it is highly unlikely that the same random variation would be found in both the training and the test data sets.

The size of the partitions differs depending on the size and complexity of the data set. For highly complex data sets, where, for example, a neural network model needs to learn about many nonlinear relations within the data, more training records would be recommended, say 75–90% of the original data. In addition, if the data set is very large, it is convenient to have more records in the training set. On the other hand, for smaller or less complex data sets, one should retain sufficient records for accurate assessment, so that the training sets would contain only 50–67% of the original data.

5.2.1 How to Partition the Data in Python

Import the following packages:

```
import pandas as pd
from sklearn.model_selection import train_test_split
import random
```

Read in the *bank_additional* data set and name it *bank*.

```
bank = pd.read_csv("C:/.../bank-additional.csv")
```

To partition the data set, we will use the command **train_test_split()**.

```
bank_train, bank_test = train_test_split(bank, test_size =
0.25, random_state = 7)
```

The command creates two data sets, **bank_train** and **bank_test**. While the names of the data sets are arbitrary, the test data set is always the second one created. The first input, **bank**, specifies that we are partitioning the *bank* data set, and the **test_size = 0.25** input states that 25% of the bank data set should be in the test data set, while the remaining 75% should be in the training data set. The **random_state** input sets the seed for the random number generator that will randomly split the data into training and test data sets. The input value itself is arbitrary. The important thing is to specify the seed and use that same number when you want to replicate your results. Setting the random seed will ensure you will get the same answer as before.

To confirm that the data set was partitioned correctly, you can compare the shapes of the original, training, and test data sets using the shape feature.

```
bank.shape
bank_train.shape
bank_test.shape
```

The first numbers given from the **bank_train.shape** and **bank_test.shape** output should sum to the first number of the **bank.shape** output. Additionally, the first number from the **bank_test.shape** output should be about 25% of the first number from the **bank.shape** output.

5.2.2   How to Partition the Data in R

Read in the *bank-additional* data set as *bank*. Next, we need to set the "seed" for the random number generator we will use later on in this section.

```
set.seed(7)
```

The number input to the **set.seed()** command is arbitrary. However, if you want to rerun the code and get the same random results, the seed (whatever it is) must match the seed used in the initial run-through. In our case, the seed is seven, **7**.

To prepare to partition the data, we identify how many records are in the data set

```
n <- dim(bank)[1]
```

The use of the **dim()** command and its additional **[1]** specification are the same as in previous chapters.

Once we have the number of records, **n**, we can determine which records will be in the training data set via a random number generator.

```
train_ind <- runif(n) < 0.75
```

The **runif()** command randomly draws numbers between zero and one, each with equal probability. The input **n** will generate **n** such numbers, one for each record in the data set. The condition **< 0.75** will look at each of the numbers generated by **runif()** and see whether the number is above or below 0.75. If the number is below 0.75, the value *TRUE* is returned, while if the number is above 0.75, the value *FALSE* is returned. You can run **train_ind** by itself to see the series of *TRUE* and *FALSE* values. While the numbers generated by **runif()** will be different each time, on average about 75% will be *TRUE*.

Now that we have a series of *TRUE* and *FALSE* values, we will use them to create the training and test data sets. We use bracket notation to break the *bank* data set into two halves by specifying the rows of interest for each partition. Remember the bracket notation specifies the rows of interest before the comma and the columns of interest after the comma.

```
bank_train <- bank[ train_ind, ]
bank_test <- bank[ !train_ind, ]
```

By running **bank[train_ind,]** we subset only those records of **bank** whose **train_ind** value equals *TRUE*. Since about 75% of the values in **train_ind** equal *TRUE*, about 75% of records from **bank** will be in the **bank_train** data set. For **bank_test** we want those records of **bank** whose **train_ind** value equals *FALSE*. By using **bank[!train_ind,]** we subset only those records of **bank** whose **train_ind** value does not equal *TRUE* (where "not" is signified by the exclamation point, !).

We now have our training and test data sets.

5.3 VALIDATING YOUR PARTITION

Because the legitimacy of the entire Data Science Methodology depends on the validity of the partition, it is important to check that the training data set and the test data set do not differ systematically from each other. We can do this by checking, on a variable-by-variable basis, whether the training and test sets differ. Because there may be many variables in the data set, we restrict ourselves to spot-checking a small set of randomly chosen variables. Depending on the variable types involved, different statistical tests are required.

- For a numerical variable, use the *two-sample t-test for the difference in means*.
- For a categorical variable with two classes, use the *two-sample Z-test for the difference in proportions*.
- For a categorical variable with more than two classes, use the *test for the homogeneity of proportions*.

For details on how to perform these tests, please see our earlier text.[1]

---

[1] *Data Mining and Predictive Analytics*, Second Edition, by Daniel T. Larose and Chantal D. Larose, John Wiley and Sons, Inc., 2015.

5.4   BALANCING THE TRAINING DATA SET

In some classification models, one of the target variable classes has a much lower relative frequency than the other classes. In such cases, balancing the training data set may be recommended. The purpose of balancing is to provide the classification algorithms with a rich selection of records for each category. In this way, the algorithms have a chance to learn about all types of records, not just those with a high frequency. For instance, suppose 1000 of 100,000 credit card transactions are fraudulent. A classification model could achieve 99% accuracy simply by predicting "non-fraudulent" for every transaction. Clearly, this model is useless.

Instead, the analyst should balance the training set so that the proportion of fraudulent transactions is increased. This balancing is achieved through resampling a number of the fraudulent (rare) records.

Resampling is the process of sampling at random and with replacement from a data set. For example, currently our fraudulent records represent 1% of our training set. Suppose we would like to increase this to 25%. Then, we would add 32,000 resampled fraudulent records, so that we had 33,000 fraudulent records in total. The total number of records in the training set would then be 100,000 + 32,000 = 132,000. We would have $\frac{33,000}{132,000} = 0.25 = 25\%$ fraudulent records, as desired.

So, how did we come up with the magic number of 32,000 resampled records? We used the following equation:

$$1000 + x = 0.25 \left(100,000 + x \right)$$

and solved for x, the required number of additional records to resample. In general, this equation is

$$rare + x = p \left(records + x \right)$$

which, solving for x gives us:

$$x = \frac{p \left(records \right) - rare}{1 - p}$$

where x is the required number of resampled records, p is the desired proportion of rare values in the balanced data set, *records* is the number of records in the unbalanced data set, and *rare* represents the current number of rare target values.

The test data set should never be balanced! Remember that the test data set represents holdout data that the models have never seen. Data sets in the real world certainly will not be conveniently rebalanced for the convenience of our classification models, so neither should our test set be rebalanced. Further, all model evaluation will be applied to the test data set, meaning that the models will be evaluated in real-world like data conditions.

5.4.1 How to Balance the Training Data Set in Python

First, we identify how many records in **bank_train** have the less common value, "yes," for *response*, using the **value_counts()** command.

```
bank_train['response'].value_counts()
```

The count of "yes" responses will change depending on the partition. For the partition using the random seed specified in the previous Python code, there are 3089 records in the training data set, with 338 having the "yes" *response* value. Thus, about 12% of the training data set has a "yes" *response* value.

Say, we want to increase the percentage of "yes" responses to 30%. Since we have $p = 0.3$, *records* = 3089, and *rare* = 338, we obtain

$$x = \frac{0.3(3089) - 338}{0.7} = 841$$

That is, we need to resample 841 records whose response is "yes" and add them to our training data set.

To begin resampling, we isolate the records which we want to resample.

```
to_resample = bank_train.loc[bank_train['response'] ==
"yes"]
```

The **loc** command subsets the **bank_train** data based on the condition **bank_train['response'] == "yes"** and saves the resulting data set under the name **to_resample**.

Next, we need to sample from our records of interest

```
our_resample = to_resample.sample(n = 841, replace = True)
```

The **sample()** command draws records at random from **to_resample**, which holds the records we want to resample. The input **n = 841** specifies how many records to draw, while the input **replace = True** specifies to sample with replacement. The output is a data set made up of these 841 randomly resampled records, which we save under the name **our_resample**.

Finally, we add the resampled records to our original training data set.

```
bank_train_rebal = pd.concat([bank_train, our_resample])
```

The **concat()** command attaches two data sets by putting the rows on top of each other. The result is a single data set made up of the records in both **bank_train** and **our_resample**, which is saved as its own data set under the name **bank_train_rebal**.

```
In [44]: bank_train_rebal['response'].value_counts()
Out[44]:
no      2751
yes     1179
Name: response, dtype: int64
```

Figure 5.1   The Python table of *response* values after rebalancing.

To check that the desired percent of "yes" responses was obtained, examine the table of the *response* variable.

```
bank_train_rebal['response'].value_counts()
```

The resulting table is shown in Figure 5.1. There are now 1179 records out of 3930 with a "yes" response, which amounts to about 30%.

5.4.2   How to Balance the Training Data Set in R

First, let us find out how many records in the **bank_train** data set have a response *value* of "yes."

```
table(bank_train$response)
```

The number of "yes" responses will be different for every partition. For the partition based on the random seed used in the previous R code, there are 3103 records in the training data set and 336 of them have "yes" response values. This gives us about 11% of the training data set having "yes" responses.

Let us resample to increase the percentage of "yes" responses to 30%. Since we have $p = 0.3$, *records* = 3103, and *rare* = 336, we obtain

$$x = \frac{0.3(3103) - 336}{0.7} = 850$$

That is, we need to resample 850 records whose *response* is "yes" and add them to our training data set.

First, we identify the record indices we want to resample using the **which()** command.

```
to.resample <- which(bank_train$response == "yes")
```

The **which()** command returns the row numbers which correspond to records that meet the specified condition. In our case, we want the row numbers of those records whose value of *y* is "yes," so our condition is **bank_train$response ==**

"yes". We save the record numbers as **to.resample**, as these are the values we want to resample.

Next, we randomly sample from the values in **to.resample**.

```
our.resample <- sample(x = to.resample, size = 850,
replace = TRUE)
```

The **x = to.resample** input specifies that we want to sample from the series of record indices we created previously. The **size = 850** input specifies how many numbers should be resampled. The **replace = TRUE** input tells the algorithm to sample with replacement. The output is a series of 850 record indices, sampled from our **to.resample** vector.

Now we want to get the records whose record numbers are those in **our. resample**.

```
our.resample <- bank_train[our.resample, ]
```

Use of the bracket notation does the job for us. The number of records in the new data set **our.resample** is 850, which is the number of records we wanted to resample.

Finally, we need to add the resampled records back onto our original training data set.

```
train_bank_rebal <- rbind(bank_train, our.resample)
```

The **rbind()** command stands for "row bind," meaning append two data sets by putting the rows on top of each other. By using **rbind()** on the original training data **bank_train** and the 850 resampled records in **our.resample**, we have created our rebalanced data set, which we name **train_bank_rebal**.

To confirm that the resampling has given the desired amount of rare records, look at the table of *response* values in our rebalanced data set.

```
t.v1 <- table(train_bank_rebal$response)
t.v2 <- rbind(t.v1, round(prop.table(t.v1), 4))
colnames(t.v2) <- c("Response = No", "Response = Yes");
rownames(t.v2) <- c("Count", "Proportion")
t.v2
```

The result is shown in Figure 5.2. The percent of "yes" responses is approximately 30%, which is the percent of rare records we wanted.

	Response = No	Response = Yes
Count	2767.0	1186.0
Proportion	0.7	0.3

Figure 5.2 The R table of *response* values after rebalancing.

5.5   ESTABLISHING BASELINE MODEL PERFORMANCE

Before evaluating model performance, data scientists should first calibrate the results against some baseline model performance. For example, in the fraud scenario above, suppose we developed a complex fraud detection model that reported 98% accuracy. Sounds impressive, until we remember that an "all negative" model that simply classifies all records as non-fraudulent would have a 99% accuracy rate. Without comparison to a baseline, our clients cannot determine whether our results are any good.

We offer the following two baseline models for the binary classification case.

Baseline Models for Binary Classification

Let one of the binary target classes represent *positive* and the other class represent *negative*.
Let p represent the proportion of positive records in the data.

- **All Positive Model.** Assign all predictions as positive.
  - The accuracy of this model will be p.
- **All Negative Model.** Assign all predictions as negative.
  - The accuracy of this model will be $1-p$.

For example, in our fraud scenario, $p = 0.01$ or 1% fraudulent records, where we let fraudulent records represent positive. Then the *All Positive Model* will have accuracy 0.01, and the *All Negative Model* will have accuracy 0.99. *Any model that we develop will need to beat this 99% accuracy*[2] *to be considered useful.*

We may extend this to the k-nary case, $k \geq 3$, as follows:

Baseline Models for k-nary Classification

Let there be k classes for the response variable, $C_1, C_2, ..., C_k$.
Let p_i represent the proportion of class C_i records in the data, $i = 1, ..., k$.

- **Biggest Category Model.** Assign all predictions as belonging to the largest category.
  - The accuracy of this model is p_{max}, the largest p_i.

For example, if your training set has 30% Democrats, 30% Republicans, and 40% Independents, the baseline model assigns all records to Independents, and has an accuracy of 40%.

---

[2] If, indeed, we are using accuracy as our method of choosing the best model. This is often not the case. See Chapter 7.

So, what kind of baseline model should we use for estimation problems? For regression, one could simply compare our estimates against the $y = \bar{y}$ model, where the estimate for each record's response is simply the mean response. But this is truly too low a bar, since almost any regression model will surely beat that. Notice that the baseline $y = \bar{y}$ model completely ignores the wealth of information residing in the predictors. Instead, we could ask a question such as, "What would a subject matter expert consider a mediocre prediction error to be?" For example, if we are a lending company trying to estimate how much our mortgage clients can afford, we might say that we could live with a model that was typically off by $50,000, which would therefore be a mediocre prediction error. Then, when we do build our regression models, we need our values of s, the standard error of the estimate, to be lower than $50,000.[3]

Of course, the optimal benchmark for calibrating any model is to compare it against the current gold standard model performance, as provided by the literature (or proprietary business models). For example, suppose our lending company had done research some years ago in which they achieved a standard error of $25,000. Then, this $s = \$25,000$ is our baseline benchmark against which the models that we build will be compared against.

To summarize, in this chapter we have learned about the Setup Phase of the Data Science Methodology, which includes the following steps:

- Partitioning the data
- Validating the data partition
- Balancing the data
- Establishing baseline model performance

Next time, we can begin the Modeling Phase, as we turn to Chapter 6.

REFERENCES

For the publication at the heart of the *random* package: M. Matsumoto and T. Nishimura, Mersenne twister: a 623-dimensionally equidistributed uniform pseudorandom number generator, *ACM Transactions on Modeling and Computer Simulation*, 8(1), 3–30, January 1998.
We will spend a lot more time with the *sklearn* package! To get more familiar with it, take a look at the following: F. Pedregosa, et al., Scikit-learn: machine learning in Python, *Journal of Machine Learning Research*, 12, 2825–2830, 2011.

EXERCISES

CLARIFYING THE CONCEPTS

1. Which four tasks should be undertaken during the Setup Phase?
2. State two reasons why the Data Science Methodology does not follow the usual statistical inference paradigm.

---

[3] See Chapter 11.

3. Describe what data dredging is and why data scientists need to avoid it.

4. How do data scientists avoid data dredging?

5. Describe the differences between the training data set and the test data set.

6. When validating the partition, does the data scientist need to check every field?

7. When validating a partition, which statistical test is used for a numerical variable?

8. What is balancing? Why is it used?

9. Describe what we mean by resampling.

10. When should the test data set be balanced?

11. Why is it important to establish baseline model performance?

12. Describe the two baseline models for binary classification.

13. True or false: there is no baseline model for k-nary classification.

14. What is the optimal benchmark for calibrating your model performance?

WORKING WITH THE DATA

For Exercises 15–20, work with the *bank_additional* data set. Use either Python or R to solve each problem.

15. Partition the data set, so that 75% of the records are included in the training data set and 25% are included in the test data set. Use a bar graph to confirm your proportions.

16. Identify the total number of records in the training data set and how many records in the training data set have "yes" for a *response* variable value.

17. Use your answers from the previous exercise to calculate how many "yes" response records you need to resample in order to have 20% of the rebalanced data set have "yes" response values.

18. Perform the rebalancing described in the previous exercise and confirm that 20% of the records in the rebalanced data set have a "yes" response value.

19. Should we balance the test data set you created above? Explain why or why not.

20. Which baseline model do we use to compare our classification model performance against? To which value does this baseline model assign all predictions? What is the accuracy of this baseline model?

HANDS-ON ANALYSIS

For Exercises 21–28, work with the *adult* data set.

21. Partition the data set, so that 50% of the records are included in the training data set and 50% are included in the test data set. Use a bar graph to confirm your proportions.

22. Identify the total number of records in the training data set, and how many records in the training data set have an income value of >50 K.

23. Use your answers from the previous exercise to calculate how many records with income >50 K you need to resample in order to have 35% of the rebalanced data set have incomes of >50 K.

24. Perform the rebalancing described in the previous exercise and confirm that 35% of the records in the rebalanced data set have incomes >50 K.

25. Which baseline model do we use to compare our classification model performance against? To which value does this baseline model assign all predictions? What is the accuracy of this baseline model?

26. Validate your partition by performing a two-sample Z-test for the difference in means for the mean *age* in the training set versus the mean *age* in the test set.[4]

27. Validate your partition by performing a two-sample Z-test for the difference in proportions for the proportion of >50 K records in the training set versus the proportion of >50 K records in the test set.

For Exercises 28–34, work with the *churn* data set.

28. Partition the data set, so that 67% of the records are included in the training data set and 33% are included in the test data set. Use a bar graph to confirm your proportions.

29. Identify the total number of records in the training data set and how many records in the training data set have a churn value of true.

30. Use your answers from the previous exercise to calculate how many true churn records you need to resample in order to have 20% of the rebalanced data set have true churn values.

31. Perform the rebalancing described in the previous exercise and confirm that 20% of the records in the rebalanced data set have true churn values.

32. Which baseline model do we use to compare our classification model performance against? To which value does this baseline model assign all predictions? What is the accuracy of this baseline model?

33. Validate your partition by testing for the difference in mean *day minutes* for the training set versus the test set.

34. Validate your partition by testing for the difference in proportion of true churn records for the training set versus the test set.

For Exercise 35, work with the *cereals* data set. Here, we are trying to estimate a numeric target, *rating* (nutritional rating), based on a set of predictors.

35. Which baseline model do we use to compare our estimation model performance against? To which value does this baseline model assign all predictions?

---

[4] Details on how to perform hypothesis tests to validate your partition may be found in *Data Mining and Predictive Analytics*, Second Edition, by Daniel T. Larose and Chantal D. Larose, John Wiley and Sons, Inc., 2015.

CHAPTER 6

DECISION TREES

6.1 INTRODUCTION TO DECISION TREES

Thus far, we have become acquainted with the first four phases of the Data Science Methodology:

1. Data Understanding Phase
2. Data Preparation Phase
3. Exploratory Data Analysis Phase
4. Setup Phase.

We are ready to finally begin modeling our data, in the Modeling Phase. Data science offers a wide variety of methods and algorithms for modeling large data sets. We begin here with one of the simplest methods: decision trees. In this chapter we will work with the *adult_ch6_training* and the *adult_ch6_test* data sets. These are adapted from the *Adult* data set from the UCI repository.[1] For simplicity, only two predictors and the target are retained, as follows:

- *Marital status*, a categorical predictor with classes *married, divorced, never-married, separated*, and *widowed*.

- *Cap_gains_losses*, a numerical predictor, equal to *capital gains* + |*capital losses*|.

- *Income*, a categorical target variable with two classes, >50k and ≤50k, representing individuals whose income is greater than $50,000 per year, and those with income less than or equal to $50,000 per year.

A *decision tree* consists of a set of *decision nodes*, connected by *branches*, extending downward from the *root node* until terminating in *leaf nodes*. Beginning at the root node, which by convention is placed at the top of the decision tree

---

[1]C.L. Blake and C.J. Merz, *UCI Repository of Machine Learning Databases*, Department of Information and Computer Science, University of California, Irvine, CA, 1998 *Adult* data set donated by Ron Kohavi.

Data Science Using Python and R, First Edition. Chantal D. Larose and Daniel T. Larose.
© 2019 John Wiley & Sons, Inc. Published 2019 by John Wiley & Sons, Inc.

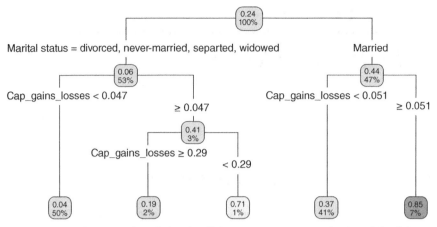

Figure 6.1   Decision tree from R for classifying response outcomes for the *adult_ch6_training* data.

diagram, variables are tested at the decision nodes, with each possible outcome resulting in a branch. Each branch then leads either to another decision node or to a terminating leaf node. Figure 6.1 provides an example of a simple decision tree, using the classification and regression trees (CART)[2] algorithm, as applied to the 18,761 records in the *adult_ch6_training* data set.

One may imagine all the data records entering the decision tree through the root node at the top of the tree, and descending through the tree based on the decisions at each decision node regarding the variable values. The 100% in the root node testifies to this. The root node also tells us that 24% (0.24) of the records in the *adult_ch6_training* data set have high income (>50 K). Thus, each node tells us the proportion of high-income records in the node, along with the percentage of the records reaching that node. At the *root node split*, CART identifies the most efficacious possible binary split as separating the records into two groups, depending on their value for the variable *marital status*, one group whose *marital status* was *married*, and the other group consisting of all the *other* marital statuses: *divorced, never-married, separated, and widowed*. Note that the *married* group contains 44% high income, while the *other* group contains only 6% high income. The married group has a sevenfold higher proportion of high-income records. This striking difference is why this split was chosen as the root node split by the CART algorithm. Note also that the root node split partitions the data nearly in half, with 47% married and 53% not married.

At the *married* node, CART then makes a second split, based on the variable, *Cap_Gains_Losses*. If the (min–max normalized) capital gains and losses exceed 0.051, then 85% of the records have high income. However, this group of records representing married people with high capital gains and losses makes up only 7%

[2]Leo Breiman, Jerome Friedman, Richard Olshen, and Charles Stone, *Classification and Regression Trees*, Chapman & Hall/CRC Press, Boca Raton, FL, 1984.

of the training data set, as shown in the leaf node in the lower right. On the other hand, those who are married but do *not* have high capital gains and losses represent 41% of the data set, but contain only 37% with high income. The two nodes in the lower right are leaf nodes because no further splits are made on them.

Back at the records from the *non-married* marital status node, we see that a split is then made, also based on the normalized capital gains and losses. Individuals who are *non-married* and who do not have high capital gains and losses make up a full 50% of the training data set. Of these, only 4% have high income. Non-married people with high capital gains and losses make up only 3% of the data set, but have a much higher proportion of high income: 41%. A final split is made on these 3% of the records, more finely tuning the level of capital gains and losses, with the higher group at 71% high income and the lower group at 19% high income. Decision trees stop growing when no further splits can be made.

So, how do decision trees work? Decision trees seek to create a set of leaf nodes that are as "pure" as possible, that is, where each of the records in a particular leaf node has the same classification. In this way, the decision tree may provide classification assignments with the highest measure of confidence available. However, how does one measure uniformity, or conversely, how does one measure heterogeneity? We shall examine two of the many methods for measuring leaf node purity, which lead to the two leading algorithms for constructing decision trees:

- CART algorithm
- C5.0 algorithm

6.2   CLASSIFICATION AND REGRESSION TREES

The CART method[3] produces decision trees that are strictly binary, containing exactly two branches for each decision node. CART recursively partitions the records in the training data set into subsets of records with similar values for the target attribute. The CART algorithm grows the tree by conducting for each decision node, an exhaustive search of all available variables and all possible splitting values, selecting the optimal split according to the Gini Index (from Kennedy et al.[4]).

Let $\Phi(s|t)$ be a measure of the "goodness" of a candidate split s at node t, where

$$\Phi(s|t) = 2P_L P_R \sum_{j=1}^{\#\text{classes}} \left| P(j|t_L) - P(j|t_R) \right|$$

[3]Leo Breiman, Jerome Friedman, Richard Olshen, and Charles Stone, *Classification and Regression Trees*, Chapman & Hall/CRC Press, Boca Raton, FL, 1984.

[4]Ruby L. Kennedy, Yuchun Lee, Benjamin Van Roy, Christopher D. Reed, and Richard P. Lippman, *Solving Data Mining Problems through Pattern Recognition*, Pearson Education, Upper Saddle River, NJ, 1995.

and where

$$t_L = \text{left child node of node } t$$

$$t_R = \text{right child node of node } t$$

$$P_L = \frac{\text{number of records at } t_L}{\text{number of records in training set}}$$

$$P_R = \frac{\text{number of records at } t_R}{\text{number of records in training set}}$$

$$P(j \mid t_L) = \frac{\text{number of class } j \text{ records at } t_L}{\text{number of records at } t}$$

$$P(j \mid t_R) = \frac{\text{number of class } j \text{ records at } t_R}{\text{number of records at } t}$$

Then, the optimal split is whichever split maximizes this measure $\Phi(s \mid t)$ over all possible splits at node t. Thus, CART identified the root node split in Figure 6.1 as maximizing $\Phi(s \mid t)$ over all candidate root node splits.

6.2.1 How to Build CART Decision Trees Using Python

Load the required packages and read in the training data set as *adult_tr*.

```
import pandas as pd
import numpy as np
import statsmodels.tools.tools as stattools
from sklearn.tree import DecisionTreeClassifier, export_
graphviz
adult_tr = pd.read_csv("C:/.../adult_ch6_training")
```

For simplicity, we save the *Income* variable as **y.**

```
y = adult_tr[['Income']]
```

We have a categorical variable, *Marital status*, among our predictors. The CART model implemented in the *sklearn* package needs categorical variables converted to a dummy variable form. Thus, we will make a series of dummy variables for *Marital status* using the **categorical()** command.

```
mar_np = np.array(adult_tr['Marital status'])
(mar_cat, mar_cat_dict) = stattools.categorical(mar_np,
drop=True, dictnames = True)
```

We turn the variable *Marital status* into an array using **array()**, then use **categorical()** command from the *stattools* package to create a matrix of dummy variables for each value of Marital status. We save the matrix and dictionary separately using **(mar_cat, mar_cat_dict)**.

The matrix **mar_cat** contains five columns, one for each category in the original *Marital status* variable. Each row represents a record in the **adult_tr** data set. Each row will have a 1 in the column which matches the value that record had in the original *Marital status* variable. You can tell which column represents which category by examining **mar_cat_dict**. In our case, the first row of **mar_cat** has a 1 in the third column. By examining **mar_cat_dict**, we know the third column represents the "Never married" category. Sure enough, the first record of **adult_tr** has "Never married" as the *Marital status* variable value.

Now, we need to add the newly made dummy variables back into the X variables.

```
mar_cat_pd = pd.DataFrame(mar_cat)
X = pd.concat((adult_tr[['Cap_Gains_Losses']], mar_cat_
pd), axis = 1)
```

We first make the **mar_cat** matrix a data frame using the **DataFrame()** command. We then use the **concat()** command to attach the predictor variable **Cap_Gains_Losses** to the data frame of dummy variables that represent marital status. We save the result as **X**.

Before we run the CART algorithm, note that the columns of **X** do not include the different values of the *Marital status* variable. Run **mar_cat_dict** to see that the first column is for the value "Divorced," the second for "Married," and so on. Since the first column of **X** is **Cap_Gains_Losses**, we can specify the names of each column of **X**.

```
X_names = ["Cap_Gains_Losses", "Divorced", "Married",
"Never-married",
    "Separated", "Widowed"]
```

It will help us when visualizing the CART model to know the levels of **y** as well.

```
y_names = ["<=50K", ">50K"]
```

Now, we are ready to run the CART algorithm!

```
cart01 = DecisionTreeClassifier(criterion = "gini", max_
leaf_nodes=5).fit(X,y)
```

To run the CART algorithm, we use the **DecisionTreeClassifier()** command. The **DecisionTreeClassifier()** command sets up the various parameters for the decision tree. For example, the **criterion = "gini"** input specifies that we are using a CART model which utilizes the Gini criterion, and the **max_leaf_nodes** input trims the CART tree to have at most the specified number of leaf nodes. For this example, we have limited our tree to five leaf nodes.

The **fit()** command tells Python to fit the decision tree that was previously specified to the data. The predictor variables are given first, followed by the target variable. Thus, the two inputs to **fit()** are the **X** and **y** objects we created. We save the decision tree as **cart01**.

Finally, to obtain the tree structure, we use the **export_graphviz()** command.

```
export_graphviz(cart01, out_file = "C:/.../cart01.dot",
feature_names=X_names, class_names=y_names)
```

The first input is the decision tree itself, which we saved as **cart01**. The **out_file** input will save the tree structure to the specified location and name the file *cart01.dot*. Run the contents of the file through the *graphviz* package to display the CART model. Specifying **feature_names = X_names** and **class_names = y_names** add the predictor variable names and the target variable values to the cart01. dot file, greatly increasing its readability.

To obtain the classifications of the *Income* variable for every variable in the training data set, use the **predict()** command.

```
predIncomeCART = cart01.predict(X)
```

Using the **predict()** command on **cart01** says that we want to use our CART model to make the classifications. Including the predictor variables **X** as input specifies that we want predictions for those records in particular. The result is the classification, according to our CART model, for every record in the training data set. We save the predictions as **predIncomeCART**.

6.2.2 How to Build CART Decision Trees Using R

Import the training data set and name it *adult_tr*. Once the data set is loaded into R, rename "Marital status" to "maritalStatus" to remove the space. This change will help our code later.

```
colnames(adult_tr)[1] <- "maritalStatus"
```

The **colnames()** command lists the names of each of the variables in the **adult_tr** data set. Run on its own, it will output the column names in order. Note that the first column contains the *Marital status* variable. Using the **[1]** at the end of **colnames(adult_tr)** isolates the variable name for *Marital status*. We then rename the variable by creating the string **"maritalStatus"** and saving it as the variable's name.

We then change both the categorical variables to factors.

```
adult_tr$Income <- factor(adult_tr$Income)
adult_tr$maritalStatus <- factor(adult_tr$maritalStatus)
```

To run and visualize the CART model, we need to install and open the required packages, **rpart** and **rpart.plot**.

```
install.packages(c("rpart", "rpart.plot"))
library(rpart); library(rpart.plot)
```

Finally, let us run the **rpart()** command to build the CART model.

```
cart01 <- rpart(formula = Income ~ maritalStatus + Cap_
Gains_Losses,
        data = adult_tr, method = "class")
```

The **formula** input has the structure *Target ~ Predictors*, where the names of the predictors are separated by plus signs. The **data** input specifies which data set the variables are coming from. The **method = "class"** input specifies that we want to use a classification (CART) model. Finally, we save the resulting model as **cart01**.

Once the CART model is built, we can plot the CART model with the default display options using the **rpart.plot** command.

```
rpart.plot(cart01)
```

The **rpart.plot()** command takes as its only required input the name under which you saved the CART model. Since we called our model **cart01**, that is our input.

Note that the plot built using the default settings of **rpart.plot()** do not replicate Figure 6.1. What other settings are there?

```
?rpart.plot
```

Run **?rpart.plot** to look at the different display options, located under the *type* and *extra* arguments. Try using **type = 4** to label each branch with its specific value, instead of a yes/no at the top of the split; and **extra = 2** to add the correct classification proportion to each node.

```
rpart.plot(cart01, type = 4, extra = 2)
```

The result is shown in Figure 6.1.

To obtain classifications for each record in the data set using the CART model, you first need to create a data frame that includes the predictor variables of the records you wish to classify.

```
X = data.frame(maritalStatus = adult_tr$maritalStatus,
Cap_Gains_Losses =
        adult_tr$Cap_Gains_Losses)
```

The data frame **X** contains the two predictor variables that were used to build the CART model. It is vitally important that the variable names in this new data frame exactly match the variable names used to build the CART model.

Once you have the predictor variables you wish to classify, use the **predict()** command.

```
predIncomeCART = predict(object = cart01, newdata = X,
type = "class")
```

The input **object = cart01** states that the classifications are made using the CART model you saved as **cart01**. The **newdata = X** sends the data in the data frame **X** down the CART model to arrive at a leaf node and classification. The **type = "class"** input specifies that we want the classification itself as the output. We save the predictions as **predIncomeCART**.

6.3 THE C5.0 ALGORITHM FOR BUILDING DECISION TREES

The C5.0 algorithm is J. Ross Quinlan's extension of his own C4.5 algorithm for generating decision trees.[5] Unlike CART, the C5.0 algorithm is not restricted to binary splits. The 5.0 algorithm uses the concept of *information gain* or *entropy reduction* to select the optimal split. Suppose that we have a variable X whose k possible values have probabilities $p_1, p_2, \ldots, p_k$. The smallest number of bits, on average per symbol, needed to transmit a stream of symbols representing the values of X observed is called the *entropy of X*, defined as

$$H(X) = -\sum_j p_j \log_2 (p_j)$$

C5.0 uses entropy as follows. Suppose that we have a candidate split S, which partitions the training data set T into several subsets, $T_1, T_2, \ldots, T_k$. The mean information requirement can then be calculated as the weighted sum of the entropies for the individual subsets, as follows:

$$H_S(T) = -\sum_{i=1}^{k} p_i H_S(T_i)$$

where P_i represents the proportion of records in subset i. We may then define our *information gain* to be gain$(S) = H(T) - H_S(T)$, that is, the increase in information produced by partitioning the training data T according to this candidate split S. At each decision node, C5.0 chooses the optimal split to be the split that has the greatest information gain, gain(S).

Figure 6.2 shows the C5.0 decision tree output from R for the *adult_ch6_training* data set. The root node split (Node 1) is on whether or not Cap_Gains_ Losses (CGL) exceeds 0.05. If it does not, then the branch immediately terminates in a leaf node (Node 2) with a majority of records having low income. Note that Node 2 contains 17,007 records, *representing 90.7% over the data set*. The remainder of the decision tree, Nodes 3–11, are together working with only 9.3% of the data set.

---

[5] J. Ross Quinlan, *C4.5: Programs for Machine Learning*, Morgan Kaufmann, San Francisco, CA, 1992.

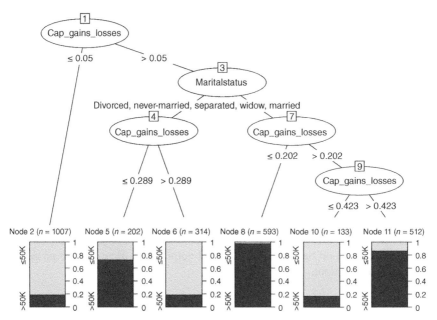

Figure 6.2   C5.0 decision tree output from R.

If CGL does exceed 0.05, then the next decision node (Node 3) is on Marital Status. If married, then the tree branches to Node 7. If some other marital status, the tree branches to Node 4, which then tests CGLs again, this time whether it exceeds 0.289. Counterintuitively, the group with CGL > 0.289 has a lower proportion of high income in its Node 6, than in the lower CGL group in Node 5. Node 7 receives the married individuals with CGL > 0.05. It then splits on whether CGL > 0.202. If not, then the leaf node (Node 8) has almost all high income. If CGL > 0.202, one final split in Node 9 tests whether CGL > 0.423. If so, the 512 records are predominantly high income, otherwise not.

There are some interesting differences between the decision trees built by CART and C5.0. In contrast with the C5.0 tree which shunted over 90% of the records to a single node, the CART tree's root node split (Figure 6.1) on marital status led to a rather balanced split, probably due to the nature of the Gini Index, which contains the $P_L P_R$ coefficient, favoring balanced branches.

6.3.1   How to Build C5.0 Decision Trees Using Python

Python packages do not directly implement C5.0. Instead, we will again use the *sklearn* package, this time changing the splitting criterion from Gini to entropy.

Before running the code in this section, run the code in the previous Python section, up to but excluding the paragraph that begins "Now we are ready to run the CART algorithm!" The code contained there will set up our variables and variable names in preparation for running this decision tree.

To obtain the decision tree using entropy as a splitting criterion, we again use the **DecisionTreeClassifier()** command.

```
c50_01 = DecisionTreeClassifier(criterion="entropy",
max_leaf_nodes=5).fit(X,y)
```

The input **criterion = "entropy"** uses information gain to identify the best candidate split.

To export the summary of the C5.0 tree, run the **export_graphviz()** command. The code is given below, with its explanation in the previous Python section.

```
export_graphviz(c50_01, out_file = "C:/.../c50_01.dot",
feature_names=X_names,
        class_names=y_names)
```

To obtain the classifications of each record in the training data set, run the predict() command on the name of the saved output, c50_01, using the predictor variables X as the input.

```
c50_01.predict(X)
```

The result is a classification for each record in the training data set.

6.3.2 How to Build C5.0 Decision Trees Using R

If you did not change the *Martial Status* variable name, or convert the categorical variables to factors, do so now by following the relevant steps in the previous R section. Then, install and load the package necessary to run C5.0.

```
install.packages("C50"); library(C50)
```

Run the algorithm, using the **C5.0()** command.

```
C5 <- C5.0(formula = Income ~ maritalStatus + Cap_Gains_
Losses, data = adult_tr,
        control = C5.0Control(minCases=75))
```

The core input value is **formula** input, which is identical to its CART counterpart. As before, the target variable is to the left of the tilde, and the predictor variables to the right, separated by plus signs. The **data = adult_tr** input specifies that we are drawing our variables from the **adult_tr** data set. The **control = C5.0Control(minCases = 75))** input requires the leaf nodes in the decision tree to have at least 75 records. We save the resulting tree as **C5**.

We can visualize the tree using the **plot()** command.

```
plot(C5)
```

The output from **plot(C5)** is shown in Figure 6.2.

To obtain classifications for each record in the data set, create the X data frame as in the previous R section and run the **predict()** command.

```
predict(object = C5, newdata = X)
```

Set **object = C5** to use the C5.0 tree you built in this section. Retain the **newdata = X** input, as in the previous R section. The result is a classification of the *Income* variable for each record in the training data set.

6.4   RANDOM FORESTS

CART and C5.0 both produce a single decision tree based on all of the records, and the specified variables, in the training data set. There is, however, a method that uses multiple trees, where the output of each tree is considered when determining the final classification of each record.

Random forests[6] build a series of decision trees and combine the trees disparate classifications of each record into one final classification. Random forests are an example of an *ensemble method*. Ensemble methods are a category of modeling techniques that take multiple models' output into account in order to arrive at a single answer. Different ensemble methods take the models' output into consideration in different ways. For more about ensemble methods, please see our earlier text.[7]

The random forests algorithm begins building each decision tree by taking a random sample, with replacement, from the original training data set. In this way, each tree will have a different data set on which to be built. For each node of the decision tree, a subset of the predictor variables is selected for consideration. It is possible, in this way, that the variable which would have given the "best" split (according to, for example, the Gini criterion) will not be available for consideration. The decision tree is completed in this way, with no restrictions on how large the tree may get.

Once the different trees are built, they are used to classify the records in the original training data set. Every record in the data set is given a classification by every tree. Since these classifications are highly unlikely to be unanimous for all records, each classification is considered a "vote" for that particular target variable value. The value with the largest number of votes is deemed the final classification of the record.

---

[6]Leo Breiman, Random forests, *Machine Learning*, 45, 5–32, 2001.

[7]*Data Mining and Predictive Analytics*, Second Edition, by Daniel T. Larose and Chantal D. Larose, John Wiley and Sons, Inc., 2015.

6.4.1 How to Build Random Forests in Python

As before, run the code in the CART Python section, up to but excluding the code in the paragraph that begins "Now we are ready to run the CART algorithm!" You will need to run the code to set up the predictor and target variables for the code in this section.

Next, load the required libraries.

```
from sklearn.ensemble import RandomForestClassifier
import numpy as np
```

The random forest command in Python requires a response variable formatted as a one-dimensional array, so we use numpy's **ravel()** command to create that format.

```
rfy = np.ravel(y)
```

We use the **RandomForestClassifier()** command to create the random forest.

```
rf01 = RandomForestClassifier(n_estimators = 100,
criterion="gini").fit(X,rfy)
```

As before, the **RandomForestClassifier()** command sets up the parameters of the algorithm. The **n_estimators** input specifies the number of trees to be built, while the **criterion = "gini"** specifies the Gini Index be used to determine the best splits. The **fit()** command uses the predictor variables **X** and target variable **y** to build the actual decision trees. Save the result as **rf01**.

To view the classifications made on the training data set by the random forests algorithm, use the **predict()** command.

```
rf01.predict(X)
```

The result is a series of classifications, one for each record in the data set.

6.4.2 How to Build Random Forests in R

If you did not change the *Martial Status* variable name, or convert the categorical variables to factors, do so now by following the relevant steps in the previous R section. Load the data.

Install and open the **randomForest** package.

```
install.packages("randomForest"); library(randomForest)
```

Now, we run the random forests algorithm, using the same **formula** input as before.

```
rf01 <- randomForest(formula = Income ~ maritalStatus +
Cap_Gains_Losses,
```

```
        data = adult_tr, ntree = 100, type =
"classification")
```

The command to build the random forests is **randomForest()**, and the first input, **formula**, is identical to the CART and C5.0 formulas in previous R sections. The **data** input specifies where the variables in **formula** come from. The **ntree** input tells the algorithm how many trees to make. For our relatively small data set, we use 100 trees. The final input, **type = "classification,"** specifies that we are classifying our data. We save the output as **rf01**.

To view the classifications made by the algorithm, look at the **predicted** values saved under **rf01**.

```
rf01$predicted
```

The result is a classification for each record in the data set.

REFERENCES

To examine the details of the *C50* package, take a look at the documentation: Max Kuhn and Ross Quinlan, C50: C5.0 Decision Trees and Rule-Based Models. R package version 0.1.2, 2018. https://CRAN.R-project.org/package=C50.

If you want to explore the entire randomForest package, start with the core publication: A. Liaw and M. Wiener, Classification and regression by randomForest, *R News*, 2(3), 18–22, 2002.

We showed some of the options the rpart.plot package has to represent the CART models. You can find the full documentation for the package here: Stephen Milborrow, rpart.plot: Plot "rpart" Models: An Enhanced Version of "plot.rpart." R package version 2.2.0, 2018. https://CRAN.R-project.org/package=rpart.plot.

Check out the proceedings that detailed the statsmodels package for Python: Skipper Seabold and Josef Perktold, "Statsmodels: Econometric and statistical modeling with python." In Proceedings of the 9th Python in Science Conference, 2010.

The package for CART models in R: Terry Therneau and Beth Atkinson, rpart: Recursive Partitioning and Regression Trees. R package version 4.1-13, 2018. https://CRAN.R-project.org/package=rpart.

EXERCISES

CLARIFYING THE CONCEPTS

1. What is a decision tree?

2. What is the difference between a decision node and a leaf node?

3. In a decision tree, where is the most powerful of all possible splits made?

4. When do decision trees stop growing?

5. How do decision trees work?

6. Would CART be a good algorithm to use if we are interested in a trinary categorical predictor?

7. Which criterion is used by CART to assess which split is optimal?

8. Which concept does the C5.0 algorithm use to select the optimal split?

9. What are random forests?

10. How do random forests work?

11. Are all the predictor variables candidates to be the "best" split for each node in a tree built by random forests?

12. Are the data sets used to build each tree in random forests the same?

13. How does the random forests algorithm give the training data set its final classification?

WORKING WITH THE DATA

For Exercises 14–20, work with the *adult_ch6_training* and *adult_ch6_test* data sets. Use either Python or R to solve each problem.

14. Create a CART model using the training data set that predicts income using marital status and capital gains and losses. Visualize the decision tree (that is, provide the decision tree output). Describe the first few splits in the decision tree.

15. Develop a CART model using the test data set that utilizes the same target and predictor variables. Visualize the decision tree. Compare the decision trees. Does the test data result match the training data result?

16. Use the training data set to build a C5.0 model to predict income using marital status and capital gains and losses. Specify a minimum of 75 cases per terminal node. Visualize the decision tree. Describe the first few splits in the decision tree.

17. How does your C5.0 model compare to the CART model? Describe the similarities and differences.

18. Construct a C5.0 model using the test data set that utilizes the same target variable, predictor variables, and minimum cases criterion. Visualize the decision tree. Does the test data result match the training data result?

19. Use random forests on the training data set to predict income using marital status and capital gains and losses.

20. Use random forests using the test data set that utilizes the same target and predictor variables. Does the test data result match the training data result?

HANDS-ON ANALYSIS

For Exercises 21–27, work with the *loans_training* and *loans_test* data sets. Use either Python or R to solve each problem.

21. Create a CART model using the training data set that predicts Approval using Debt to Income Ratio, FICO Score, and Request Amount. Visualize the decision tree. Describe the first few splits in the decision tree.

22. Develop a CART model using the test data set that uses the same target and predictor variables. Visualize the decision tree. Investigate the splits in the decision tree. Does the tree built using the test data match the tree built using the training data?

23. Build a C5.0 model using the training data set that predicts Approval using Debt to Income Ratio, FICO Score, and Request Amount. Specify a minimum of 1000 cases per terminal node. Visualize the decision tree. Describe the first few splits in the decision tree.

24. How does your C5.0 model compare to your CART model for the *loans_training* data? Describe the similarities and differences.

25. Create a C5.0 model using the test data set that utilizes the same target variable, predictor variables, and minimum cases criterion. Visualize the decision tree. Does the tree built using the test data match the tree built using the training data?

26. Use random forests on the training data set to obtain the predicted value of Approval using the same predictor variables as in the CART and C5.0 models.

27. Use random forests on the test data set to obtain the predicted value of Approval in the test data set. Build a table comparing the predictions from the training and test data sets. How do they compare?

For Exercises 28–34, work with the *bank_marketing_training* and *bank_marketing_test* data sets. Use either Python or R to solve each problem.

28. Create a CART model using the training data set that predicts Response using whatever predictors you think appropriate. Visualize the decision tree. Describe the first few splits in the decision tree.

29. Develop a CART model using the test data set and the same target and predictor variables. Visualize the decision tree. Investigate the splits in the decision tree. Does the tree built using the test data match the tree built using the training data?

30. Build a C5.0 model using the training data set that predicts Response and the same target and predictor variables. Specify a minimum of 1000 cases per terminal node. Visualize the decision tree. Describe the first few splits in the decision tree.

31. How does your C5.0 model compare to your CART model for the *bank_marketing_training* data? Describe the similarities and differences.

32. Create a C5.0 model using the test data set that utilizes the same target variable, predictor variables, and minimum cases criterion. Visualize the decision tree. Does the tree built using the test data match the tree built using the training data?

33. Use random forests on the training data set to obtain the predicted value of Response using the same predictor variables as in the CART and C5.0 models.

34. Use random forests on the test data set to obtain the predicted value of Response in the test data set. Build a table comparing the predictions from the training and test data sets. How do they compare?

For Exercises 35–41, work with the training and test data sets that you obtained by partitioning the *Churn* data set in the Chapter 5 Exercises. Use either Python or R to solve each problem.

35. Create a CART model using the training data set that predicts Churn using whatever predictors you think appropriate. Visualize the decision tree. Describe the first few splits in the decision tree.

36. Develop a CART model using the test data set and the same target and predictor variables. Visualize the decision tree. Investigate the splits in the decision tree. Does the tree built using the test data match the tree built using the training data?

37. Build a C5.0 model using the training data set that predicts Churn and the same target and predictor variables. Specify a minimum of 1000 cases per terminal node. Visualize the decision tree. Describe the first few splits in the decision tree.

38. How does your C5.0 model compare to your CART model for the *churn_training* data? Describe the similarities and differences.

39. Create a C5.0 model using the test data set that utilizes the same target variable, predictor variables, and minimum cases criterion. Visualize the decision tree. Does the tree built using the test data match the tree built using the training data?

40. Use random forests on the training data set to obtain the predicted value of Churn using the same predictor variables as in the CART and C5.0 models.

41. Use random forests on the test data set to obtain the predicted value of Churn in the test data set. Build a table comparing the predictions from the training and test data sets. How do they compare?

CHAPTER 7

MODEL EVALUATION

7.1 INTRODUCTION TO MODEL EVALUATION

So far in *Data Science Using Python and R*, we have covered the first five phases of the Data Science Methodology:

1. Data Understanding Phase
2. Data Preparation Phase
3. Exploratory Data Analysis Phase
4. Setup Phase
5. Modeling Phase (at least a little bit)

But, so far we have not examined whether our models are any good. That is, we have not evaluated their usefulness in making predictions. Note the difference between evaluation and validation. Model validation simply makes sure that our model results are consistent between the training and test data sets. But, model validation does not tell us how accurate our models are, or what their error rate is. For measures like these, we need to turn to model evaluation. Since the only models we have learned so far are decision trees for classification, we shall restrict our discussion to evaluative measures for classification models.

7.2 CLASSIFICATION EVALUATION MEASURES

We will develop classification evaluation measures for the case where we have a binary target variable. In order to apply the measures we will learn in this chapter, we will need to denote (arbitrarily, if desired) one of the two target outcomes as positive and one as negative. For example, suppose we are trying to predict *income*,

Data Science Using Python and R, First Edition. Chantal D. Larose and Daniel T. Larose.

TABLE 7.1 General form of contingency table for binary classifications

		Predicted Category		
		0	**1**	**Total**
Actual category	**0**	True negatives: Predicted 0 Actually 0	False positives: Predicted 1 Actually 0	**Total actually negative**
	1	False negatives: Predicted 0 Actually 1	True positives: Predicted 1 Actually 1	**Total actually positive**
	Total	**Total Predicted negative**	**Total Predicted positive**	**Grand total**

a binary variable with values *high income* and *low income*. We could denote *high income* as positive and *low income* as negative.[1]

Now, the classification model evaluation measures we will learn in this chapter are functions of the entries in the *contingency table*[2] generated by the classification model, the general form of which is shown in Table 7.1. Note that, by convention, the actual values are represented by the rows, while the predicted values are represented by the columns. The upper-left cell in Table 7.1 represents the number of records where the model predicted a negative response and the actual response value was indeed negative, making this prediction a *true negative*. The cell below that represents the number of records where the model predicted a negative response, but the actual response value was positive, making this prediction a *false negative*. The other cells are similarly defined.

Let *TN*, *FN*, *FP*, and *TP* represent the numbers of true negatives, false negatives, false positives, and true positives, respectively, in our contingency table. Also, let

$$TAN = Total\ Actually\ Negative = TN + FP$$

$$TAP = Total\ Actually\ Positive = FN + TP$$

$$TPN = Total\ Predicted\ Negative = TN + FN$$

$$TPN = Total\ Predicted\ Positive = FP + TP$$

Further, let $GT = TN + FN + FP + TP$ represent the grand total of the counts in the four cells. Then, we may reexpress Table 7.1 as Table 7.2.

Then, using the notation in Table 7.2, we define our set of classification evaluation measures.

$$Accuracy = \frac{TN + TP}{TN + FN + FP + TP} = \frac{TN + TP}{GT}$$

[1] There is no positive or negative connotation to these labels. They simply allow us to apply these measures for any binary classification problem.

[2] Also referred to as the *confusion matrix* or the *error matrix*.

TABLE 7.2 General form of contingency table, reexpressed

		Predicted Category		
		0	**1**	**Total**
	0	*TN*	*FP*	**TAN**
Actual category	**1**	*FN*	*TP*	**TAP**
	Total	**TPN**	**TPP**	**GT**

$$Error\ Rate = 1 - Accuracy = \frac{FN + FP}{TN + FN + FP + TP} = \frac{FN + FP}{GT}$$

Accuracy represents an overall measure of the proportion of correct classifications being made by the model, while error rate measures the proportion of incorrect classifications, across all cells in the contingency table. However, these measures do not distinguish between the various types of errors or the various types of correct decisions. We begin to do so using sensitivity and specificity, as follows.

7.3   SENSITIVITY AND SPECIFICITY

$$Sensitivity = \frac{Number\ of\ true\ positives}{Total\ actually\ positive} = \frac{TP}{TAP} = \frac{TP}{TP + FN}$$

$$Specificity = \frac{Number\ of\ true\ negatives}{Total\ actually\ negative} = \frac{TN}{TAN} = \frac{TN}{FP + TN}$$

Sensitivity measures the ability of the model to classify a record positively, while specificity measures the ability to classify a record negatively. Sensitivity measures what proportion of all positive records are captured by your model, while specificity measures what proportion of all the negative records are captured by your model. Of course, a perfect classification model would have sensitivity = 1.0 = 100%. However, a model which simply classified all customers as positive would also have sensitivity = 1.0. Clearly, it is not sufficient to identify the positive responses alone. A classification model also needs to be *specific*, meaning that it should identify a high proportion of the customers who are negative. Of course, a perfect classification model would have specificity = 1.0. But, so would a model which classifies all customers as negative. A good classification model should have acceptable levels of both sensitivity and specificity, but what constitutes acceptable varies greatly from domain to domain.

7.4   PRECISION, RECALL, AND F_β SCORES

Of the records classified by our model as positive, what proportion are true positives? The metric addressing this question is called *precision*, and is defined as follows:

$$Precision = \frac{TP}{TPP}$$

In the field of information retrieval (e.g. search engines) the precision metric answers the question, "What proportion of the selected items is relevant?" This metric is often paired with *recall*, which is just another name for *sensitivity*.

$$Recall = Specificity = \frac{TN}{TAN}$$

It would be useful to combine precision and recall into a single measure. To do so, we may use F_β scores, defined as follows:

$$F_\beta = \left(1 + \beta^2\right) \cdot \frac{precision \cdot recall}{\left(\beta^2 \cdot precision\right) + recall}$$

for $\beta > 0$.

- When $\beta = 1$, this is called the *harmonic mean* of precision and recall, which are thus equally weighted in the metric F_1.
- When $\beta > 1$, F_β weights recall higher than precision.
- When $\beta < 1$, F_β weights recall lower than precision.
- Thus, F_2 would weight recall twice as high as precision, while $F_{0.5}$ would weight recall half as much as precision.

7.5 METHOD FOR MODEL EVALUATION

The general Method for Model Evaluation is given as follows. This applies to any classification or estimation model.

Method for Model Evaluation

1. Develop the model using the training data set.
2. Evaluate the model using the test data set. That is, take the model developed using the training data set and apply it to the test data set. Put another way, pass the test set through the model generated by the training set.

7.6 AN APPLICATION OF MODEL EVALUATION

We will be working with the *clothing_data_driven_training* and *clothing_data_driven_test* data sets. The task is to predict whether or not customers will respond to a phone/mail marketing campaign, based on three continuous predictors:

- *Days since Purchase*
- *# of Purchase Visits*
- *Sales per Visit*

The target variable is a flag, *Response*, coded 1 for positive response and 0 for negative.

We develop a C5.0 model for classifying response using the *clothing_data_ driven_training* data set. Call this Model 1. We will use the *clothing_data_driven_ test* data set to evaluate Model 1. This is performed as follows:

Method for Evaluating Model 1

1. Obtain the predicted values for *Response*, generated by Model 1 on the training data set.
2. Apply Model 1 to the test data set and compare the predicted *Response* values from Step 1 to the actual *Response* values from test data set.

When we compare the predicted *Response* values from Model 1 to the actual *Response* values from the *clothing_data_driven_test* data set, we obtain the contingency table in Table 7.3.

Note that $TAN = 9,614$, $TAP = 1,940$, and $GT = 11,554$ would be true across any model, because these are actual values, not predictions. The remaining numbers vary across different models, depending on the predictions. The results of our eight evaluation measures are shown in Table 7.4.

Model 1 has an accuracy of 0.8410 or 84.10%. Is this any good? Well, recall from Chapter 5 that we should always calibrate our results against the baseline performance. In this case, there are $TAN = 9614$ negative records, out of a total of $GT = 11,554$ records, so that the baseline *All Negative Model*, which assigns all predictions as negative, would have accuracy of

$$Accuracy_{All\,Negative\,Model} = \frac{9614}{11,554} = 0.8321$$

So, indeed Model 1 does manage, barely, to edge out the accuracy of the baseline All Negative Model. (Surely, we can do better? See below.)

Model 1's specificity of 0.9541 is brilliant, meaning that the model managed to correctly classify

$$\frac{TN}{TAN} = \frac{9173}{9614} = 95.41\%$$

TABLE 7.3   Contingency table for evaluating Model 1

		Predicted Category		
		0	**1**	**Total**
	0	$TN = 9173$	$FP = 441$	**TAN = 9614**
Actual category	**1**	$FN = 1396$	$TP = 544$	**TAP = 1940**
	Total	**TPN = 10,569**	**TPP = 985**	**GT = 11,554**

TABLE 7.4   Evaluation measures of the R C5.0 model

Evaluation Measure	Formula	Value
Accuracy	$\dfrac{TN+TP}{GT}=\dfrac{9173+544}{11{,}554}$	0.8410
Error rate	$1-Accuracy$	0.1590
Sensitivity	$\dfrac{TP}{TAP}=\dfrac{544}{1940}$	0.2804
Specificity	$\dfrac{TN}{TAN}=\dfrac{9173}{9614}$	0.9541
Precision	$\dfrac{TP}{TPP}=\dfrac{544}{985}$	0.5523
F_1	$2\cdot\dfrac{precision\cdot recall}{precision+recall}$	0.3720
F_2	$5\cdot\dfrac{precision\cdot recall}{\left(4\cdot precision\right)+recall}$	0.3110
$F_{0.5}$	$1.25\cdot\dfrac{precision\cdot recall}{\left(0.25\cdot precision\right)+recall}$	0.4626

of the actual negative records as negative. That is, the model is doing great at correctly identifying customers who would not respond to the marketing campaign. However, the model's sensitivity of 0.2804 is rather poor, meaning that only

$$\frac{TP}{TAP}=\frac{544}{1940}=28.04\%$$

of the actual positive records were classified as positive by the model. In other words, the model is not doing a very good job of correctly identifying customers who would respond positively to the campaign.

The model's precision is not much better than a coin flip:

$$\frac{TP}{TPP}=\frac{544}{985}=55.23\%$$

meaning that, of the customers classified as positive by the model, 55.23% actually would respond positively to the marketing. Notice that the three F_β scores range between the values for precision and recall, as they must. F_1, the harmonic mean of precision and recall, has a value of 0.372. The value of F_2, which weights recall higher than precision, is closer to recall, while the value of $F_{0.5}$ is closer to precision. Note that we do not provide thumbnail interpretations of these values as we do for the others. Instead, these metrics are used for model selection, comparing the F_β values directly to choose the best model.

7.6.1 How to Perform Model Evaluation Using R

To validate the model, we need to

1. Develop Model 1 using the training data, and

2. Then run the test data through Model 1.

Read in the *clothing_data_driven_training* data set as *clothing_train* and the *clothing_data_driven_test* data set as *clothing_test*. Load the required package, if necessary, using **library(C50)**. Run the training data set through C5.0 to obtain Model 1, using the code given here.[3] Save the result as **C5**.

```
C5 <- C5.0(Response ~ Days.since.Purchase + Number.of.
Purchase.Visits + Sales.per.Visit, data = clothing_train)
```

Next, subset the predictor variables from the test data set into their own data frame.

```
test.X <- subset(x = clothing_test, select = c("Days.
since.Purchase",
        "Number.of.Purchase.Visits", "Sales.per.Visit"))
```

The **subset()** command takes input **x = clothing_test** to specify what object to subset. For our case, we are subsetting from the *clothing_test* data set. The **select** input specifies the names of the variables to subset from the data. We are subsetting all three predictor variables, so we give the names of those variables in double quotes and list them inside a **c()** command. We save the resulting data set as **test.X**.

Now, we are ready to run the test data through the training data model (Model 1).

```
ypred <- predict(object = C5, newdata = test.X)
```

The **predict()** command requires as input the model you are using to make predictions, labeled **object**, and the data you are using to make the predictions, labeled **newdata**. In our case, we are using **C5** from the training data set as our model and the predictor variables from the test data set.

The output of the **predict()** command when using a C5.0 model as the **object** is a list of predicted target variable labels, one for each record in the test data set. We save this series of predictions under the name **ypred**. Since the response variable in the C5.0 model has values 0 and 1, the contents of **ypred** will be 0 or 1 values for each record in the *clothing_test* data set.

Now that we have the predictions, we can compare them to the actual income values in the test data set. We do this using a table.

```
t1 <- table(clothing_test$Response, ypred)
row.names(t1) <- c("Actual: 0", "Actual: 1")
```

[3] For an explanation of the code, see the R section on C5.0 in Chapter 6.

```
colnames(t1) <- c("Predicted: 0", "Predicted: 1")
t1 <- addmargins(A = t1, FUN = list(Total = sum), quiet =
TRUE); t1
```

We build the table itself using the **table()** command, followed by the target variable from the test data set **clothing_test$Response** for the rows and the predicted target variable values **ypred** for the columns. For clarity, we add row and column names to the table, to differentiate between the actual and predicted values. We use **row.names()** to name the rows **"Actual: 0"** and **"Actual: 1"** and **colnames()** to name the columns **"Predicted: 0"** and **"Predicted: 1"** in order to make the resulting table as readable as possible. The **addmargins()** command, as we have seen before, adds a *Total* row and column. The resulting table is equivalent to Table 7.3.

7.7 ACCOUNTING FOR UNEQUAL ERROR COSTS

Now, the intrinsic assumption in Model 1 was that the two types of classification errors, false positive and false negative, are equally costly. But, as a clothing retailer, with millions of dollars potentially at stake, we need to ask ourselves, is this assumption valid? Let us investigate, by positing some costs associated with the various contingencies. These are shown in Table 7.5.

The rationale for these costs is as follows:

- **True Negative.** This represents a nonresponder being correctly classified as a nonresponder. The retailer will not go to the trouble of contacting this customer, who would not have responded if contacted. No money lost or gained. $Cost_{TN} = \$0$.

- **False Positive.** This represents a nonresponder being incorrectly classified as a responder. This is not a very serious error for the retailer, as the cost of contacting each customer, by phone and with a mailing is, say, \$10. $Cost_{FP} = \$10$.

- **False Negative.** This represents a positive responder being incorrectly classified as a nonresponder. Sad, but no costs directly incurred. $Cost_{FN} = \$0$.

- **True Positive.** This represents a positive responder being correctly classified as a positive responder. The retailer would contact this customer, and the customer would come and spend, on average, say, \$40. Since profit equals negative cost, we have $Cost_{TP} = -\$40$.

TABLE 7.5 Cost matrix for the retailer

		Predicted Category	
		0	**1**
Actual category	**0**	$Cost_{TN} = \$0$	$Cost_{FP} = \$10$
	1	$Cost_{FN} = \$0$	$Cost_{TP} = -\$40$

TABLE 7.6   Adjusted cost matrix for the lender

		Predicted Category	
		0	**1**
Actual category	**0**	$Cost_{TN} = 0$	$Cost_{FP} = 1$
	1	$Cost_{FN} = 4$	$Cost_{TP} = 0$

We may[4] add \$40 across the bottom row, and then divide all cells by \$10, so that our adjusted cost matrix becomes Table 7.6.

In other words, the retailer's false negative cost is four times higher than the false positive cost. So, clearly, Model 1's assumption that the two errors are equally costly is invalid. Instead, we should turn to a new model, Model 2, which incorporates the unequal error costs in Table 7.6.

7.7.1   Accounting for Unequal Error Costs Using R

Once you create a cost matrix as in Table 7.6, you can add the matrix into your C5.0 model. First, create the matrix itself.

```
cost.C5 <- matrix(c(0,4,1,0), byrow = TRUE, ncol=2)
dimnames(cost.C5) <- list(c("0", "1"), c("0", "1"))
```

It is important to note that C5.0 defines its cost matrix using the rows as the predicted values and the columns as the actual values (the details of this are contained in the C5.0 help page, which can be found by running **?C5.0**). This is the reverse of how our cost matrix in Table 7.6 was defined. When we create the cost matrix for the C5.0 model, it will have a "1" where the "4" is in Table 7.6, and a "4" where the "1" is. Save the cost matrix as **cost.C5**. Specifying the **dimnames()** of the cost matrix will ensure that the C5.0 algorithm identifies the different costs correctly.

Now we rerun the C5.0 model, this time adding the matrix of unequal error costs.

```
C5.costs <- C5.0(Response ~ Days.since.Purchase +
Number.of.Purchase.Visits + Sales.per.Visit, data =
clothing_train, costs = cost.C5)
```

The code above differs from the previous R code for C5.0 in two ways. First, we save the model under a different name, so we do not lose the information from our previous model. Second, we add the input **costs = cost.C5** into the **C5.0()** command to add the cost matrix to the model.

---

[4] For details on the rationale behind these actions, please see Chapter 16 of *Data Mining and Predictive Analytics*.

7.8 COMPARING MODELS WITH AND WITHOUT UNEQUAL ERROR COSTS

When we develop Model 2 using R (see the previous section for code details) and evaluate it, we obtain the contingency table shown in Table 7.7.

Because the error costs for Model 2 are unequal, the evaluative measures introduced earlier are now *superseded* by a new evaluation measure, *model cost per record* (or its additive inverse, *overall model profit per record*).

Model Cost per Record and Model Profit per Record

When error costs are unequal, one of the most important evaluation measures for the purpose of model selection is the *model cost per record*. First, calculate the *Overall Model Cost*, as follows:

$$Overall\ Model\ Cost = TN \cdot Cost_{TN} + FP \cdot Cost_{FP} + FN \cdot Cost_{FN} + TP \cdot Cost_{TP}$$

Often, the error costs for true negatives and false negatives equal zero, since no action is taken. In this case, the overall model cost simplifies to:

$$Overall\ Model\ Cost = FP \cdot Cost_{FP} + TP \cdot Cost_{TP}$$

Then,

$$Model\ Cost\ per\ Record = \frac{Overall\ Model\ Cost}{GT}$$

Finally,

$$Model\ Profit\ per\ Record = -Model\ Cost\ per\ Record$$

For model selection, choose the model which minimizes the model cost per record, or, conversely, maximizes model profit. It is important to report the per-record cost or profit, because overall cost varies with the size of the data set.

Using the costs delineated in Table 7.5, we calculate the overall model costs for Model 1 and Model 2 as follows:

$$Overall\ Model\ Cost_{Model1}$$
$$= FP \cdot Cost_{FP} + TP \cdot Cost_{TP}$$
$$= 441 \cdot \$10 + 544 \cdot -\$40$$
$$= -\$17,350$$

TABLE 7.7 Contingency table for evaluating Model 2, which incorporates asymmetric error costs

		Predicted Category		
		0	**1**	**Total**
	0	$TN = 7163$	$FP = 2451$	**TAN = 9614**
Actual category	**1**	$FN = 618$	$TP = 1322$	**TAP = 1940**
	Total	**TPN = 7781**	**TPP = 3773**	**GT = 11,554**

$$Overall\ Model\ Cost_{Model2}$$
$$= FP \cdot Cost_{FP} + TP \cdot Cost_{TP}$$
$$= 2451 \cdot \$10 + 1322 \cdot -\$40$$
$$= -\$28,370$$

Then, the model profit per customer for each model is given as:

$$Profit\ per\ Customer_{Model1} = \frac{-Overall\ Model\ Cost_{Model1}}{GT} = \frac{\$17,350}{11,554} = \$1.5016$$

$$Profit\ per\ Customer_{Model2} = \frac{-Overall\ Model\ Cost_{Model2}}{GT} = \frac{\$28,370}{11,554} = \$2.4554$$

In other words, *we increased the retailer's profits by almost 64%, simply from accounting for the unequal error costs!*

7.9 DATA-DRIVEN ERROR COSTS

In this era of big data, businesses should leverage the information in their existing databases in order to help uncover the optimal predictive models. In other words, as an alternative to assigning error costs because "these cost values seem right to our consultant" or "that's how we have always modeled them," we would instead be well advised to listen to the data and learn from the data itself what the error costs should be. Let us illustrate the power of data-driven error costs by continuing our example.

Recall that our only nonzero costs were $Cost_{FP} = \$10$ and $Cost_{TP} = -\$40$. Fortunately, however, we have access to data that would give us a better idea of $Cost_{TP}$, namely the predictor *Sales per Visit*. This predictor provides the average amount of money spent per visit for each customer. So, if we calculate the mean *Sales per Visit* across all customers, we could use this as a better estimate of how much the customers would come and spend, on average. Our previous estimate was $40. But the mean *Sales per Visit* for all records in the training data set is $113.58. Our data-derived or data-driven cost for true positives is therefore updated to $Cost_{TP} = -\$113.58$. Unfortunately, there is no analogous data for us to better estimate $Cost_{FP} = \$10$, which therefore remains at $10.

This gives us the revised cost matrix in Table 7.8.

TABLE 7.8 Data-driven cost matrix for the clothing store problem

		Predicted Category	
		0	**1**
Actual category	**0**	$Cost_{TN} = \$0$	$Cost_{FP} = \$10$
	1	$Cost_{FN} = \$0$	$Cost_{TP} = -\$113.58$

TABLE 7.9 Simplified data-driven cost matrix for the clothing store problem.

		Predicted Category	
		0	**1**
Actual category	**0**	0	$Cost_{FP} = 1$
	1	$Cost_{FN} = 11.358$	0

TABLE 7.10 Contingency table for Model 3 with data-driven error costs

		Predicted Category		
		0	**1**	**Total**
Actual category	**0**	$TN = 4237$	$FP = 5377$	**TAN = 9614**
	1	$FN = 201$	$TP = 1739$	**TAP = 1940**
	Total	**TPN = 4438**	**TPP = 7116**	**GT = 11,554**

Subtracting $Cost_{TP} = -\$113.58$ from the bottom row and then dividing each cell by \$10 gives us the simplified data-driven cost matrix in Table 7.9.

Thus, our false negatives are 11.358 times as costly as our false positives.

Another C5.0 model is developed using the training set, called Model 3, which is then evaluated using the test data set. The resulting contingency table is shown in Table 7.10.

We calculate the overall model costs for Model 3 as follows:

$$Overall\,Model\,Cost_{Model3}$$
$$= FP \cdot Cost_{FP} + TP \cdot Cost_{TP}$$
$$= 5377 \cdot \$10 + 1739 \cdot -\$113.58$$
$$= -\$143,745.62$$

Then, the model profit per customer for Model 3 is given as:

$$Profit\,per\,Customer_{Model3} = \frac{-Overall\,Model\,Cost_{Model3}}{GT} = \frac{\$143,745.62}{11,554} = \$12.4412$$

This is a great increase in profitability compared to the previous models. However, much of this increase is due to the data-driven increase in $Cost_{TP}$ to \$113.58. To be fair, we should compare all three models according to the new model costs. This is shown for all our evaluation measures in Table 7.11.

Table 7.11 contains the evaluation measures for Models 1–3, with the best performing model's results in **bold**. Note that Model 1, the least profitable model (without error costs), is the most accurate model, at 84.10%, while Model 3, our most profitable model (with the data-driven error costs), is the least accurate model, at a mere 51.72%. Thus, *accuracy is not the proper metric to compare models which have unequal error costs.*

TABLE 7.11 Model evaluation metrics for all models

Evaluation Measure	C5.0 Model		
	Model 1: No error Costs	Model 2: Error costs 4x	Model 3: Error costs 11.358x
Accuracy	**0.8410**	0.7344	0.5172
Error rate	**0.1590**	0.2656	0.4828
Sensitivity	0.2804	0.6814	**0.8964**
Specificity	**0.9541**	0.7451	0.4407
Precision	**0.5523**	0.3504	0.2444
F_1	0.3720	**0.4628**	0.3841
F_2	0.3110	0.5731	**0.5845**
$F_{0.5}$	**0.4626**	0.3881	0.2860
Overall model cost	−$57,377.52	−$125,642.76	−$143,745.62
Profit per customer	$4.97	$10.87	**$12.44**

Because every true positive gives us $113.58, the models which tended to make more positive predictions did better. Sensitivity (recall), the proportion of all the positive responders that the model captured, thus turned out to be more important than specificity (capturing the nonresponders). Thus, our best-performing model had the highest sensitivity, while our worst performing model had the lowest sensitivity. The reverse relationship held for specificity.

Precision did not appear to be very important either, as Model 1's solid precision was partly due to its few positive predictions. F_2, which favors recall (sensitivity) over precision, was highest with Model 3, while $F_{0.5}$, which favors precision over recall, was highest with losing Model 1.

Finally, we should also make sure that our models outperformed the baseline models: the All Positive Model and the All Negative Model. Since no customers were contacted in the All Negative Model, then there is no profit. On the other hand, the All Positive Model did quite well, with an Overall Model Profit of $124,205.20 and a Profit per Customer of $10.75, nearly beating Model 2 above.

To summarize, data scientists should always evaluate their models. In this chapter we learned a series of metrics for evaluating classification models. We discovered that error costs were not always equal, and when unequal, the model cost per record may be the best metric. Finally, we illustrated how data-driven error costs can further enhance the profitability of our classification models.

EXERCISES

CLARIFYING THE CONCEPTS

1. Explain the difference between model evaluation and model validation.

2. What does a contingency table consist of?

3. Show that $GT = TPN + TPP$ and that $TAP = GT - TAN$.

4. Show that *Error Rate* $= 1 - Accuracy$.

5. What do sensitivity and specificity measure?

6. Explain the Method for Model Evaluation.

7. Why did we choose the All Negative model as a baseline to calibrate the accuracy of Model 1, rather than the All Positive model?

8. When error costs are unequal, what is the most important evaluation measure for the purpose of model selection?

9. Explain how a naïve analyst would erroneously prefer Model 1 to Model 2.

10. For the All Positive and All Negative models, calculate the evaluation metrics from Table 7.11.

WORKING WITH THE DATA

For Exercises 11–22, work with the *clothing_data_driven_training* and *clothing_data_driven_test* data sets. Use R to solve each problem.

11. Using the training data set, create a C5.0 model (Model 1) to predict a customer's *Response* using *Days since Purchase*, *# of Purchase Visits*, and *Sales per Visit*. Obtain the predicted responses.

12. Evaluate Model 1 using the test data set. Construct a contingency table to compare the actual and predicted values of *Response*.

13. For Model 1, recapitulate Table 7.4 from the text, calculating all of the model evaluation measures shown in the table. Call this table the *Model Evaluation Table*. Leave space for Models 2 and 3.

14. Clearly and completely interpret each of the Model 1 evaluation measures from the Model Evaluation Table.

15. Create a cost matrix, called the *4x* cost matrix, that specifies a false positive is four times as bad as a false negative.

16. Using the training data set, build a C5.0 model (Model 2) to predict a customer's *Response* using *Days since Purchase*, *# of Purchase Visits*, and *Sales per Visit*, using the *4x* cost matrix.

17. Evaluate your predictions from Model 2 using the actual response values from the test data set. Add *Overall Model Cost* and *Profit per Customer* to the Model Evaluation Table. Calculate all the measures from the Model Evaluation Table.

18. Compare the evaluation measures from Model 1 and Model 2 using the *4x* cost matrix. Discuss the strengths and weaknesses of each model.

19. Construct the simplified *data-driven cost matrix* as follows:

   a. Obtain the mean of the *Sales per Visit* variable from the training data set and set the negative of that value to be the "cost" of a true positive. Let the false positive cost equal $10.

b. Construct the appropriate cost matrix, and simplify it, to obtain the simplified *data-driven cost matrix*.

20. Using the training set, build a C5.0 model (Model 3) to predict a customer's *Response* using *Days since Purchase*, *# of Purchase Visits*, and *Sales per Visit*, using the data-driven cost matrix.

21. Populate the Model Evaluation Table with the evaluation measures for Model 3, using the data-driven cost matrix.

22. Compare Model 1, Model 2, and Model 3 using the Model Evaluation Table.

HANDS-ON ANALYSIS

For the following exercises, work with the *adult_ch6_training* and *adult_ch6_test* data sets. Use R to solve each problem.

23. Using the training data set, create a C5.0 model (Model 1) to predict a customer's *Income* using *Marital Status* and *Capital Gains and Losses*. Obtain the predicted responses.

24. Evaluate Model 1 using the test data set. Construct a contingency table to compare the actual and predicted values of *Income*.

25. For Model 1, recapitulate Table 7.4 from the text, calculating all of the model evaluation measures shown in the table. Call this table the *Model Evaluation Table*. Leave space for Model 2.

26. Clearly and completely interpret each of the Model 1 evaluation measures from the Model Evaluation Table.

27. Create a cost matrix, called the *3x* cost matrix, that specifies a false positive is four times as bad as a false negative.

28. Using the training data set, build a C5.0 model (Model 2) to predict a customer's *Income* using *Marital Status* and *Capital Gains and Losses*, using the *3x* cost matrix.

29. Evaluate your predictions from Model 2 using the actual response values from the test data set. Add *Overall Model Cost* and *Profit per Customer* to the Model Evaluation Table. Calculate all the measures from the Model Evaluation Table.

30. Compare the evaluation measures from Model 1 and Model 2 using the *3x* cost matrix. Discuss the strengths and weaknesses of each model.

For the following exercises, work with the *Loans_Training* and *Loans_Test* data sets. Use R to solve each problem.

31. Using the training data set, create a C5.0 model (Model 1) to predict a loan applicant's *Approval* using *Debt-to-Income Ratio, FICO Score*, and *Request Amount*. Obtain the predicted responses.

32. Evaluate Model 1 using the test data set. Construct a contingency table to compare the actual and predicted values of *Approval*.

33. For Model 1, recapitulate Table 7.4 from the text, calculating all of the model evaluation measures shown in the table. Call this table the *Model Evaluation Table*. Leave space for Model 2.

34. Clearly and completely interpret each of the Model 1 evaluation measures from the Model Evaluation Table.

35. Do the following to construct the simplified *data-driven cost matrix*.

    a. Compute the mean of the *Interest* per loan applicant from the training data set. Set the negative of that value to be the "cost" of a true positive.

    b. Calculate the mean *Request Amount* per loan applicant from the training data set. Set this value to be the cost of a false positive.

    c. Obtain the simplified *data-driven cost matrix*.

36. Using the training set, build a C5.0 model (Model 2) to predict a loan applicant's *Approval* using *Debt-to-Income Ratio, FICO Score*, and *Request Amount*, using the simplified data-driven cost matrix.

37. Populate the Model Evaluation Table with the evaluation measures for Model 2, using the data-driven cost matrix.

38. Clearly and completely interpret each of the Model 2 evaluation measures from the Model Evaluation Table.

39. Compare Model 1 and Model 2 using the Model Evaluation Table. Discuss the strengths and weaknesses of each model.

40. How much money did we make for our bank by using *data-driven error costs* to evaluate our models?

CHAPTER 8

NAÏVE BAYES CLASSIFICATION

8.1 INTRODUCTION TO NAÏVE BAYES

Of course, classification modeling is not restricted to decision trees. Many other classification methods are available, including Naïve Bayes classification. Naïve Bayes classification methods are based on Bayes Theorem, developed by the Reverend Thomas Bayes.[1] Bayes Theorem updates our knowledge about the data parameters by combining our previous knowledge (called the *prior distribution*) with new information obtained from observed data, resulting in updated parameter knowledge (called the *posterior distribution*).

8.2 BAYES THEOREM

Consider a data set made up of two predictors $X = X_1, X_2$ and a response variable Y, where the response variable takes one of three possible class values: y_1, y_2, and y_3. Our objective is to identify which of y_1, y_2, and y_3 is the most likely for a particular combination of predictor variable values. Let us call this most likely combination $X^* = \{X_1 = x_1, X_2 = x_2\}$.

We can use Bayes Theorem to identify which class is the most likely for a particular combination of predictor variable values by:

1. calculating the posterior probability for each of y_1, y_2, and y_3, for the combination of predictors x_1 and x_2 and

2. selecting the value of y with the highest posterior probability.

Let y^* be one of the three potential values of Y. Bayes Theorem tells us:

$$p\left(Y = y^*|X^*\right) = \frac{p\left(X^*|Y = y^*\right)p\left(Y = y^*\right)}{p\left(X^*\right)} \tag{8.1}$$

[1] Thomas Bayes, *Essay Toward Solving a Problem in the Doctrine of Changes, Philosophical Transactions of the Royal Society of London*, 1793.

Data Science Using Python and R, First Edition. Chantal D. Larose and Daniel T. Larose.
© 2019 John Wiley & Sons, Inc. Published 2019 by John Wiley & Sons, Inc.

Now, $p(Y = y^*)$ represents the knowledge we have about how likely the class value y^* is, before we even begin. Since that information is known prior to our analysis, we call $p(Y = y^*)$ the *prior probability*. This prior information is combined with $p(X^* \mid Y = y^*)$, which represents how the data behave, when the response equals y^*. The denominator, $p(X^*)$, is how the data behave without reference to the response class values, otherwise known as the *marginal probability* of the data.

The result of the formula, $p(Y = y^* \mid X^*)$, represents the information or idea we have about how likely our class value y^* is if we observe the particular predictor variable values X^*. Since the information is updated from $P(Y = y^*)$ after examining the data, we call $p(Y = y^* \mid X^*)$ the *posterior probability*.

What if you have no prior knowledge about the parameters? In this case, you can use a *noninformative prior*, which says that every class value is equally likely. By using a noninformative prior, your posterior probabilities are based solely on the data.

8.3 MAXIMUM A POSTERIORI HYPOTHESIS

How can we use the Bayes Theorem probabilities to classify a record? In our example above, we have three different possible values of y^*. For a fixed value of X^*, we calculate a Bayes Theorem probability for each of the three possible values of Y:

$$p\left(Y = y_1 \mid X^*\right) = \frac{p\left(X^* \mid Y = y_1\right) p\left(Y = y_1\right)}{p\left(X^*\right)}$$

$$p\left(Y = y_2 \mid X^*\right) = \frac{p\left(X^* \mid Y = y_2\right) p\left(Y = y_2\right)}{p\left(X^*\right)}$$

$$p\left(Y = y_3 \mid X^*\right) = \frac{p\left(X^* \mid Y = y_3\right) p\left(Y = y_3\right)}{p\left(X^*\right)}$$

The *maximum* a posteriori *hypothesis* tells us to classify the record X^* as the value of Y which has the highest posterior probability. In other words, choose the class value of Y that corresponds with the largest of the three posterior probabilities we calculated.

8.4 CLASS CONDITIONAL INDEPENDENCE

If we have more than one predictor variable, then the class conditional independence assumption allows us to write $p(X^* \mid Y = y^*)$ as the product of independent events. For example, say we have two predictor variables $X^* = \{X_1 = x_1, X_2 = x_2\}$. To write $p(X^* \mid Y = y^*)$, we would write $p(X_1 = x_1 \mid Y = y^*) \times p(X_2 = x_2 \mid Y = y^*)$. We will see a demonstration of this in the Section 8.5.

8.5 APPLICATION OF NAÏVE BAYES CLASSIFICATION

We will use the *wine_ flag_training* and *wine_flag_test* data sets to demonstrate how we use Naïve Bayes to classify a response variable. Let us say we want to predict whether a wine is red or white based on whether the wine has high or low alcohol and sugar content. Alcohol and sugar content values are considered low if they are below the median for that variable, and high if they are above the median.

First, we construct two contingency tables, one for *Type* and *Alcohol_flag* and another for *Type* and *Sugar_flag*. Recall that the class values of target variable constitute the rows, and the class values of predictor variables constitute the columns. The contingency table for *Type* and *Alcohol_flag* is shown in Figure 8.1, while the contingency table for *Type* and *Sugar_flag* is shown in Figure 8.2.

We can use Figures 8.1 and 8.2 to calculate the values required to perform Naïve Bayes classification. Let us start by examining the response variable, *Type*. *Type* has two class levels: Red and White. Using either contingency table, we can calculate the prior probability of each *Type* class level:

- $p(Type = Red) = 500/1000 = 0.5$
- $p(Type = White) = 500/1000 = 0.5$

The two *Type* probabilities make up the two possible values of $p(Y)$, the prior distribution of *Type*. For example, we now know that any randomly selected wine from this data set has a 50% chance of being a red wine.

We use Figure 8.1 to calculate the marginal probability of the predictor variable *Alcohol_flag*. *Alcohol_flag* has two levels: High and Low. These two values will make up the distribution of the first predictor variable, $p(X_1)$:

- $p(Alcohol\_flag = High) = 486/1000 = 0.486$
- $p(Alcohol\_flag = Low) = 514/1000 = 0.514$

We now know, for example, that a randomly chosen wine from this data set has a 48.6% probability of having a high alcohol content. Notice that this marginal distribution takes no account of the response values Y.

```
              Alcohol = High Alcohol = Low Total
Type = Red         218            282        500
Type = White       268            232        500
Total              486            514       1000
```

Figure 8.1   Contingency table from R for *Type* and *Alcohol_flag*.

```
              Sugar = High Sugar = Low Total
Type = Red        116          384       500
Type = White      300          200       500
Total             416          584      1000
```

Figure 8.2   Contingency table from R for *Type* and *Sugar_flag*.

We use Figure 8.2 to calculate the marginal probability of the predictor variable *Sugar_flag*. *Sugar_flag* also has two levels: High and Low. These two values will make up the distribution of the second predictor variable, $p(X_2)$:

- $p(Sugar\_flag = High) = 416/1000 = 0.416$
- $p(Sugar\_flag = Low) = 584/1000 = 0.584$

We now know, for example, that a randomly chosen wine from this data set has a 41.6% probability of having a high sugar content.

What about $p(X^* | Y)$, the conditional probabilities of each predictor variable given the target variable? For each predictor variable we have four different probabilities, one for each of the four pairs of predictor and target variable levels.

From Figures 8.1 and 8.2, we may calculate the four conditional probabilities for *Alcohol_flag* and *Type*, as follows:

- $p(Alcohol\_flag = High | Type = Red) = 218 / 500 = 0.436$
- $p(Alcohol\_flag = Low | Type = Red) = 282 / 500 = 0.564$
- $p(Alcohol\_flag = High | Type = White) = 268 / 500 = 0.536$
- $p(Alcohol\_flag = Low | Type = White) = 232 / 500 = 0.464$

We now know, for example, that if a wine is red, it has a 56.4% chance of having a low alcohol content, compared to a 43.6% chance of having a high alcohol content. To visualize this difference we can use a normalized bar graph, as on the left-hand side of Figure 8.1.

The four conditional probabilities for *Sugar_flag* and *Type* are given below.

- $p(Sugar\_flag = High | Type = Red) = 116 / 500 = 0.232$
- $p(Sugar\_flag = Low | Type = Red) = 384 / 500 = 0.768$
- $p(Sugar\_flag = High | Type = White) = 300 / 500 = 0.6$
- $p(Sugar\_flag = Low | Type = White) = 200 / 500 = 0.4$

We now know, for example, that if a wine is red, it has a 76.8% chance of having a low sugar content, compared to a 23.2% chance of having a high sugar content. To visualize this difference we can use a normalized bar graph, as on the right-hand side of Figure 8.3.

Now that we have all values of $p(Y)$, $p(X^*)$, and $p(X^* | Y)$, we are ready to calculate the posterior probability of each level of *Type*, $p(Y = y^* | X^*)$. In other words, we can finally address the question at hand: How would Naïve Bayes classify a wine, given the alcohol and sugar content? To find that out, we use the *maximum* a posteriori *hypothesis*. We examine the posterior probability of each possible *Type* given a particular value of *Alcohol_flag* and *Sugar_flag and* select the *Type* that has the highest posterior probability.

First, let us consider a wine with low alcohol and low sugar content. Using our probability notation, we want to know each of the following:

- $p(Y = y_1 | X^*) = p(Red | Alcohol\_flag = Low, Sugar\_flag = Low)$
- $p(Y = y_2 | X^*) = p(White | Alcohol\_flag = Low, Sugar\_flag = Low)$

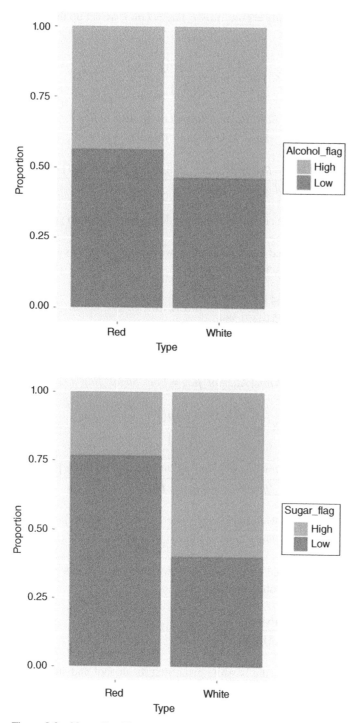

Figure 8.3   Normalized bar graphs of *Type* with an overlay of *Alcohol_flag* (on the top) and *Sugar_flag* (on the bottom).

To find $p(Red \mid Alcohol\_flag = Low, Sugar\_flag = Low)$, we set up the Bayes Theorem:

$$p\left(Y = y_1 \mid X^*\right) = \frac{p\left(X^* \mid Y = y_1\right) p\left(Y = y_1\right)}{p\left(X^*\right)}$$

$$= \frac{p(Alcohol\_flag = Low, Sugar\_flag = Low \mid Red) \times p\left(Red\right)}{p\left(Alcohol\_flag = Low, Sugar\_flag = Low\right)}$$

$$= \frac{p\left(Alcohol\_flag = Low \mid Type = Red\right) \times p\left(Sugar\_flag = Low \mid Type = Red\right) \times p\left(Red\right)}{p\left(Alcohol\_flag = Low\right) \times p\left(Sugar\_flag = Low\right)}$$

Note that we are using the conditional independence assumption to get to this last step.

We have already calculated every probability we need to solve this equation, so we plug each value in and crunch the numbers:

$$\frac{0.564 \times 0.768 \times 0.5}{0.514 \times 0.584} = 0.7215$$

The probability that the wine is red given that its alcohol and sugar contents are low is about 72.15%.

Next, we need to find $p(White \mid Alcohol\_flag = Low, Sugar\_flag = Low)$:

$$p\left(Y = y_2 \mid X^*\right) = \frac{p\left(X^* \mid Y = y_2\right) p\left(Y = y_2\right)}{p\left(X^*\right)}$$

$$= \frac{p(Alcohol\_flag = Low, Sugar\_flag = Low \mid White) \times p\left(White\right)}{p\left(Alcohol\_flag = Low, Sugar\_flag = Low\right)}$$

$$= \frac{p\left(Alcohol\_flag = Low \mid Type = White\right) \times p\left(Sugar\_flag = Low \mid Type = White\right) \times p\left(White\right)}{p\left(Alcohol\_flag = Low\right) \times p\left(Sugar\_flag = Low\right)}$$

We have already calculated every probability we need to solve this equation, so we plug each value in and crunch the numbers:

$$\frac{0.464 \times 0.4 \times 0.5}{0.514 \times 0.584} = 0.3092$$

The probability that the wine is white given that its alcohol and sugar contents are low is about 30.92%. Since the posterior probability of a low alcohol, low sugar wine being red is higher than the posterior probability of the same wine being white, the Naïve Bayes algorithm will classify the wine as red.

Let us compare the prior probability of a wine being red to the posterior probability of a wine being red given its alcohol and sugar contents are low. The probability of a randomly selected wine being red is $p(Type = Red) = 50\%$. However, after we took into account that the wine had low alcohol and sugar content, the probability of it being a red wine rose to 72.15%! Why? Because the data told us that red wines were more likely to be low in alcohol content compared to their white wine counterparts (56.4% compared to 46.4%) and that they were also more likely to be low in sugar content compared to their white wine counterparts (76.8% compared to 40%). Naïve Bayes took this information into account and used it to say that a wine low in sugar and alcohol is more likely to be red than white.

What about a wine that has a high alcohol and high sugar content? We use the same formulas as above, changing the X^* values to reflect our new values. We want to compare two posterior probabilities:

- $p(Y = y_1 | X^*) = p(Red | Alcohol\_flag = High, Sugar\_flag = High)$
- $p(Y = y_2 | X^*) = p(White | Alcohol\_flag = High, Sugar\_flag = High)$

Let us start with $p(Red | Alcohol\_flag = High, Sugar\_flag = High)$.

$$p\left(Y = y_1 | X^*\right) = \frac{p\left(X^* | Y = y_1\right) p\left(Y = y_1\right)}{p\left(X^*\right)}$$

$$= \frac{p(Alcohol\_flag = High, Sugar\_flag = High | Red) \times p\left(Red\right)}{p\left(Alcohol\_flag = High, Sugar\_flag = High\right)}$$

$$= \frac{p\left(Alcohol\_flag = High | Type = Red\right) \times p\left(Sugar\_flag = High | Type = Red\right) \times p\left(Red\right)}{p\left(Alcohol\_flag = High\right) \times p\left(Sugar\_flag = High\right)}$$

Plugging in the specific probabilities into the above formula, we obtain our posterior probability:

$$\frac{0.436 \times 0.232 \times 0.5}{0.486 \times 0.416} = 0.2502$$

The probability that the wine is red given that its alcohol and sugar contents are high is about 25.02%.

Next, $p(White | Alcohol\_flag = High, Sugar\_flag = High)$.

$$p\left(Y = y_2 | X^*\right) = \frac{p\left(X^* | Y = y_2\right) p\left(Y = y_2\right)}{p\left(X^*\right)}$$

$$= \frac{p(Alcohol\_flag = High, Sugar\_flag = High | White) \times p\left(White\right)}{p\left(Alcohol\_flag = High, Sugar\_flag = High\right)}$$

$$= \frac{p\left(Alcohol\_flag = High | Type = White\right) \times p\left(Sugar\_flag = High | Type = White\right) \times p\left(White\right)}{p\left(Alcohol\_flag = High\right) \times p\left(Sugar\_flag = High\right)}$$

Plugging in the specific probabilities into the above formula, we obtain our posterior probability:

$$\frac{0.536 \times 0.6 \times 0.5}{0.486 \times 0.416} = 0.7953$$

The probability that the wine is white given that its alcohol and sugar contents are high is about 79.53%. Since the posterior probability of a high alcohol, high sugar wine being white is higher than the posterior probability of the same wine being red, the Naïve Bayes algorithm will classify the wine as white.

There are two more combinations of the predictor variables we have yet to cover: low alcohol and high sugar, and high sugar and low alcohol. The Naïve Bayes classification for a low alcohol, high sugar wine is white, and the Naïve Bayes classification for a high alcohol, low sugar wine is red. The details of the posterior probability calculations for these wines are left as exercises. Taken all together, our Naïve Bayes classification model can be summarized by Table 8.1.

We can evaluate the Naïve Bayes model we uncovered in the above example using a test data set. For this example, we evaluate the model built using the *wine_flag_training* data set using the *wine_flag_test* data. The contingency table for the actual and predicted values of *Type* is shown in Figure 8.4.

From Figure 8.4, we can see that the accuracy of the model is $(464 + 1082)/2345 = 0.6593$. Using our Naïve Bayes model, we correctly predict the type of wine 65.93% of the time. Our model correctly classifies red wines $464/585 = 0.7932$, or 79.32% of the time, and correctly classifies white wines $1082/1760 = 0.6148$, or 61.48% of the time. Since half our wines are red and half are white, our baseline accuracy is 50%, and therefore our Naïve Bayes model outperforms the baseline model.

TABLE 8.1   A summary of the Naïve Bayes model for predicting wine type based on alcohol and sugar content

If a wine has...		... then we classify that wine as a...
... alcohol content that is...	... and sugar content that is...	
... High...	... High...	White wine
... High...	... Low...	Red wine
... Low...	... High...	White wine
... Low...	... Low...	Red wine

```
               Predicted: Red  Predicted: White  Total
Actual: Red           464               121      585
Actual: White         678              1082     1760
Total                1142              1203     2345
```

Figure 8.4   Contingency table from R of actual wine *Type* versus predicted wine *Type* for the Naïve Bayes model evaluated on the test data set.

8.5.1 Naïve Bayes in Python

Start by importing all required libraries.

```
import pandas as pd
import numpy as np
from sklearn.naive_bayes import MultinomialNB
import statsmodels.tools.tools as stattools
```

Load in the training and test data sets, and call them *wines_tr* and *wines_test*, respectively.

```
wine_tr = pd.read_csv("C:/.../wine_flag_training.csv")
wine_test = pd.read_csv("C:/.../wine_flag_test.csv")
```

First, we look at the data using contingency tables. These tables will allow us to obtain the marginal and conditional probabilities we need to perform the Naïve Bayes calculations by hand, if we so choose.

```
t1 = pd.crosstab(wine_tr['Type'], wine_tr['Alcohol_flag'])
t1['Total'] = t1.sum(axis=1)
t1.loc['Total'] = t1.sum()
t1
```

The tables are shown in Figure 8.5. From these, we can obtain the marginal probabilities for *Type Alcohol_flag* and *Sugar_flag*, and the conditional probabilities *Alcohol_flag* given *Type* and *Sugar_flag* given *Type*.

We can also create bar charts to visualize the probabilities from our tables. To do so, we need to tweak the code for our contingency table, as explained in Chapter 4.

```
t1_plot = pd.crosstab(wine_tr['Alcohol_flag'], wine_tr['Type'])
t1_plot.plot(kind='bar', stacked = True)
```

Now we move to the Naïve Bayes algorithm itself. As before, *sklearn* does not automatically handle categorical variables. This means we need to convert *Alcohol_flag* and *Sugar_flag* into dummy variables versions of themselves before we can run the algorithm. We follow the same approach as in Chapter 6.

```
X_Alcohol_ind = np.array(wine_tr['Alcohol_flag'])
(X_Alcohol_ind , X_Alcohol_ind_dict) = stattools.
categorical(X_Alcohol_ind,
```

Alcohol_flag	High	Low	Total		Sugar_flag	High	Low	Total
Type					Type			
Red	218	282	500		Red	116	384	500
White	268	232	500		White	300	200	500
Total	486	514	1000		Total	416	584	1000

Figure 8.5   Contingency tables from Python for *Type* and *Alcohol_flag* (left), and *Type* and *Sugar_flag* (right).

```
        drop=True, dictnames = True)
X_Alcohol_ind = pd.DataFrame(X_Alcohol_ind)
X_Sugar_ind = np.array(wine_tr['Sugar_flag'])
(X_Sugar_ind , X_Sugar_ind_dict) = stattools.
categorical(X_Sugar_ind,
        drop=True, dictnames = True)
X_Sugar_ind = pd.DataFrame(X_Sugar_ind)
X = pd.concat((X_Alcohol_ind, X_Sugar_ind), axis = 1)
```

In **X**, our matrix of predictor dummy variables, we have four columns. The first two correspond to *Alcohol_flag*, where the first column has a 1 if the alcohol content is high, and zero otherwise. Similarly, the second column has a 1 if the alcohol content is low, and zero otherwise. The third and fourth columns similarly correspond to a high sugar content and a low sugar content.

We also save the target variable as **Y**, for clarity.

```
Y = wine_tr['Type']
```

Finally, we move on to the Naïve Bayes algorithm.

```
nb_01 = MultinomialNB().fit(X, Y)
```

As with previous algorithms, there are two steps: Specifying the parameters of the algorithm and fitting the parameter-specific algorithm to the data. For the **NultinomialNB()** algorithm in this case, there are no extra parameters to set. When we **fit()** the model to our **X** and **Y** variables, we save the output as **nb_01**.

To test the Naïve Bayes estimator on the test data, we first need to set up the X variables in the test data set as dummy variables. We follow the same steps as for the training data, which are given below.

```
X_Alcohol_ind_test = np.array(wine_test['Alcohol_flag'])
(X_Alcohol_ind_test, X_Alcohol_ind_dict_test) =
stattools.categorical(X_Alcohol_ind_test,
        drop=True, dictnames = True)
X_Alcohol_ind_test = pd.DataFrame(X_Alcohol_ind_test)
X_Sugar_ind_test = np.array(wine_test['Sugar_flag'])
(X_Sugar_ind_test, X_Sugar_ind_dict_test) = stattools.
categorical(X_Sugar_ind_test,
        drop=True, dictnames = True)
X_Sugar_ind_test = pd.DataFrame(X_Sugar_ind_test)
X_test = pd.concat((X_Alcohol_ind_test, X_Sugar_ind_
test), axis = 1)
```

Once we have set up the predictor variables for the test data set, we can generate predictions.

```
Y_predicted = nb_01.predict(X_test)
```

```
Predicted    Red   White   Total
Actual
Red          464    121     585
White        678   1082    1760
Total       1142   1203    2345
```

Figure 8.6   Contingency table from Python of actual and predicted wine types from Python.

Using the **predict()** command on our Naïve Bayes object **nb_01** will generate an array of labels, Red or White, for each record in the test data set.

Finally, we want a contingency table of the actual and predicted wine types. We utilize the **crosstab()** command once more.

```
ypred = pd.crosstab(wine_test['Type'], Y_predicted,
rownames = ['Actual'],
        colnames = ['Predicted'])
ypred['Total'] = ypred.sum(axis=1); ypred.loc['Total'] =
ypred.sum(); ypred
```

The true wine types located in the variable **wine_test['Type']** form the rows, and the predicted wine types **Y_predicted** form the columns. The optional input values **rownames** and **colnames** label the start of the rows and columns to increase the readability of the table. The total row and column are added following the same steps as were used with the contingency table that started this section. The results are shown in Figure 8.6.

8.5.2   Naïve Bayes in R

Import the *wine_flag_training* and *wine_flag_test* data set into R. Name them *wine_tr* and *wine_test*, respectively.

We first create the tables that will allow us to calculate the necessary probabilities by hand, if we choose to. The first table will be the contingency table of *Type* and *Alcohol_flag*.

```
ta <- table(wine_tr$Type, wine_tr$Alcohol_flag)
colnames(ta) <- c("Alcohol = High", "Alcohol = Low")
rownames(ta) <- c("Type = Red", "Type = White")
addmargins(A = ta, FUN = list(Total = sum), quiet = TRUE)
```

The result of the **addmargins()** command is shown in the contingency table in Figure 8.1.

The second table will be the contingency table of *Type* and *Sugar_flag*.

```
ts <- table(wine_tr$Type, wine_tr$Sugar_flag)
colnames(ts) <- c("Sugar = High", "Sugar = Low")
rownames(ts) <- c("Type = Red", "Type = White")
addmargins(A = ts, FUN = list(Total = sum), quiet = TRUE)
```

The result of the **addmargins()** command is shown in the contingency table in Figure 8.2.

We can also create the side-by-side bar graphs shown in Figure 8.3. The core code is **ggplot()** code, covered previously in this text. However, to place the graphs side by side, we will tweak the core code.

First, install the package that will let us place graphs side by side: the **gridExtra** package.

```
install.packages("gridExtra"); library(gridExtra)
```

Then, run the **ggplot()** code as shown.

```
plot1 <- ggplot(wine_tr, aes(Type)) + geom_bar( aes(fill =
Alcohol_flag), position = "fill") +
      ylab("Proportion")
plot2 <- ggplot(wine_tr, aes(Type)) + geom_bar( aes(fill =
Sugar_flag), position = "fill") +
      ylab("Proportion")
grid.arrange(plot1, plot2, nrow = 1)
```

The **ggplot()** code itself will be familiar from Chapter 4. Note that we save each graph under its own name; **plot1** for the *Alcohol_flag* overlay and **plot2** for the *Sugar_flag* overlay. After we save each graph, we run the **grid.arrange()** command, with three input values: **plot1**, **plot2**, and **nrow = 1** to specify that we want the graphs side by side on one row. The result is shown in the side-by-side graphs in Figure 8.3.

Now that we have our contingency tables and graphs, we move on to the Naïve Bayes algorithm. The package **e1071** contains the Naïve Bayes classification algorithm. Install and open the package.

```
install.packages("e1071"); library(e1071)
```

Run the Naïve Bayes estimator.

```
nb01 <- naiveBayes(formula = Type ~ Alcohol_flag +
Sugar_flag, data = wine_tr)
```

The **naiveBayes()** command will build the model. The **formula** input takes the target variable **Type** on the left of the tilde and the two predictor variables **Alcohol_flag** and **Sugar_flag** on the right of the tilde, separated by a plus sign. The **data** input specifies the data set where these variables come from. We save the model as **nb01**.

To observe the prior and conditional probabilities used in the Naïve Bayes model, run the name of the model by itself.

```
nb01
```

```
Naïve Bayes Classifier for Discrete Predictors

Call:
naiveBayes.default(x = X, y = Y, laplace = laplace)

A-priori probabilities:
Y
  Red White
  0.5   0.5

Conditional probabilities:
        Alcohol_flag
Y          High   Low
    Red   0.436 0.564
  White   0.536 0.464

        Sugar_flag
Y          High   Low
    Red   0.232 0.768
  White   0.600 0.400
```

Figure 8.7   The output from the Naïve Bayes model in R.

The output is shown in Figure 8.7.

The two main items of interest in the output are **A-priori probabilities** and **Conditional probabilities**. The A-priori probabilities are the values of $p(Y)$ and the Conditional probabilities are the resulting values of $p(Y|X)$.

To predict the type of wine for each wine in our test data set, we use the **predict()** command

```
ypred <- predict(object = nb01, newdata = wine_test)
```

The **object = nb01** specifies that we are using our Naïve Bayes model and **newdata = wine_test** states the test data set to use. The algorithm classifies each record in the test data set as either a white or red wine and saves the string of classifications as **ypred**.

Finally, we create the contingency table of actual versus predicted wine types.

```
t.preds <- table(wine_test$Type, ypred)
rownames(t.preds) <- c("Actual: Red", "Actual: White")
colnames(t.preds) <- c("Predicted: Red", "Predicted: White")
addmargins(A = t.preds, FUN = list(Total = sum), quiet = TRUE)
```

The result of the **addmargins()** command is shown in Figure 8.4.

REFERENCES

We used a new package, *gridExtra*, to format multiple *ggplot* graphs. If you want more detail on the inner workings of the new package, look here: Baptiste Auguie, gridExtra: Miscellaneous Functions for "Grid" Graphics. R package version 2.3, 2017. https://CRAN.R-project.org/package=gridExtra.

The *e1071* package holds a lot more than Naïve Bayes! See the citation for a full description: David Meyer, Evgenia Dimitriadou, Kurt Hornik, Andreas Weingessel, and Friedrich Leisch, e1071: Misc Functions of the Department of Statistics, Probability Theory Group (Formerly: E1071), TU Wien. R package version 1.6-8., 2017. http://CRAN.R-project. org/package=e1071.

EXERCISES

CLARIFYING THE CONCEPTS

1. With what information does Bayes Theorem update our previous knowledge about the data parameters?

2. What does the prior probability represent?

3. What formula represents how the data behave within the target variable's class values?

4. What formula represents how the data behave without reference to the class values?

5. What is the formula from the previous exercise called?

6. What does the posterior probability represent?

7. What do we use for a prior probability if we have no prior knowledge about the parameters?

8. How does the maximum a posteriori hypothesis help us to classify a record?

9. What is the class conditional independence assumption?

10. If we have more than one predictor, how do we write $p(X^* | Y = y^*)$ if we have two predictor variables $X^* = \{X_1 = x_1, X_2 = x_2\}$?

WORKING WITH THE DATA

For the following exercises, work with the *wine_flag_training* and *wine_flag_test* data sets. Use either Python or R to solve each problem.

11. Create two contingency tables, one with *Type* and *Alcohol_flag* and another with *Type* and *Sugar_flag*.

12. Use the tables in the previous exercise to calculate:

    a. The prior probability of *Type = Red* and *Type = White*.

    b. The probability of high and low alcohol content.

    c. The probability of high and low sugar content.

    d. The conditional probabilities $p(Alcohol\_flag = High | Type = Red)$ and $p(Alcohol\_flag = Low | Type = Red)$.

    e. The conditional probabilities $p(Alcohol\_flag = High | Type = White)$ and $p(Alcohol\_flag = Low | Type = White)$.

f. The conditional probabilities $p(Sugar\_flag = High | Type = Red)$ and $p(Sugar\_flag = Low | Type = Red)$.

g. The conditional probabilities $p(Sugar\_flag = High | Type = White)$ and $p(Sugar\_flag = Low | Type = White)$.

13. Use the probabilities in the previous exercise to discuss

   a. How likely it is that a randomly selected wine is red.

   b. How likely it is that a randomly selected wine has a high alcohol content.

   c. How likely it is that a randomly selected wine has a low sugar content.

14. Use the conditional probabilities found earlier to discuss

   a. What a typical white wine might have as its alcohol and sugar content.

   b. What a typical red wine might have as its alcohol and sugar content.

15. Create side-by-side bar graphs for *Type*, one with an overlay of *Alcohol_flag* and the other with an overlay of *Sugar_flag*. Compare the graphs to the conditional probabilities you calculated.

16. Compute the posterior probability of *Type = Red* for a wine that is low in alcohol content and high in sugar content. Compute the posterior probability of *Type = White* for the same wine.

17. Use your answers to the previous exercise to determine which type, red or white, is more probable for a wine with low alcohol and high sugar content. What would the Naïve Bayes classifier classify this wine as?

18. Compute the posterior probability of *Type = Red* for a wine that is high in alcohol content and low in sugar content. Compute the posterior probability of *Type = White* for the same wine.

19. Use your answers to the previous exercise to determine which type, red or white, is more probable for a wine with high alcohol and low sugar content. What would the Naïve Bayes classifier classify this wine as?

20. Run the Naïve Bayes classifier to classify wines as white or red based on alcohol and sugar content.

21. Evaluate the Naïve Bayes model on the *wines_test* data set. Display the results in a contingency table. Edit the row and column names of the table to make the table more readable. Include a total row and column.

22. According to your table in the previous exercise, find the following values for the Naïve Bayes model:

   a. Accuracy

   b. Error rate

23. According to your contingency table, find the following values for the Naïve Bayes model:

   a. How often it correctly classifies red wines.

   b. How often it correctly classifies white wines.

HANDS-ON ANALYSIS

For the following exercises, work with the *framingham_nb_training* and *framingham_nb_test* data sets. Use either Python or R to solve each problem.

24. Convert all variables (*Death, Sex,* and *Educ*) to factors.

25. Create two contingency tables, one with *Death* and *Sex* and another with *Death* and *Educ*.

26. Use the tables in the previous exercise to calculate:

    a. The probability a randomly selected person is alive or is dead.

    b. The probability a randomly selected person is a male.

    c. The probability a randomly selected person has an *Educ* value of 3.

    d. The probabilities that a dead person is male with education level 1, and that a living person is male with education level 1.

    e. The probabilities that a living person is female with education level 2, and that a dead person is female with education level 2.

27. Create side-by-side bar graphs for *Death,* one with an overlay of *Sex* and the other with an overlay of *Educ.*

28. Use the graphs from the previous exercise to answer the following questions:

    a. If we know a person is dead, are they more likely to be male or female?

    b. If we know a person is alive, are they more likely to be male or female?

    c. If we know a person is dead, what education level are they most likely to have?

    d. If we know a person is alive, what education level are they most likely to have?

    e. Which education levels are more prevalent for dead persons? For living persons?

29. Compute the posterior probability of *Death = 0* (person is living) for a male with education level 1. Compute the posterior probability of *Death = 1* (person is dead) for a male with education level 1.

30. Compute the posterior probability of *Death = 0* (person is living) for a female with education level 2. Compute the posterior probability of *Death = 1* (person is dead) for a female with education level 2.

31. Run the Naïve Bayes classifier to classify persons as living or dead based on sex and education.

32. Evaluate the Naïve Bayes model on the *framingham_nb_test* data set. Display the results in a contingency table. Edit the row and column names of the table to make the table more readable. Include a total row and column.

33. According to your table in the previous exercise, find the following values for the Naïve Bayes model:

    a. Accuracy

    b. Error rate

34. According to your contingency table, find the following values for the Naïve Bayes model:

    a. How often it correctly classifies dead persons.

    b. How often it correctly classifies living persons.

CHAPTER 9

NEURAL NETWORKS

9.1 INTRODUCTION TO NEURAL NETWORKS

Neural networks represent an attempt at a very basic level to imitate the type of non-linear learning that occurs in the networks of neurons found in nature, such as the human brain. As shown in Figure 9.1, a neuron from the human brain uses dendrites to gather inputs from other neurons and combines the input information, generating a nonlinear response ("firing") when some threshold is reached, which it sends to other neurons using the axon. Figure 9.1 also shows an artificial neuron model used in most neural networks. The inputs (x_i) are collected from upstream neurons (or the data set) and combined through a combination function such as summation (Σ), which is then input into a (usually nonlinear) activation function to produce an output response (y), which may then be channeled downstream to other neurons.

The main benefit of neural networks is that they are quite *robust* for noisy, complicated, or nonlinear data, due to the nonlinear nature of the activation function. On the other hand, the main drawback of neural networks is that they are relatively opaque to human interpretation, as opposed to, say, decision trees.

9.2 THE NEURAL NETWORK STRUCTURE

Let us examine the simple neural network shown in Figure 9.2.

A neural network consists of a *layered, feedforward, completely connected* network of artificial neurons or *nodes*.

- The *feedforward* nature of the network restricts the network to a single direction of flow and does not allow looping or cycling.

- Most networks consist of three layers: an *input layer*, a *hidden layer*, and an *output layer*.

  ○ There may be more than one hidden layer, although most networks contain only one, which is sufficient for most purposes.

Data Science Using Python and R, First Edition. Chantal D. Larose and Daniel T. Larose.
© 2019 John Wiley & Sons, Inc. Published 2019 by John Wiley & Sons, Inc.

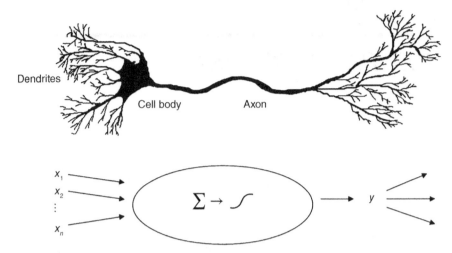

Figure 9.1   Real neuron and artificial neuron model.

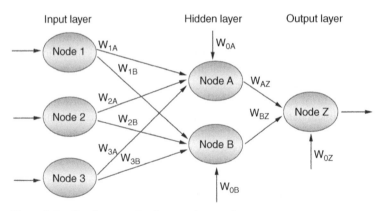

Figure 9.2   Simple example of a neural network.

- The neural network is *completely connected*, meaning that every node in a given layer is connected to every node in adjoining layers, although not to other nodes in the same layer.
  - Each connection between nodes has a weight (e.g. W_{1A}) associated with it.
  - At initialization, these weights are randomly assigned to values between 0 and 1.

The number of input nodes depends on the number and type of attributes in the data set. The input layer accepts inputs from the data set, such as attribute values, and simply passes these values along to the hidden layer without further processing.

The number of hidden layers and the number of nodes in each hidden layer are both configurable by the analyst. How many nodes should one have in the hidden layer? Since having more nodes in the hidden layer increases the power and flexibility of the network for identifying complex patterns, one might be tempted to have a large number of nodes in the hidden layer. However, an overly large hidden layer leads to overfitting, memorizing the training set at the expense of generalizability to the validation set. If overfitting is occurring, one may consider reducing the number of nodes in the hidden layer. Conversely, if the training accuracy is unacceptably low, one may consider increasing the number of nodes in the hidden layer.

9.3 CONNECTION WEIGHTS AND THE COMBINATION FUNCTION

The nodes in the hidden layer and the output layer collect the inputs from the previous layer and combine them using a *combination function*. This combination function (usually summation, Σ) produces a linear combination of the node inputs and the connection weights into a single scalar value, which we will term *net*. Thus, for a given node j,

$$net_j = \sum_i W_{ij} x_{ij} = W_{0j} x_{0j} + W_{1j} x_{1j} + \cdots + W_{Ij} x_{Ij}$$

where x_{ij} represents the ith input to node j, W_{ij} represents the weight associated with the ith input to node j, and there are $I+1$ inputs to node j. Note that $x_1, x_2, \ldots, x_I$ represent inputs from upstream nodes, while x_0 represents a *constant* input, analogous to the constant factor in regression models, which by convention uniquely takes the value $x_{0j} = 1$. Thus, each hidden layer or output layer node j contains an "extra" input equal to a particular weight $W_{0j} x_{0j} = W_{0j}$, such as W_{0B} for node B.

We illustrate the structure of hidden layer nodes and output layer nodes using the toy sample data provided in Table 9.1.

For example, for node A in the hidden layer, we have

$$net_A = \sum_i W_{iA} x_{iA} = W_{0A}(1) + W_{1A} x_{1A} + W_{2A} x_{2A} + W_{3A} x_{3A}$$
$$= 0.5 + 0.6(0.4) + 0.80(0.2) + 0.6(0.7) = 1.32$$

So, in Figure 9.3, we see that node A has combined its inputs into a *net input* of 1.32. Within node A, this combination function $net_A = 1.32$ is then used as an input to an activation function. In biological neurons, signals are sent between

TABLE 9.1   Data inputs and initial values for neural network weights

$x_0 = 1.0$	$W_{0A} = 0.5$	$W_{0B} = 0.7$	$W_{0Z} = 0.5$
$x_1 = 0.4$	$W_{1A} = 0.6$	$W_{1B} = 0.9$	$W_{AZ} = 0.9$
$x_2 = 0.2$	$W_{2A} = 0.8$	$W_{2B} = 0.8$	$W_{BZ} = 0.9$
$x_3 = 0.7$	$W_{3A} = 0.6$	$W_{3B} = 0.4$	—

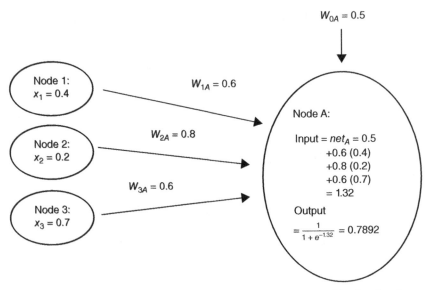

Figure 9.3   Details of neural network, showing input to node A, combination function, and output from node A.

neurons when the combination of inputs to a particular neuron crosses a certain threshold and the neuron "fires." This is nonlinear behavior, since the firing response is not necessarily linearly related to the increment in input stimulation.

The most common activation function is the sigmoid function:

$$y = \frac{1}{1 + e^{-x}}$$

where e is the base of natural logarithms, equal to about 2.718281828. Thus, within node A, the activation would take $net_A = 1.32$ as an input to the sigmoid activation function and produce an output value of

$$y = f\left(net_A\right) = \frac{1}{1 + e^{-1.32}} = 0.7892$$

Node A's work is done (for the moment) and this output value would then be passed along the connection to the output node Z, where it would form (via another linear combination) a component of net_Z.

It is left as an exercise to calculate $net_B = 1.5$ and $f\left(net_B\right) = \frac{1}{1 + e^{-1.5}} = 0.8176$.

Node Z then combines these outputs from nodes A and B, through net_Z, a weighted sum, using the weights associated with the connections between these nodes. Note that the inputs x_i to node Z are not data-attribute values but the outputs from the sigmoid functions from upstream nodes:

$$net_Z = \sum_i W_{iZ} x_{iZ} = W_{0Z}(1) + W_{AZ} x_{AZ} + W_{BZ} x_{BZ}$$
$$= 0.5 + 0.9(0.7892) + 0.9(0.8176) = 1.9461$$

Finally, net_Z is input into the sigmoid activation function in node Z, resulting in

$$f(net_Z) = \frac{1}{1 + e^{-1.9461}} = 0.8750$$

This value of 0.8750 is the *output* from the neural network for this first pass through the network and represents the value predicted for the target variable for the first observation.

9.4 THE SIGMOID ACTIVATION FUNCTION

A common activation function is the sigmoid function

$$y = f(x) = \frac{1}{1 + e^{-x}}$$

Why use the sigmoid function? Because it combines *nearly linear* behavior, *curvilinear* behavior, and *nearly constant* behavior, depending on the value of the input. Figure 9.4 shows the graph of the sigmoid function for $-5 < x < 5$. Through much of the center of the domain of the input x (e.g. $-1 < x < 1$), the behavior of $f(x)$ is *nearly linear*. As the input moves away from the center, $f(x)$ becomes *curvilinear*. By the time the input reaches extreme values, $f(x)$ becomes *nearly constant*.

Moderate increments in the value of x produce varying increments in the value of $f(x)$, depending on the location of x. Near the center, moderate increments in the

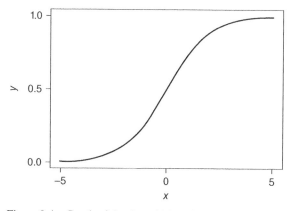

Figure 9.4   Graph of the sigmoid function $y = f(x) = 1/(1 + e^{-x})$.

value of x produce moderate increments in the value of $f(x)$; however, near the extremes, moderate increments in the value of x produce tiny increments in the value of $f(x)$.

9.5 BACKPROPAGATION

How does the neural network learn? As each observation from the training set is processed through the network, an output value is produced from the output node. This output value is then compared to the actual value of the target variable for this training set observation and the error (actual – output) is calculated. This prediction error is analogous to the prediction error in linear regression models. To measure how well the output predictions fit the actual target values, most neural network models use the sum of squared errors (SSE):

$$\text{SSE} = \sum_{\text{records}} \sum_{\text{output nodes}} \left(\text{actual} - \text{output}\right)^2$$

where the squared prediction errors are summed over all the output nodes and over all the records in the training set. The problem is therefore *to construct a set of model weights that will minimize the SSE*. In this way, the weights are analogous to the parameters of a regression model. The "true" values for the weights that will minimize SSE are unknown and our task is to estimate them, given the data.

However, due to the nonlinear nature of the sigmoid functions permeating the network, there exists no closed-form solution for minimizing SSE as exists for least-squares regression. Optimization methods, specifically gradient-descent methods, are therefore used.

The backpropagation algorithm does the following:

1. It takes the prediction error (actual – output) for a particular record and percolates the error back through the network.

2. Assigning partitioned responsibility for the error to the various connections.

3. The weights on these connections are then adjusted to decrease the error, using gradient descent.[1]

9.6 AN APPLICATION OF A NEURAL NETWORK MODEL

We next turn to an example of a neural network model using a subset of the Framingham Heart Study data.[2] The data set, *Framingham_training*, contains information on three variables for 7953 patients. *Sex* is a binary predictor with

---

[1] For further information regarding gradient-descent methods and the details of backpropagation, see *Data Mining and Predictive Analytics*, Chapter 12.

[2] www.framinghamheartstudy.org.

1 = Male and 2 = Female. *Age* is a continuous predictor. The target variable is *Death*, with values 0 = survival and 1 = death.

Clues to the relationship between the predictors and the target are obtained through exploratory data analysis, namely through Figures 9.5 and 9.6, and Tables 9.2 and 9.3. The histograms in Figures 9.5 and 9.6 show that, as *Age* increases, the proportion of *Death* increases. Tables 9.2 and 9.3 show that a larger proportion of males died, compared to females. Thus, these interrelationships should be reflected in our neural network model results.

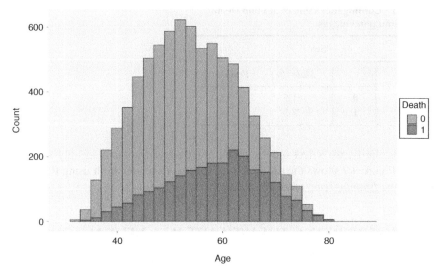

Figure 9.5   Histogram from R of Age, with Death overlay.

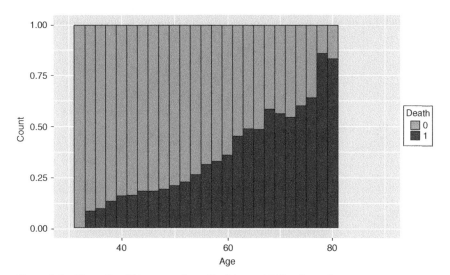

Figure 9.6   Normalized histogram from R of Age, with Death overlay.

TABLE 9.2 Contingency table of Sex and Death

		Sex		
		Male	*Female*	Total
Death	**0**	2113	3422	5535
	1	1324	1094	2418
	Total	3437	4516	7953

TABLE 9.3 Contingency table of Sex and Death with column percentages

		Sex	
		Male (%)	*Female (%)*
Death	**0**	61.5	75.8
	1	38.5	24.2

For clarity, we select only a single hidden layer, containing only a single neuron. Figure 9.7 shows the resulting neural network model, built using R, generated by the *Framingham_training* data set.

9.7 INTERPRETING THE WEIGHTS IN A NEURAL NETWORK MODEL

The weights in a neural network model represent what the model is trying to tell you, given the data. These weights are analogous to the predictor coefficients in a regression model. Let us glean what information we can from the weights in Figure 9.7.

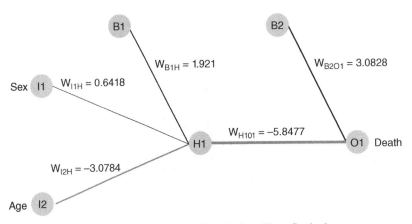

Figure 9.7   Neural network model from Framingham Heart Study data.

First, let us ignore the bias (constant term) weights $B1$ and $B2$, since they do not affect the relationship between the predictors and the response. Next, recall our exploratory data analysis (EDA), where we found that greater age and being male were both associated with higher probability of death in the Framingham Heart Study. Also, *Sex* is a binary predictor with 1 = Male and 2 = Female, so that an increase in the value of *Sex* should be associated with a decrease in probability of death. Let us see how and whether these EDA results are reflected in the neural network weights.

Now, the weight between the hidden layer node $H1$ and the output node $O1$ takes a negative value, $W_{H1O1} = -5.8477$. Thus, when the hidden layer node $H1$ is excited to a high value, it actually has a protective effect against death, lowering its probability, because of this negative weight.

Next, the weight from the *Sex* predictor to the hidden layer node takes a positive value, $W_{I1H} = 0.6418$. This means that larger values of *Sex* (females) will tend to excite the hidden layer neuron $H1$ to a higher value. As we just learned, such a high value for $H1$ lowers the probability of death. Thus, *the weights are telling us that being female protects against the probability of death*, just as we saw in the EDA.

Finally, the weight from the *Age* predictor to the hidden layer node takes a negative value, $W_{I2H} = -3.0784$. This means that higher values of *Age* will result in a lower value for the hidden layer neuron $H1$. Low values from $H1$ to output node $O1$ result in a high probability of death because its weight is negative as well. Thus, *the weights are telling us that an increase in age is associated with an increase in the probability of death*, exactly as we saw in the EDA.

9.8 HOW TO USE NEURAL NETWORKS IN R

First, read in the *Framingham_training* data set as *fram_train*, and convert the binary and ordinal variables *Death* and *Sex* to factors.

```
fram_train$Death <- as.factor(fram_train$Death)
fram_train$Sex <- as.factor(fram_train$Sex)
```

Perform min–max standardization on the Age variable

```
fram_train$Age.mm <- (fram_train$Age - min(fram_train$Age)) /
(max(fram_train$Age) - min(fram_train$Age))
```

Install the *nnet* and *NeuralNetTools* packages, and open both packages.

```
install.packages("nnet"); install.packages("NeuralNetTools")
library(nnet); library(NeuralNetTools)
```

Run the neural network algorithm.

```
nnet01 <- nnet(Death ~ Sex + Age.mm, data = fram_train, size = 1)
```

Note the formula structure, with the target variable *Death* on the left side of the tilde, and the two predictor variables *Sex* and *Age* on the right side. The

data = fram_train input specifies where the three variables come from. The **size = 1** command states that there is one unit in the hidden layer.

Note that the neural network output is saved as **nnet01**. Saving the output is required in order to obtain the plot and weights of the neural network.

Next, plot the neural network.

```
plotnet(nnet01)
```

The output from the **plotnet()** command with the **nnet01** input will match Figure 9.7.

Finally, obtain the weights.

```
nnet01$wts
```

REFERENCES

The *NeuralNetTools* package visualized our neural network model. To see the options and other features, check out the documentation for the package:M. Beck, _NeuralNetTools: Visualization and Analysis Tools for Neural Networks_. R package version 1.5.1, 2018. http://CRAN.R-project.org/package=NeuralNetTools.

The *nnet* package was used to create the neural network. For more information, see the publication: W. N. Venables and B. D. Ripley, *Modern Applied Statistics with S*, Fourth Edition, Springer, New York, 2002.

EXERCISES

CLARIFYING THE CONCEPTS

1. Neural networks classification represents an attempt to imitate what?

2. Using Figure 9.1, explain how an artificial neuron model imitates the actions of real neurons.

3. What is the main benefit of neural networks for modeling? What gives neural networks this power?

4. Describe the main drawback of neural network modeling.

5. Explain what we mean when we say that a neural network is completely connected.

6. Describe the benefits and drawbacks of using more or fewer nodes in the hidden layer.

7. Referring to the example in the text, calculate $net_B = 1.5$ and $f(net_B) = \dfrac{1}{1+e^{-1.5}} = 0.8176$.

8. Explain how the sigmoid function combines nearly linear behavior, curvilinear behavior, and nearly constant behavior.

9. Describe the process of backpropagation.

10. The essential problem for the neural network is to construct a set of weight that will minimize what?

WORKING WITH THE DATA

For the following exercises, work with the *Framingham_training* and *Framingham_test* data sets. Use either Python or R to solve each problem.

11. Convert the binary and ordinal variables *Death*, *Sex*, and *Educ* to factors.

12. Run the neural network algorithm to predict *Death* using *Sex* and *Educ*.

13. Plot the neural network.

14. Obtain the weights for the neural network. Identify which part of the network has which weight.

15. Evaluate your neural network model using the *Framingham_test* data set. Construct a contingency table to compare the actual and predicted values of *Death*.

16. Which baseline model do we compare your neural network model against? Did it outperform the baseline according to accuracy?

HANDS-ON ANALYSIS

For the following exercises, work with the *adult_ch6_training* and the *adult_ch6_test* data set. Use either Python or R to solve each problem.

17. Prepare the data set for neural network modeling by doing the following:

    a. Create a binary variable that equals one if *Cap_Gains_Losses* is greater than zero, and zero otherwise. Call it *CapGainsLossesPositive*.

    b. Convert the *Marital.status*, *Income*, and *CapGainsLossesPositive* to factors.

18. Using the training data set, create a neural network model to predict a customer's *Income* using *Marital.status* and *CapGainsLossesPositive*. Call this *NNM1* (For *neural network Model 1*). Obtain the predicted responses.

19. Plot the NNM1 neural network.

20. Evaluate NNM1 using the test data set. Construct a contingency table to compare the actual and predicted values of *Income*.

21. Which baseline model do we compare NNM1 against? Did NNM1 outperform the baseline according to accuracy?

22. Gather the results (contingency tables) from your earlier modeling of the *adult_ch6_training* and *adult_ch6_test* data sets in the Chapter 6 and Chapter 8 exercises. From Chapter 6, call the CART model *CARTM1* and call the C5.0 model *C5M1*. From Chapter 8, call the Naïve Bayes model *NBM1*.

23. Compare the NNM1 results with the three models from the previous exercise, according to the following criteria. Discuss in detail which model performed best and worst according to each criterion.

    a. Accuracy

    b. Sensitivity

    c. Specificity

For the following exercises, work with the *bank_marketing_training* and the *bank_marketing_test* data set. Use either Python or R to solve each problem.

24. Prepare the data set for neural network modeling, including standardizing the variables.

25. Using the training data set, create a neural network model to predict a customer's *Response* using whichever predictors you think appropriate. Obtain the predicted responses.

26. Plot the neural network.

27. Evaluate the neural network model using the test data set. Construct a contingency table to compare the actual and predicted values of *Response*.

28. Which baseline model do we compare your neural network model against? Did it outperform the baseline according to accuracy?

29. Using the same predictors you used for your neural network model, build models to predict *Response* using the following algorithms:

    a. CART

    b. C5.0

    c. Naïve Bayes

30. Compare the results of your neural network model with the three models from the previous exercise, according to the following criteria. Discuss in detail which model performed best and worst according to each criterion.

    a. Accuracy

    b. Sensitivity

    c. Specificity

CHAPTER *10*

CLUSTERING

10.1 WHAT IS CLUSTERING?

Clustering refers to the grouping of records, observations, or cases into classes of similar objects. A *cluster* is a collection of records that are similar to one another and dissimilar to records in other clusters. Clustering differs from classification in that there is no target variable for clustering. The clustering task does not try to classify, estimate, or predict the value of a target variable. Instead, clustering algorithms seek to segment the entire data set into relatively homogeneous subgroups or clusters, where the similarity of the records within the cluster is maximized and the similarity to records outside this cluster is minimized.

For example, the Nielsen PRIZM segments, developed by Claritas, Inc., represent demographic profiles of each geographic area in the United States, in terms of distinct lifestyle types, as defined by zip code. For example, the clusters identified for zip code 90210, Beverly Hills, California, are:

- Cluster 01: Upper Crust Estates
- Cluster 03: Movers and Shakers
- Cluster 04: Young Digerati
- Cluster 07: Money and Brains
- Cluster 16: Bohemian Mix

The description for Cluster 01: Upper Crust is "The nation's most exclusive address, Upper Crust is the wealthiest lifestyle in America, a Haven for empty-nesting couples between the ages of 45 and 64. No segment has a higher concentration of residents earning over $100,000 a year and possessing a postgraduate degree. And none has a more opulent standard of living."

Examples of clustering tasks in business and research include:

- Target marketing of a niche product for a small-capitalization business that does not have a large marketing budget.

Data Science Using Python and R, First Edition. Chantal D. Larose and Daniel T. Larose.
© 2019 John Wiley & Sons, Inc. Published 2019 by John Wiley & Sons, Inc.

141

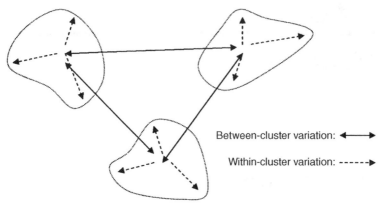

Between-cluster variation: ◄────►

Within-cluster variation: ------►

Figure 10.1 Clusters should have small within-cluster variation compared to the between-cluster variation.

- For accounting auditing purposes, to segment financial behavior into benign and suspicious categories.
- For gene expression clustering, where very large quantities of genes may exhibit similar behavior.

Clustering is often performed as a preliminary step in a data mining process, with the resulting clusters being used as further inputs into a different technique downstream, such as neural networks. Due to the enormous size of many present-day databases, it is often helpful to apply clustering analysis first, to reduce the search space for the downstream algorithms.

All clustering methods have as their goal the identification of groups of records such that similarity within a group is very high, while the similarity to records in other groups is very low. In other words, as shown in Figure 10.1, clustering algorithms seek to construct clusters of records such that the *between-cluster variation* is large compared to the *within-cluster variation*.

10.2 INTRODUCTION TO THE *K*-MEANS CLUSTERING ALGORITHM

There are many different clustering methods, including hierarchical clustering, Kohonen networks clustering, and BIRCH clustering.[1] Here, we shall focus on the *k*-means clustering algorithm. The *k*-means clustering algorithm[2] is a

---

[1] For details on these clustering methods, see *Data Mining and Predictive Analytics*, Second Edition, by Daniel T. Larose and Chantal D. Larose, John Wiley and Sons, Inc., 2015.

[2] James B. MacQueen, Some methods for classification and analysis of multivariate observations. In *Proceedings of the 5th Berkeley Symposium on Mathematical Statistics and Probability*, Vol. 1, pp. 281–297, University of California Press, Berkeley, CA, 1967.

straightforward and effective algorithm for finding clusters in data. The algorithm proceeds as follows:

- *Step 1:* Ask the user how many clusters k the data set should be partitioned into.
- *Step 2:* Randomly assign k records to be the initial cluster center locations.
- *Step 3:* For each record, find the nearest cluster center. Thus, in a sense, each cluster center "owns" a subset of the records, thereby representing a partition of the data set. We therefore have k clusters, $C_1, C_2, ..., C_k$.
- *Step 4:* For each of the k clusters, find the cluster *centroid* and update the location of each cluster center to the new value of the centroid.
- *Step 5:* Repeat steps 3–5 until convergence or termination.

The "nearest" criterion in step 3 is usually Euclidean distance, although other criteria may be applied as well. The cluster centroid in step 4 is found as follows. Suppose that we have n data points $(a_1, b_1, c_1), (a_2, b_2, c_2), ..., (a_n, b_n, c_n)$, the *centroid* of these points is the center of gravity of these points and is located at point $(\Sigma a_i/n, \Sigma b_i/n, \Sigma c_i/n,)$. For example, the points $(1,1,1), (1,2,1), (1,3,1)$, and $(2,1,1)$ would have centroid

$$\left(\frac{1 + 1 + 1 + 2}{4}, \frac{1 + 2 + 3 + 1}{4}, \frac{1 + 1 + 1 + 1}{4} \right) = \left(1.25, 1.75, 1.00 \right)$$

The algorithm terminates when the centroids no longer change. In other words, the algorithm terminates when for all clusters $C_1, C_2, ..., C_k$, all the records "owned" by each cluster center remain in that cluster. For much more on k-means clustering, see *Data Mining and Predictive Analytics*.

10.3 AN APPLICATION OF *K*-MEANS CLUSTERING

We apply the k-means clustering algorithm to the *white_wine_training* and the *white_wine_test* data sets. These data sets are adapted from the Wine Quality data set at UCI.[3] The data consist of chemical and quality characteristics of a collection of Portuguese white wines. The predictors are *alcohol* and *sugar*. The target variable is *quality*, a measure of how good the wine is, according to a professional taster. When constructing clusters, it is important to *not* include the target variable as an input to the clustering algorithm. Doing so would bias the results if we later use the clusters to predict the target. It is also important to standardize or normalize all the predictors, so that the greater variability of one predictor does not dominate the cluster construction process.

Now, the k-means algorithm requires the analyst to specify the desired number of clusters. For simplicity, we specify $k = 2$ clusters and proceed to apply

[3] https://archive.ics.uci.edu/ml/datasets/wine+quality. Also P. Cortez, A. Cerdeira, F. Almeida, T. Matos, and J. Reis, Modeling wine preferences by data mining from physicochemical properties, *Decision Support Systems*, Elsevier, 47(4), 547–553, 2009.

TABLE 10.1   Mean variable value, by cluster, for the *white_wine_training* data sets

Variable	Cluster 1 : 712 wines "Sweet Wines"	Cluster 2 : 1097 wines "Dry Wines"
Sugar_z	0.96	−0.62
Alcohol_z	−0.76	0.49

The Python results in Figure 10.2 were copied here in Table 10.1

the k-means clustering algorithm to the predictor variables *alcohol* and *sugar*. Python was used. Table 10.1 shows the mean variable value for each predictor, for the two resulting clusters. Cluster 1 contains 712 wines, with a mean sugar content 0.96 standard deviations above the overall mean sugar content for all the white wines in the training data set. (That is, the mean Cluster 1 value for the standard normal *sugar_z* variable is 0.96.) Cluster 1's mean alcohol content, however, lies 0.76 standard deviations below the mean alcohol level for all wines. On the other hand, Cluster 2 contains 1097 wines, with lower mean sugar content than Cluster 1 (0.62 standard deviations below the overall mean) but with higher alcohol content, at 0.49 standard deviations above the overall mean.

So, we may identify Cluster 1 as containing "Sweet Wines," high in sugar but low in alcohol, while Cluster 2 contains "Dry Wines," low in sugar but packing a higher alcohol punch. Perhaps, the most important cluster validation method is to *obtain clusters that make sense* to a subject matter expert. A quick Internet search shows how we obtain these different wines in the real world: "During fermentation, yeasts transform sugars … into ethanol [alcohol]…"[4] So, it is no surprise that our clustering algorithm has uncovered these two "natural" clusters of white wines: sweet wines and dry wines. The dry wines have, on the whole, evidently undergone longer fermentation than the sweet wines.

10.4   CLUSTER VALIDATION

Cluster solutions should be validated. Since no predictions were made using the training data set, we simply reapply the k-means algorithm, this time to the *white_wine_test* data set, and compare the results obtained with the training set. Table 10.2

TABLE 10.2   Mean variable value, by cluster, for the *white_wine_test* data sets

Variable	Cluster 1 : 638 wines "Sweet Wines"	Cluster 2 : 1122 wines "Dry Wines"
Sugar_z	1.07	−0.61
Alcohol_z	−0.80	0.46

The Python results in Figure 10.3 are used for this table. The cluster labels "Cluster 1" and "Cluster 2" were reversed, for ease of interpretation. These cluster labels are arbitrarily assigned by the algorithm

[4] https://en.wikipedia.org/wiki/Fermentation_in_winemaking

TABLE 10.3   Difference in variable means, training set minus test set, by cluster

Variable	Training – Test "Sweet Wines"	Training – Test "Dry Wines"
Sugar_z	$0.96 - 1.07 = -0.11$	$-0.62 - (-0.61) = -0.01$
Alcohol_z	$-0.76 - (-0.80) = 0.04$	$0.49 - 0.46 = 0.03$

contains the resulting mean variable values, by cluster. As shown in Table 10.3, the difference in mean values (training minus test sets) is relatively small. Analysts wishing further validation may perform two-sample t-tests here.

10.5 HOW TO PERFORM *K*-MEANS CLUSTERING USING PYTHON

Load the required packages.

```
import pandas as pd
from scipy import stats
from sklearn.cluster import KMeans
```

Read in the *white_wine_training* data set as *wine_train*.

```
wine_train = pd.read_csv("C:/.../white_wine_training")
```

For simplicity, let us isolate the predictor variables and save them as **X**.

```
X = wine_train[['alcohol', 'sugar']]
```

Once we have our predictor variables, standardize them using the z-score transformation and save the result as a data frame.

```
Xz = pd.DataFrame(stats.zscore(X), columns=['alcohol', 'sugar'])
```

As in Chapter 3, the **stats.zscore** command will convert the variables in **X** into their z-scores. We save the new standardized variables as a data frame using the **DataFrame()** command. The optional input **columns** use the given names as the column names. We save the result as **Xz**.

Now, we run k-means clustering on the training data set.

```
kmeans01 = KMeans(n_clusters = 2).fit(Xz)
```

The **KMeans()** command sets up the parameters of the k-means algorithm. In our case, the input **n_cluster = 2** specifies that we want two clusters. The **fit()** command runs the specified k-means algorithm on our data, with the input **Xz** giving the data set we want to cluster. The clustering result is saved under the name **kmeans01**.

To investigate the clustering results, we need to save the cluster membership as its own variable.

```
cluster = kmeans01.labels_
```

The cluster membership information is contained under **labels_** within the **kmeans01** result we saved previously. For simplicity, we save it as its own object, **cluster**.

Once we have cluster membership information, we can separate the records into two groups based on cluster membership.

```
Cluster1 = Xz.loc[cluster == 0]
Cluster2 = Xz.loc[cluster == 1]
```

The results are two data sets, one for the records in Cluster 1 and another for the records in Cluster 2.

Finally, we compute summary statistics of the two clusters using the **describe()** command.

```
Cluster1.describe()
Cluster2.describe()
```

The **describe()** command prints various statistics for the variables in each cluster, shown in Figure 10.2. The means from Figure 10.2 are copied into Table 10.1.

To validate the clustering result, run the *k*-means clustering algorithm on test data set. The code is given below and is analogous to the training set case. The describe results for the test data set are shown in Figure 10.3, with the means copied into Table 10.2.

```
wine_test = pd.read_csv("C:/.../white_wine_test")
X_test = wine_test[['alcohol', 'sugar']]
Xz_test = pd.DataFrame(stats.zscore(X_test),
columns=['alcohol', 'sugar'])
```

```
In [106]: Cluster1.describe()          In [107]: Cluster2.describe()
Out[106]:                               Out[107]:
          alcohol_z      sugar_z                  alcohol_z       sugar_z
count   712.000000   712.000000        count   1097.000000   1097.000000
mean     -0.755428     0.961034        mean       0.490305     -0.623752
std       0.580989     0.818726        std        0.905663      0.475694
min      -1.826971    -0.908740        min       -1.576448     -1.122791
25%      -1.158911     0.354160        25%       -0.156821     -0.951551
50%      -0.908388     0.867883        50%        0.427732     -0.844525
75%      -0.407343     1.488630        75%        1.179299     -0.352208
max       2.014374     5.512788        max        2.891203      1.477928
```

Figure 10.2   The Python descriptions of Cluster 1 (left) and Cluster 2 (right) from the training data set.

```
In [115]: Cluster1_test.describe()      In [116]: Cluster2_test.describe()
Out[115]:                               Out[116]:
           alcohol_z      sugar_z                  alcohol_z      sugar_z
count   1122.000000  1122.000000        count    638.000000   638.000000
mean       0.456397    -0.605782        mean      -0.802630     1.065341
std        0.903287     0.459740        std        0.561207     0.779670
min       -1.675754    -1.089453        min       -2.080483    -1.037949
25%       -0.218729    -0.945241        25%       -1.190079     0.396441
50%        0.368129    -0.821632        50%       -0.947241     1.032518
75%        1.157351    -0.285988        75%       -0.542512     1.583612
max        2.776268     1.423949        max        1.562080     3.298700
```

Figure 10.3   The Python descriptions of Cluster 1 (left) and Cluster 2 (right) from the test data set.

```
kmeans_test = KMeans(n_clusters = 2).fit(Xz_test)
cluster_test = kmeans_test.labels_  # Cluster membership
Cluster1_test = Xz_test.loc[cluster_test == 0]
Cluster2_test = Xz_test.loc[cluster_test == 1]
Cluster1_test.describe()
Cluster2_test.describe()
```

10.6   HOW TO PERFORM *K*-MEANS CLUSTERING USING R

Read in the *white_wine_training* data set as *wine_train* and subset the predictor variables into their own matrix.

```
X <- subset(wine_train, select = c("alcohol", "sugar"))
```

The **subset()** command will **select** the two variables named **alcohol** and **sugar** from the **wine_train** data set, and store them under their own name, **X**.

Now, we standardize both predictor variables and save the output as a data frame. Data frame format is required for running the **kmeans()** command.

```
Xs <- as.data.frame(scale(X))
colnames(Xs) <- c("alcohol_z", "sugar_z")
```

The **scale()** command turns the variables in **X** into their respective *z*-scores, while **as.data.frame** saves the result as a data frame. The result is saved as **Xs**. We edit the column names using colnames() to emphasize that the variables are now standardized.

The **kmeans()** command is included in the base installation of R. However, if you do get an error that says "*Could not find function 'kmeans'*," install and open the *stats* package using **install. packages("stats"); library(stats)**.

Run the *k*-means clustering algorithm.

```
kmeans01 <- kmeans(Xs, centers = 2)
```

The required inputs are **Xs**, the data frame, and **centers = 2**, the number of clusters the algorithm will look for. Note that we save the clustering algorithm output as **kmeans01**.

We need to save the cluster membership of each record as its own variable.

```
cluster <- as.factor(kmeans01$cluster)
```

The code **kmeans01$cluster** will get each record's cluster membership. Since we have two clusters in this example, the values of **kmeans01$cluster** will be either 1 or 2. The command **as.factor()** will save that string of numbers as a factor.

Now let us look at the descriptive statistics of each cluster. First, we separate the records into two groups, based on which cluster they belong to.

```
Cluster1 <- Xs[ which(cluster == 1), ]
Cluster2 <- Xs[ which(cluster == 2), ]
```

The **which()** command, used in the bracket notation on the left side of the comma, chooses only those records whose cluster membership is **1** (for **Cluster1**) or **2** (for **Cluster2**). Then, we run the **summary()** command on each group individually and note the output of interest.

```
summary(Cluster1)
summary(Cluster2)
```

The results are shown in Figure 10.4.

To validate the clusters, input the *white_wine_test* data set as *wine_test* and subset the alcohol and sugar variables. Perform variable standardization and *k*-means clustering on the test data set. The code is given below. The results are shown in Figure 10.5.

```
X_test <- subset(wine_test, select = c("alcohol", "sugar"))
Xs_test <- as.data.frame(scale(X_test))
colnames(Xs_test) <- c("alcohol_z", "sugar_z")
kmeans01_test <- kmeans(Xs_test, centers = 2)
cluster_test <- as.factor(kmeans01_test$cluster)
Cluster1_test <- Xs[ which(cluster_test == 1), ]
Cluster2_test <- Xs[ which(cluster_test == 2), ]
summary(Cluster1_test); summary(Cluster2_test)
```

```
> summary(Cluster1)                         > summary(Cluster2)
    alcohol_z          sugar_z                  alcohol_z          sugar_z
 Min.   :-1.5760   Min.    :-1.1225         Min.   :-1.8265   Min.    :-0.9085
 1st Qu.:-0.1568   1st Qu.:-0.9513         1st Qu.:-1.1586   1st Qu.: 0.3541
 Median : 0.4276   Median :-0.8443         Median :-0.9081   Median : 0.8676
 Mean   : 0.4902   Mean    :-0.6236         Mean   :-0.7552   Mean    : 0.9608
 3rd Qu.: 1.1790   3rd Qu.:-0.3521         3rd Qu.:-0.4072   3rd Qu.: 1.4882
 Max.   : 2.8904   Max.    : 1.4775         Max.   : 2.0138   Max.    : 5.5113
```

Figure 10.4   The R descriptions of Cluster 1 and Cluster 2 from the training data set.

```
> summary(Cluster1_test)                      > summary(Cluster2_test)
    alcohol_z              sugar_z                 alcohol_z              sugar_z
 Min.   :-1.8265    Min.    :-1.1011          Min.    :-1.7430    Min.    :-1.1225
 1st Qu.:-1.2421    1st Qu.:-0.7801          1st Qu.:-0.2403    1st Qu.:-0.9245
 Median :-0.9081    Median : 0.3327          Median : 0.3441    Median :-0.5019
 Mean   :-0.8267    Mean    : 0.3606          Mean    : 0.3697    Mean    :-0.1869
 3rd Qu.:-0.5742    3rd Qu.: 1.2100          3rd Qu.: 1.0120    3rd Qu.: 0.3327
 Max.   : 1.4294    Max.    : 5.5113          Max.    : 1.9303    Max.    : 3.5853
```

Figure 10.5   The R descriptions of Cluster 1 (left) and Cluster 2 (right) from the test data set.

EXERCISES

CLARIFYING THE CONCEPTS

1. Explain what clustering is trying to accomplish, using the concepts of between-cluster variation and within-cluster variation.

2. Which, records or variables, does clustering seek to group?

3. Why is it helpful to apply clustering fairly early in the modeling process?

4. True or false: k-means clustering automatically selects the optimal number of clusters.

5. Why do we omit the target variable as an input to the clustering algorithm?

6. Explain how we proceed to perform cluster validation.

7. Why do we standardize the numerical predictors prior to clustering?

8. What is perhaps the most important cluster validation method?

9. What is the centroid of the points (1, 5), (2, 4), and (3, 3)?

10. Provide an example of clustering in the everyday world that is not discussed in this chapter.

WORKING WITH THE DATA

For the following exercises, work with the *white_wine_training* and *white_wine_test* data sets. Use either Python or R to solve each problem.

11. Input and standardize both the training and test data sets.

12. Run k-means clustering on the training data set, using two clusters.

13. Give the mean of each variable within each cluster and use the means to identify a "Dry wines" and a "Sweet wines" cluster.

14. Validate the clustering results by running k-means clustering on the test data set, using two clusters, and identifying a "Dry wines" and a "Sweet wines" cluster.

HANDS-ON ANALYSIS

For the following exercises, work with the *cereals* data set. Use either Python or R to solve each problem.

15. Subset the *Fat* and *Sodium* variables into their own data frame, X. Standardize the data set.

16. Run *k*-means clustering on the data set, using three clusters.

17. Obtain the summary of each variable within each cluster and use the summaries to identify:

    a. A low fat, low sodium cluster.

    b. A low fat, high sodium cluster.

    c. A high fat, high sodium cluster.

For the following exercises, work with the *Framingham_training* and *Framingham_test* data sets. Use only the *Sex* and *Age* fields. Standardize *Age*.

18. Run *k*-means clustering on the *Framingham_training* data set, requesting $k = 2$ clusters.

19. Construct a table of statistics summarizing your clusters. Describe what these two clusters consist of.

20. Perform *k*-means clustering on the *Framingham_test* data set, requesting $k = 2$ clusters.

21. Report the results from your test set. Are your clusters validated?

22. Again run *k*-means clustering on the *Framingham_training* data set, this time specifying $k = 3$ clusters.

23. Construct a table of statistics summarizing your clusters. Describe which records belong to each cluster.

24. Perform *k*-means clustering on the *Framingham_test* data set, specifying $k = 3$ clusters.

25. Report the results from your test set. Are your clusters validated?

26. Run *k*-means clustering on the *Framingham_training* data set. Specify $k = 4$ clusters.

27. Construct a table of statistics summarizing your four clusters. Clearly describe your four clusters.

28. Perform *k*-means clustering on the *Framingham_test* data set, requesting $k = 4$ clusters.

29. Report the results from your test set. Are your clusters validated?

30. Which of the clustering solutions, $k = 2$, 3, or 4, do you prefer, and why?

CHAPTER *11*

REGRESSION MODELING

11.1 THE ESTIMATION TASK

Thus far in the Modeling Phase we have covered the following tasks:

- Classification task
- Clustering task

There remain two tasks left to cover:

- Estimation task
- Association task

In this chapter, we cover the estimation task; later, in Chapter 14, we will cover the association task.

The most widespread method for performing the estimation task is linear regression. Simple linear regression approximates the relationship between a numeric predictor and a continuous target, using a straight line. Multiple regression modeling approximates the relationship between a set of $p > 1$ predictors and a single continuous target, using a p-dimensional plane or hyperplane.

11.2 DESCRIPTIVE REGRESSION MODELING

The usual multiple regression model is a parametric model, defined by the following equation:

$$y = \beta_0 + \beta_1 x_1 + \beta_2 x_2 + \cdots + \beta_p x_p + \varepsilon$$

where the x's represent the predictor variables, and the β's represent the unknown model parameters, whose values are estimated using the data.[1] Now, estimating

---

[1] For much more on inferential regression modeling, see *Data Mining and Predictive Analytics*.

Data Science Using Python and R, First Edition. Chantal D. Larose and Daniel T. Larose.
© 2019 John Wiley & Sons, Inc. Published 2019 by John Wiley & Sons, Inc.

151

model parameters using sample data represents classical statistical inference. The Data Science Methodology outlined in Chapter 1, however, employs cross-validation rather than classical statistical inference to validate model results. Thus, in this book, *we will bypass the parametric regression equation above, in favor of a descriptive approach to regression modeling*, using the following regression equation:

$$\hat{y} = b_0 + b_1 x_1 + b_2 x_2 + \cdots + b_p x_p$$

In this regression equation, $\hat{y}$ represents the estimated value of the target variable y, the b's represent the *known* values of the regression coefficients, and the x's represent the predictor variables.

11.3 AN APPLICATION OF MULTIPLE REGRESSION MODELING

To illustrate multiple regression, we turn to the *clothing_sales_training* and *clothing_sales_test* data sets. The client has some data on customer spending and would like to estimate *Sales_per_Visit*, given three predictors:

- *Days between purchases* ("Days," Continuous: Average number of days between purchases.)
- *Credit Card* ("CC," Flag: Does the customer have a store credit card?)
- *Web Account* ("Web," Flag: Does the customer have a web account?)

So, our provisional regression equation will be:

$$\widehat{Sales\ per\ Visit} = b_0 + b_1(Days\ between\ purchases) + b_2(Credit\ Card) + b_3(Web\ Account)$$

Because there is only one continuous predictor, it is not necessary to standardize the predictors. The results of the regression of *Sales per Visit* vs the three predictors for the training set are shown in Figure 11.1. We use the p-values as a guide to tell us which variables belong in the model. Note that we are not performing inference as such (the usual domain of p-values), because we will be careful to cross-validate these results with the test data set. The usual p-value cutoff for retaining variables in a regression model is about 0.05, though cutoff values differ from field to field. Variables with p-values lower than the cutoff are retained in the model.

From Figure 11.1, we see that *Web Account*, with a p-value of 0.533, does not belong in the model. The regression results for the test data set in Figure 11.2 concur that *Web Account* does not belong in the model. This leaves us with our regression equation as:

$$\widehat{Sales\ per\ Visit} = b_0 + b_1(Days\ between\ purchases) + b_2(Credit\ Card)$$

```
=================================================================================
                coef      std err         t      P>|t|      [0.025      0.975]
---------------------------------------------------------------------------------
const        73.3654        4.676    15.689      0.000      64.192      82.538
CC           21.8175        4.766     4.578      0.000      12.468      31.167
Days          0.1644        0.017     9.802      0.000       0.131       0.197
Web           7.2755       11.658     0.624      0.533     -15.593      30.144
=================================================================================
```

Figure 11.1   Python regression results for the training data set.

```
=================================================================================
                coef      std err         t      P>|t|      [0.025      0.975]
---------------------------------------------------------------------------------
const        80.2877        4.000    20.071      0.000      72.441      88.135
CC           20.8955        4.170     5.011      0.000      12.716      29.075
Days          0.1261        0.014     9.120      0.000       0.099       0.153
Web          12.4811        9.054     1.378      0.168      -5.280      30.242
=================================================================================
```

Figure 11.2   Python validation of the regression results with the test data set.

```
=================================================================================
                coef      std err         t      P>|t|      [0.025      0.975]
---------------------------------------------------------------------------------
const        73.6209        4.657    15.808      0.000      64.485      82.757
CC           22.1357        4.738     4.672      0.000      12.842      31.429
Days          0.1637        0.017     9.784      0.000       0.131       0.197
=================================================================================
```

Figure 11.3   Final regression model for the training data set using Python.

```
=================================================================================
                coef      std err         t      P>|t|      [0.025      0.975]
---------------------------------------------------------------------------------
const        80.7656        3.986    20.260      0.000      72.946      88.586
CC           21.5262        4.146     5.192      0.000      13.393      29.659
Days          0.1254        0.014     9.071      0.000       0.098       0.152
=================================================================================
```

Figure 11.4   Validating the final regression model with the test data set using Python.

We therefore rerun the regression model, this time omitting *Web Account* from the model. The results for the training set and test set are shown in Figures 11.3 and 11.4. Using the coefficients from the training set, we obtain our final regression model as:

$$\widehat{Sales\ per\ Visit} = 73.6209 + 0.1637(Days\ between\ purchases) \\ + 22.1357(Credit\ Card)$$

That is, the estimated sales per visit for our customer base is $73.6209 plus $0.1637 times the number of days between purchases plus $22.1357 if they have a store credit card. We see that customers tend to spend more if they have a store credit card. Also, the longer it has been between visits, the more customers tend to spend.

We interpret these *regression coefficients* as follows:

- **Credit Card.** The estimated increase in Sales per Visit for a customer with a store credit card (compared to a customer without a store credit card) is $22.1357, when Days between Purchase is held constant.

- **Days Between Purchase.** For each increase of one day in the average days between purchases, the estimated increase in Sales per Visit is $0.1637, when Credit Card is held constant. This can be better understood if we compare two shoppers, Customer A and Customer B, where Customer A has an average number of days between purchases one month (30 days) longer than Customer B. Then, Customer A's Sales per Visit is $30 \times \$0.1637 = \$4.91$ greater than Customer B, holding Credit Card constant.

11.4 HOW TO PERFORM MULTIPLE REGRESSION MODELING USING PYTHON

First, as always, we load the required packages.

```
import pandas as pd
import numpy as np
import statsmodels.api as sm
```

Next, we import the *clothing_sales_training* and *clothing_sales_test* data sets as *sales_train* and *sales_test*, respectively.

```
sales_train = pd.read_csv("C:/.../clothing_sales_
training.csv")
sales_test = pd.read_csv("C:/.../clothing_sales_test.csv")
```

For simplicity, we separate the predictor variables and the target variable. We call the data frame of predictor variables **X** and the target variable **y**.

```
X = pd.DataFrame(sales_train[['CC', 'Days', 'Web']])
y = pd.DataFrame(sales_train[['Sales per Visit']])
```

To have a constant term b_0 in our regression model, we need to add a constant variable to our predictor variables.

```
X = sm.add_constant(X)
```

Running the **add_constant**() command on the **X** variables will add a column to the data frame filled with the value one (1.0).

Finally, we run the multiple regression model.

```
model01 = sm.OLS(y, X).fit()
```

OLS stands for "Ordinary Least Squares," which is the method used to fit this regression model. Note that the two inputs of the **OLS**() command are the target variable **y** and the predictor variables **X**. Save the fitted model as **model01**. To obtain the results of the regression model, run the **summary()** command on **model01**.

```
model01.summary()
```

An excerpt from the output of the **summary()** command is shown in Figure 11.1. The regression coefficients are located in the *coef* column.

To verify the regression model results, we run the same code on the *sales_test* data set. The code is given below, the explanations equivalent to those given earlier in this section.

```
X_test = pd.DataFrame(sales_test[['CC', 'Days', 'Web']])
y_test = pd.DataFrame(sales_test[['Sales per Visit']])
X_test = sm.add_constant(X_test)
model01_test = sm.OLS(y_test, X_test).fit()
model01_test.summary()
```

An excerpt from the results from the **summary()** command run on **model01_test** is given in Figure 11.2. The results validate the results from **model01**.

To remove the variable *Web* from the regression model, we redefine the **X** data frame to include only the remaining two predictor variables. After doing so, we also need to add the constant term back into our predictor variable data frame.

```
X = pd.DataFrame(sales_train[['CC', 'Days']])
X = sm.add_constant(X)
```

Once the predictor variable data frame is ready, we run the **OLS()** and **fit()** commands on the target variable **y** and new **X** data frame again. Note that we did not change the **y** input, since only the **X** input needed to change. Save the new model as **model02** and run the **summary()** command on **model02** to view the results.

```
model02 = sm.OLS(y, X).fit()
model02.summary()
```

An excerpt from the output of the **model02.summary()** command is shown in Figure 11.3.

To verify this smaller model, we run similar code on the test data. Once again, the explanations are similar to those for the preceding example.

```
X_test = pd.DataFrame(sales_test[['CC', 'Days']])
X_test = sm.add_constant(X_test)
model02_test = sm.OLS(y_test, X_test).fit()
model02_test.summary()
```

An excerpt of the output from the **model02_test.summary()** command is shown in Figure 11.4.

11.5 HOW TO PERFORM MULTIPLE REGRESSION MODELING USING R

Load the *clothing_sales_training* and *clothing_sales_test* data sets as *sales_train* and *sales_test*, respectively. Next, make sure the binary variables are factors in both data sets.

```
sales_train$CC <- as.factor(sales_train$CC)
sales_train$Web <- as.factor(sales_train$Web)
sales_test$CC <- as.factor(sales_test$CC)
sales_test$Web <- as.factor(sales_test$Web)
```

Now, run the full model for the training data set.

```
model01 <- lm(formula = Sales.per.Visit ~ Days + Web +
CC, data = sales_train)
```

Notice the two pieces of input that are required: **formula** and **data**. The **formula** takes the same *Target ~ Predictors* form we have seen before. The **data = sales_train** input specifies the data set that our variables come from. We save the results of the regression modeling under the name **model01**. To view a summary of the model results, run the **summary()** command on **model01**.

```
summary(model01)
```

An excerpt of the output generated by **summary(model01)** is shown in Figure 11.5.

To validate the model, change the data input to specify that the variables now come from the *sales_test* data set.

```
model01_test <- lm(formula = Sales.per.Visit ~ Days +
Web + CC, data = sales_test)
```

To view the regression summary of this new model, run **summary (model01_test)**. An excerpt of the output generated by this command is shown in Figure 11.6.

To remove variables from the model, remove their names from the series of predictor variables to the right of the tilde within the **lm()** command.

```
Coefficients:
            Estimate Std. Error t value Pr(>|t|)
(Intercept) 73.36537    4.67621  15.689  < 2e-16 ***
Days         0.16438    0.01677   9.802  < 2e-16 ***
Web1         7.27550   11.65786   0.624    0.533
CC1         21.81750    4.76607   4.578 5.1e-06 ***
---
Signif. codes:  0 '***' 0.001 '**' 0.01 '*' 0.05 '.' 0.1 ' ' 1
```

Figure 11.5   Regression results from R for the training data set.

```
Coefficients:
             Estimate Std. Error t value Pr(>|t|)
(Intercept) 80.28768    4.00016  20.071  < 2e-16 ***
Days         0.12610    0.01383   9.120  < 2e-16 ***
Web1        12.48109    9.05412   1.378    0.168
CC1         20.89548    4.16987   5.011 6.11e-07 ***
---
Signif. codes:  0 '***' 0.001 '**' 0.01 '*' 0.05 '.' 0.1 ' ' 1
```

Figure 11.6   Validating the regression results from R with the test data set.

```
Coefficients:
             Estimate Std. Error t value Pr(>|t|)
(Intercept) 73.62090    4.65727  15.808  < 2e-16 ***
Days         0.16374    0.01674   9.784  < 2e-16 ***
CC1         22.13570    4.73772   4.672 3.26e-06 ***
---
Signif. codes:  0 '***' 0.001 '**' 0.01 '*' 0.05 '.' 0.1 ' ' 1
```

Figure 11.7   Final regression results from R for the training data set.

```
Coefficients:
             Estimate Std. Error t value Pr(>|t|)
(Intercept) 80.76564    3.98640  20.260  < 2e-16 ***
Days         0.12538    0.01382   9.071  < 2e-16 ***
CC1         21.52618    4.14603   5.192 2.39e-07 ***
---
Signif. codes:  0 '***' 0.001 '**' 0.01 '*' 0.05 '.' 0.1 ' ' 1
```

Figure 11.8   Validating the final regression results from R with the test data set.

The commands to run the new models and generate the summary output are given below.

```
model02 <- lm(formula = Sales.per.Visit ~ Days + CC,
data = sales_train)
summary(model02)
model02_test <- lm(formula = Sales.per.Visit ~ Days +
CC, data = sales_test)
summary(model02_test)
```

Notice that excerpts of the output generated by **summary(model02)** and **summary(model02_test)** are shown in Figures 11.7 and 11.8, respectively.

11.6   MODEL EVALUATION FOR ESTIMATION

We can use the regression equation to make predictions (estimates) of sales per visit. For example, consider Customer 1 in the training set, who goes 333 days between purchases and who does not have a store credit card (*Credit Card* = 0). Plugging these values into the regression equation, we obtain:

$$\widehat{Sales\ per\ Visit} = 73.62 + 0.1637(333) + 22.14(0) = \$128.13$$

```
In [194]: np.sqrt(model02.scale)
Out[194]: 87.54136112817613
```

Figure 11.9   The standard error of the estimate from Python.

That is, using the regression model, we would estimate the average sales per visit for this customer to be $\hat{y} = \$128.13$. However, the *actual* sales per visit for this customer is $y = \$184.23$. So, the *prediction error* (residual) for this customer is:

$$prediction\ error = (y - \hat{y}) = 184.23 - 128.13 = \$56.10$$

So, this customer spends $56.10 more than expected, given his or her days between visits and credit card status.

The typical size of the prediction error is given by the statistic s, the standard error of the estimate.

$$s = \sqrt{MSE} = \sqrt{\frac{SSE}{n-p-1}} = \sqrt{\frac{\sum(y-\hat{y})^2}{n-p-1}}$$

Here, $s = \$87.54$, meaning that the size of the model's typical prediction error is about $87.54, as can be seen in Figure 11.9. This large value is due to the fact that our data is excerpted from a much larger data set, including dozens more predictors, useful for making our model's estimates more precise. Usually, however, s is a very important metric for measuring the efficacy of a regression model.

In its derivation, s squares the prediction errors, thereby possibly endowing outliers with undue influence in the magnitude of the statistic. Data scientists should therefore compare s with the *Mean Absolute Error* (MAE), given by

$$Mean\ Absolute\ Error = \frac{\sum|y-\hat{y}|}{n}$$

The MAE takes the *distance* between the actual and predicted values of y and finds the average of these distances. There is no squaring going on. As for any model evaluation statistics, we should do the following:

1. Develop the regression model using the training data set.
2. Calculate the *MAE* by passing the test data set through the model trained on the training data set.

For the training data set, we have $MAE = \$53.39$.

Estimation Model Metrics

When evaluating estimation models, always report both s and *MAE*.

OLS Regression Results

```
=================================================================================
Dep. Variable:        Sales per Visit   R-squared:                    0.065
Model:                            OLS   Adj. R-squared:               0.064
Method:                 Least Squares   F-statistic:                  50.72
Date:               Mon, 13 Aug 2018   Prob (F-statistic):        5.12e-22
Time:                        12:33:41   Log-Likelihood:             -8546.4
No. Observations:                1451   AIC:                      1.710e+04
Df Residuals:                    1448   BIC:                      1.711e+04
Df Model:                           2
Covariance Type:            nonrobust
```

Figure 11.10 R^2_{adj} from Python for the final regression model.

Finally, R^2 is a well-known regression metric. It is interpreted as the proportion of the variability in the response that is accounted for by the predictors in the model. For multiple regression models, analysts should use R^2_{adj}, which penalizes R^2 for having too many unhelpful predictors in the model. Our regression model has $R^2_{adj} = 0.064$, as seen in Figure 11.10. That is, 6.4% of the variability in *Sales per Visit* is accounted for by the predictors *Days since Purchase* and *Credit Card*. This small proportion is not surprising, since there are many other factors affecting how much customers spend.

11.6.1   How to Perform Estimation Model Evaluation Using Python

To use the regression model to predict customer sales per visit, we first need to specify the variable values for the first customer for the Python regression model. As the variables in the model are in the order *Constant, CC, Days*, this is the order in which we specify the values.

```
cust01 = np.column_stack((1, 0, 333))
```

The first input in the **column_stack()** command is 1, for the constant term in the model.

Once you have constructed the customer in question, run the **predict()** command on **cust01**. Since we are predicting the sales using the results stored in **model02**, we use **model02.predict()**.

```
model02.predict(cust01)
```

To obtain the predicted values of all customers in the test data set, change the input of the **predict()** command to the test data predictor variable data frame, **X_test**.

```
ypred = model02.predict(X_test)
```

The result is a column of predictions, one for each record in the test data set. These values will allow us to calculate the MAE later in this section.

```
In [191]: met.mean_absolute_error(y_true = ytrue, y_pred = ypred)
Out[191]: 53.386395553029432
```

Figure 11.11   The MAE from Python.

Python does not automatically supply the standard error of the estimate. However, it can be calculated using the square root of the scale parameter of the model.

```
np.sqrt(model02.scale)
```

To calculate the MAE, we need both the predicted and actual values of y. The actual values are the values of the target variable, renamed below as **ytrue** for clarity. The **ypred** values come from the code above.

```
ytrue = sales_train[['Sales per Visit']]
met.mean_absolute_error(y_true = ytrue, y_pred = ypred)
```

The final output from the code is about 53.39, the value of the MAE. The code, with this result, is shown in Figure 11.11.

To obtain the value of R^2_{adj}, examine the output from the **summary()** command demonstrated in the previous Python section, and shown in Figure 11.10.

11.6.2   How to Perform Estimation Model Evaluation Using R

To use our model to predict the sales per visit of a particular customer, we build a data frame containing that customer's information.

```
cust01 <- data.frame(CC = as.factor(0), Days = 333)
```

The command **data.frame()** will create a data frame using the input contents. The variables' names must exactly match the names of the predictor variables in the model. Since the credit card variable were factors when we built the model, make sure they are factors when creating this new customer. Save this new customer data as **cust01**. Note that we did not include the target variable.

```
predict(object = model02, newdata = cust01)
```

When we run the **predict()** command using **object = model02** and **newdata = cust01**, the output is the predicted number of sales per visit.

The standard error of the estimate is given as part of the output generated by the **summary()** command. Figure 11.12 shows an excerpt of the output generated by **summary(model02)**. The important statistic *s* is called the "Residual standard error" in this output, and is reported for this model as 87.54 in Figure 11.12, along with the value of R^2_{adj}, called "Adjusted R-squared."

To calculate the MAE, we need the actual and predicted values for all records in the test data set using the training data model.

```
X_test <- data.frame(Days = sales_test$Days, CC = sales_
test$CC)
ypred <- predict(object = model02, newdata = X_test)
```

```
Residual standard error: 87.54 on 1448 degrees of freedom
Multiple R-squared:  0.06547,   Adjusted R-squared:  0.06418
F-statistic: 50.72 on 2 and 1448 DF,  p-value: < 2.2e-16
```

Figure 11.12   Standard error and Adjusted R-squared from R.

```
> MAE(y_pred = ypred, y_true = ytrue)
[1] 53.3864
```

Figure 11.13   The MAE from R.

> ytrue <- sales_test$Sales.per.Visit
>
> We also need to install and open the *MLmetrics* package.
>
> install.packages("MLmetrics"); library(MLmetrics)
>
> Once the package is open, you can calculate the MAE.
>
> MAE(y_pred = ypred, y_true = ytrue)

The two inputs of the **MAE()** command are **y_pred** and **y_true**. Set **y_pred = ypred**, the values you obtained from the regression model; and set **y_true = ytrue**, the target variable from the training data set. The result of running this command is the MAE, the code and output for which are shown in Figure 11.13.

11.7   STEPWISE REGRESSION

In this small example, we had only three predictors. But, most data science projects use dozens if not hundreds of predictors. We therefore need a method to ease the selection of the best regression model. This method is called *stepwise regression*. In stepwise regression, helpful predictors are entered into the model one at a time, starting with the most helpful predictor. Because of multicollinearity or other effects, when several helpful variables are entered, one of them may no longer be considered helpful any more, and should be dropped. For this reason, stepwise regression adds the most helpful predictors into the model one at a time and then checks to see if they all still belong. Finally, the stepwise algorithm can find no further helpful predictors and converges to a final model.

The application of stepwise regression (not shown) to the *clothing_sales_training* and *clothing_sales_test* data sets converged on the final models displayed in Figures 11.3 and 11.4. It is important to understand that stepwise regression is not guaranteed to uncover the optimal model, as its search algorithm does not perform all possible regressions. To guarantee the optimal model, you can use *best subsets regression*,[2] though the software may limit the number of predictors to the best subsets algorithm.

---

[2] See *Data Mining and Predictive Analytics*.

```
Start:  AIC=12982.67
Sales.per.Visit ~ Days + Web + CC

         Df Sum of Sq      RSS    AIC
- Web    1      2986 11096733  12981
<none>              11093747  12983
- CC     1    160657 11254404  13002
- Days   1    736574 11830321  13074

Step:  AIC=12981.06
Sales.per.Visit ~ Days + CC

         Df Sum of Sq      RSS    AIC
<none>              11096733  12981
- CC     1    167291 11264025  13001
- Days   1    733593 11830326  13072
```

Figure 11.14 The output from stepwise regression in R.

11.7.1 How to Perform Stepwise Regression Using R

To run stepwise regression, you first need to install and open the *MASS* package.

```
install.packages("MASS"); library(MASS)
```

Run the regression model, including all variables under consideration. Save the model under a name. For this example, we will use **model01**, which we know to have a variable, *Web*, that does not belong in the model.

Once you have saved the model, it is time for stepwise regression.

```
model01_step <- stepAIC(object = model01)
```

The **stepAIC()** command will run stepwise regression on the object specified. For our example, we want to run stepwise regression on **model01**. We save the result under the name **model01_step**.

Even saving the **stepAIC()** output under the name will show some output, given in Figure 11.14. The output shows the steps taken to converge on a model. Moving from the top half to the bottom half of the output shows that the stepwise algorithm took one step. Namely, it removed the variable *Web*.

If you run the name **model01_step** by itself, it will give you the regression coefficients of the final model. If you run **summary(model01_step)**, it will give the full summary of the final model, which will match the output given by **summary(model02)**, since the final model converged to by stepwise is the regression model we saved as **model02**.

11.8 BASELINE MODELS FOR REGRESSION

The usual baseline model to compare your regression model against is the simple $y = \bar{y}$ model. If any of the predictors are helpful at all in estimating the response, then the model will beat the $y = \bar{y}$ model. Nevertheless, we should still formally verify that our regression model (or any estimation model) is outperforming the $y = \bar{y}$ model, as follows:[3]

Baseline Model Comparison for Estimation Models

1. Calculate the errors made by the baseline model. These take the form $Error = y - \bar{y}$.
2. Compute the MAE for the baseline model, as follows:

$$MAE_{Baseline} = \frac{\sum |y - \bar{y}|}{n}$$

3. Compare $MAE_{Baseline}$ to the MAE for the estimation model.

$$MAE_{Regression} = \frac{\sum |y - \hat{y}|}{n}$$

4. The estimation model outperforms the baseline model when

$$MAE_{Regression} < MAE_{Baseline}$$

We apply the Baseline Model Comparison to our final regression model (Figure 11.3) as follows:

1. We calculate the errors for the baseline model using the $\bar{y} = \$112.57$ provided by the test data set.
2. We compute $MAE_{Baseline} = \$55.53$.
3. The $MAE_{Regression}$ we obtained by passing the test data set through the model developed by the training data set is $53.39.
4. Since $\$53.39 = MAE_{Regression} < MAE_{Baseline} = \$55.53$, our regression model did beat the baseline model.

REFERENCES

The *MASS* package shares the same core publication that we have seen for the *nnet* package: W. N. Venables and B. D. Ripley, *Modern Applied Statistics with S*, Fourth Edition, Springer, New York, 2002.

The *MLmetrics* package, which allowed us to obtain the MAE in R, can be further explored here: Yachen Yan, MLmetrics: Machine Learning Evaluation Metrics. R package version 1.1.1. 2016. https://CRAN.R-project.org/package=MLmetrics

---

[3] Some data scientists may prefer to compare $MSE_{Regression}$ with $MSE_{Baseline}$.

EXERCISES

CLARIFYING THE CONCEPTS

1. How does multiple regression approximate the relationship between a set of two predictors and a single numeric target?

2. Explain how we are bypassing the classical statistical inference approach to regression.

3. Explain why it is not necessary to standardize the predictors when there is only one continuous predictor and the others are flags?

4. True or false: Our use of p-values as guides for determining inclusion in the model means that we are using statistical inference. If false, explain why not.

5. For the training set results in Figure 11.3, suppose two customers both had a store credit card, but Customer A had 100 more days between purchases than Customer B. Describe the difference in the two customers' estimated sales per visit.

6. For the training set results in Figure 11.3, suppose two customers both had the same days between purchases, but Customer C had a store credit card and Customer D did not. Describe the difference in the two customers' estimated sales per visit.

7. Calculate the prediction error for Customer 2 in the training set.

8. Calculate s for the test data set.

9. Calculate the MAE for the test data set.

10. True or false: Stepwise regression always finds the optimal set of predictors.

WORKING WITH THE DATA

For the following exercises, work with the *clothing_sales_training* and *clothing_sales_test* data sets. Use either Python or R to solve each problem.

11. Use the training set to run a regression model to predict Sales per Visit using Days between purchases, Credit card, and Web account. Identify which predictor variable should not be in the model.

12. Validate the model from the previous exercise, by running the regression using the test data set.

13. Suppose someone said, "There is no evidence for a relationship between *Sales per Visit* and whether the customer has a store credit card." How would you respond?

14. Suppose someone said, "There is no evidence for a relationship between *Sales per Visit* and whether the customer has a store web account." How would you respond?

15. Run a regression model to predict Sales per Visit, using only the variables found to be significant in the previous regression model.

16. Validate the model from the previous exercise.

17. Use the regression equation to complete this sentence: "The estimated Sales per Visit equals...."

18. Calculate and interpret the standard error of the estimate for the regression.

19. Find and interpret R^2_{adj}.

20. Calculate and interpret the MAE for the regression model. Compare it to the standard error.

21. Perform stepwise regression on the model in Exercise 11. Confirm that it converges to the model in Exercise 13.

22. Calculate $MAE_{Baseline}$.

23. Compute $MAE_{Regression}$.

24. Determine whether the regression model outperformed its baseline model.

HANDS-ON ANALYSIS

For the following exercises, work with the *adult* data set. Use either Python or R to solve each problem.

25. Partition the data set into a training set and a test set, each containing about half of the records.

26. Run a regression model to predict Hours per Week using Age and Education Num. Obtain a summary of the model. Are there any predictor variables that should not be in the model?

27. Validate the model from the previous exercise.

28. Use the regression equation to complete this sentence: "The estimated Hours per Week equals…."

29. Interpret the coefficient for *Age*.

30. Interpret the coefficient for *Education Num*.

31. Find and interpret the value of *s*.

32. Find and interpret R^2_{adj}.

33. Find $MAE_{Baseline}$ and $MAE_{Regression}$, and determine whether the regression model outperformed its baseline model.

For the following exercises, work with the *bank_reg_training* and the *bank_reg_test* data sets. Use either Python or R to solve each problem.

34. Use the training set to run a regression predicting *Credit Score*, based on *Debt-to-Income Ratio* and *Request Amount*. Obtain a summary of the model. Do both predictors belong in the model?

35. Validate the model from the previous exercise.

36. Use the regression equation to complete this sentence: "The estimated Credit Score equals…."

37. Interpret the coefficient for *Debt-to-Income Ratio*.

38. Interpret the coefficient for *Request Amount*.

39. Find and interpret the value of *s*.

40. Find and interpret R^2_{adj}. Comment.

41. Find $MAE_{Baseline}$ and $MAE_{Regression}$, and determine whether the regression model outperformed its baseline model.

42. Construct a regression model for predicting *Interest*, using *Request Amount*. Obtain a summary of the model.

43. Explain what is unusual with your results from the previous exercise.

44. Construct a scatterplot of *Interest* against *Request Amount*. Describe the relationship between the variables. Explain how this relationship explains the unusual results from your regression model.

For the following exercises, work with the *Framingham_training* and the *Framingham_test* data sets. Reexpress *Sex* so that it is a flag variable with 0 for males and 1 for females. Use either Python or R to solve each problem.

45. Use the training set to run a regression predicting *Age*, based on *Sex* and *Education*. Obtain a summary of the model. Do both predictors belong in the model?

46. Validate the model from the previous exercise.

47. Use the regression equation to complete this sentence: "The estimated Age equals…."

48. Interpret the coefficient for *Sex*.

49. Interpret the coefficient for *Education*.

50. Find and interpret the value of *s*.

51. Find and interpret R^2_{adj}.

52. Find $MAE_{Baseline}$ and $MAE_{Regression}$, and determine whether the regression model outperformed its baseline model.

For the following exercises, work with the *white_wine_training* and the *white_wine_test* data sets. Use either Python or R to solve each problem.

53. Use the training set to run a regression predicting *Quality*, based on *Alcohol* and *Sugar*. Obtain a summary of the model. Do both predictors belong in the model?

54. Validate the model from the previous exercise.

55. Use the regression equation to complete this sentence: "The estimated Quality equals…."

56. Interpret the coefficient for *Alcohol*.

57. Interpret the coefficient for *Sugar*.

58. Find and interpret the value of *s*.

59. Find and interpret R^2_{adj}.

60. Find $MAE_{Baseline}$ and $MAE_{Regression}$, and determine whether the regression model outperformed its baseline model.

CHAPTER 12

DIMENSION REDUCTION

12.1 THE NEED FOR DIMENSION REDUCTION

High dimensionality in data science refers to when there are a large number of predictors in the data set. For example, 100 predictors describe a 100-dimensional space. So, why do we need dimension reduction in data science?

1. **Multicollinearity.** Typically, large databases have many predictors. It is unlikely that all of these predictors are uncorrelated. Multicollinearity, which occurs when there is substantial correlation among the predictors, can lead to unstable regression models.

2. **Double-Counting.** Inclusion of predictors which are highly correlated tends to overemphasize a particular aspect of the model, that is, essentially double-counting this aspect. For example, suppose we are trying to estimate the age of youngsters using math knowledge, height, and weight. Since height and weight are correlated, the model is essentially double-counting the physical component of the youngster, as compared to the intellectual component.

3. **Curse of Dimensionality.** As dimensionality increases, the volume of the predictor space grows exponentially, that is, faster than the number of predictors itself. Thus, even for huge sample sizes, the high-dimension space is *sparse*. For example, the empirical rule states that about 68% of normally distributed data lies within one standard deviation of the mean. But, this is for one dimension. For 10 dimensions, only 2% of the data lies within the analogous hypersphere.

4. **Violates Parsimony.** The use of too many predictors also violates the principle of *parsimony*, the scientific principle one sees in many branches of science, that things often behave in a quite economical way. In data science, simplicity (parsimony) should be considered when comparing models, keeping the number of predictors to such a size that would be easily interpreted.

5. **Overfitting.** Keeping too many predictors in the model tends to lead to *overfitting*, in which the generality of the findings is hindered because new data do not behave the same as the training data for all the many predictors.

Data Science Using Python and R, First Edition. Chantal D. Larose and Daniel T. Larose.
© 2019 John Wiley & Sons, Inc. Published 2019 by John Wiley & Sons, Inc.

6. **Miss the Bigger Picture.** Further, analysts should try to keep an eye on the big picture, and analysis solely at the variable level might miss the fundamentals underlying relationships among the predictors. Instead, several predictors might fall naturally into a single group (a *factor* or *component*), which addresses a single aspect of the data. For example, the variables savings account balance, checking account balance, home equity, stock portfolio value, and 401 k balance might all fall together under the single component, *assets*.

In summary, dimension reduction methods use the correlation structure among the predictor variables to accomplish the following:

1. Reduce the number of predictor items.
2. Help ensure that these predictors items are uncorrelated.
3. Provide a framework for interpretability of the results.

12.2 MULTICOLLINEARITY

Data scientists need to guard against *multicollinearity*, a condition where some of the predictor variables are correlated with each other. Multicollinearity leads to instability in the solution space, leading, for example, to regression coefficients you cannot trust, because the coefficient variability is so large. Multicollinearity is an occupational hazard for data scientists, because many of the data sets have dozens if not hundreds of predictors, some of which are often correlated.

Consider Figures 12.1 and 12.2. Figure 12.1 illustrates a situation where the predictors x_1 and x_2 are not correlated with each other; that is, they are orthogonal, or independent. In such a case, the predictors form a solid basis, upon which the response surface y may rest sturdily, thereby providing stable coefficient estimates b_1 and b_2 each with small variability. On the other hand, Figure 12.2 illustrates a multicollinear situation where the predictors x_1 and x_2 are correlated with each

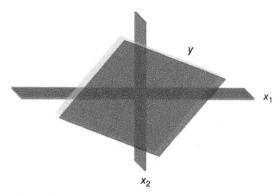

Figure 12.1   When the predictors x_1 and x_2 are uncorrelated, the response surface y rests on a solid basis, providing stable coefficient estimates.

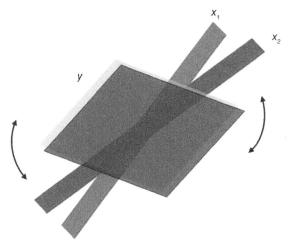

Figure 12.2 Multicollinearity: when the predictors are correlated, the response surface is unstable, resulting in dubious and highly variable coefficient estimates.

other, so that as one of them increases, so does the other. In this case, the predictors no longer form a solid basis upon which the response surface may firmly rest. Instead, when the predictors are correlated, the response surface is unstable, providing highly variable coefficient estimates b_1 and b_2.

The high variability associated with the estimates means that *different samples may produce coefficient estimates with widely different values*. For example, one sample may produce a positive coefficient estimate for x_1, while a second sample may produce a negative coefficient estimate. This situation is unacceptable when the analytic task calls for an explanation of the relationship between the response and the predictors, individually.

Let us look at a toy example to help us understand the problem. Consider the tiny population in Table 12.1.

Clearly, x_1 and x_2 are correlated, with $r = 0.938$, p-value about 0.

Now, split into two samples, as shown in Tables 12.2 and 12.3.

The regression equation for sample 1 is:

$$\hat{y} = -0.542 + 2.552\,x_1 - \mathbf{0.206}\,x_2$$

The regression equation for sample 2 is:

$$\hat{y} = -1.08 + 0.547\,x_1 + \mathbf{1.759}\,x_2$$

Note that the coefficient for x_2 is negative in sample 1 and positive in sample 2. This represents unstable behavior in the regression coefficients, caused by the correlation between the predictors. Essentially, *we cannot trust the values, or even the signs, of the regression coefficients*. So, interpreting the regression coefficients for our clients

TABLE 12.1 **Tiny population for our toy example**

	Population	
x_1	x_2	**Target, y**
1	1	2.0693
1	2	2.6392
2	2	3.7501
2	3	5.6432
3	3	5.8925
3	4	6.4308
4	4	8.3950
4	5	8.4947
5	5	11.3236
5	5	10.1562

TABLE 12.2 **Sample 1 from our tiny population**

	Sample 1	
x_1	x_2	**Target, y**
1	1	2.0693
2	2	3.7501
3	4	6.4308
4	5	8.4947
5	5	11.3236

TABLE 12.3 **Sample 2 from our tiny population**

	Sample 2	
x_1	x_2	**Target, y**
1	2	2.6392
2	3	5.6432
3	3	5.8925
4	4	8.3950
5	5	10.1562

is probably not a good idea. The values and signs might change from sample to sample, so that interpreting the coefficients from just one sample may cost your client big bucks. This is why we need methods for dealing with this multicollinearity.

We shall use a subset of the *Cereals* data set, where we estimate the nutrition rating of breakfast cereals, using fiber, potassium, and sugar. Our regression equation is as follows:

$$\widehat{rating} = b_0 + b_1 \cdot fiber + b_2 \cdot potassium + b_3 \cdot sugars$$

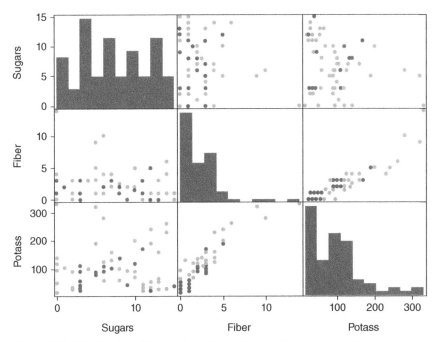

Figure 12.3   Matrix plot of the predictors from Python. Fiber and potassium are correlated.

To be aware of possible multicollinearity, the analyst should investigate the correlation structure among the predictor variables. Figure 12.3 provides the matrix plot of the predictors. Clearly, *potassium and fiber are positively correlated.* In fact, their correlation coefficient is $r = 0.912$ (not shown). This strong correlation will inflate the variability of the regression coefficients, making our regression model unstable.

12.3   IDENTIFYING MULTICOLLINEARITY USING VARIANCE INFLATION FACTORS

However, suppose we did not check for the presence of correlation among our predictors, and went ahead and performed the regression anyway. Is there some way that the regression results can warn us of the presence of multicollinearity? The answer is yes: We may ask for the *variance inflation factors* (VIFs) to be reported.

The VIF for the ith predictor is given by:

$$VIF_i = \frac{1}{1 - R_i^2}$$

```
> vif(model03)
   Fiber   Potass   Sugars
6.850050 6.693982 1.158761
```

Figure 12.4 Regression results, with variance inflation factors from R indicating a multicollinearity problem.

where R_i^2 represents the R^2 value obtained by regressing x_i on the other predictor variables. Note that R_i^2 will be large when x_i is highly correlated with the other predictors, thus making VIF_i large.

A rough rule of thumb for interpreting the value of the VIF is to consider $VIF_i \geq 5$ to be an indicator of moderate multicollinearity, and to consider $VIF_i \geq 10$ to be an indicator of severe multicollinearity. A VIF of five corresponds to $R_i^2 = 0.80$, while $VIF_i = 10$ corresponds to $R_i^2 = 0.80$.

For the regression of *nutritional rating* on *fiber*, *potassium*, and *sugars*, we have the output provided in Figure 12.4. The VIF for fiber is 6.85 and the VIF for potassium is 6.69, with both values indicating moderate-to-strong multicollinearity.

12.3.1 How to Identify Multicollinearity Using Python

First, we load the required packages and read in the *cereals* data set under the name *cereals*.

```
import pandas as pd
import statsmodels.api as sm
import statsmodels.stats.outliers_influence as inf
cereals = pd.read_csv("C:/.../cereals.csv")
```

Once the data set is in Python, pull out the three predictor variables and put them in their own data frame. Call the data frame **X**.

```
X = pd.DataFrame(cereals[['Sugars', 'Fiber', 'Potass']])
```

Now that we have the predictor variables all together, use the **scatter_matrix()** command with **X** as the input to create a scatterplot matrix.

```
pd.plotting.scatter_matrix(X)
```

The result of the **scatter_matrix()** command is shown in Figure 12.3 above. Notice that the command creates both scatterplots and histograms.

To obtain the VIF values, we need to do a little data cleaning first. Use the **dropna()** command on the X data frame to remove any records with missing values.

```
X = X.dropna()
```

Then, make sure you add the constant term in the X data frame.

```
X = sm.add_constant(X)
```

Finally, run the **variance_inflation_factor()** command as given below to obtain the VIF values for all four columns in the X data frame.

```
[inf.variance_inflation_factor(X.values, i) for i in
range(X.shape[1])]
```

The output will include a VIF value for the constant term we added; ignore it. The VIF values of interest are for the three predictor variables, which are the second, third, and fourth numbers output by the **variance_inflation_factor()** command.

12.3.2   How to Identify Multicollinearity in R

To build a scatterplot matrix in R, we first need to identify which columns in the data set hold our predictor variables.

```
names(cereals)
```

You can see that the Sugars, Potass, and Fiber variables are in columns 10, 8, and 11, respectively. These are the columns you will put in the scatterplot matrix in Figure 12.5.

```
pairs(x = cereals[, c(10, 8, 11)], pch = 16)
```

The command for the scatterplot matrix is **pairs()**. The required input is **x**, which asks for the columns to include in the scatterplot matrix. We specify the columns using **cereals[, c(10, 8, 11)]**. An optional input **pch = 16** will change the scatterplot points from open circles to closed circles.

To calculate VIFs, we first need to install and open the *car* package.

```
install.packages("car"); library(car)
```

Once the *car* package is open, we build the model whose coefficients we want to examine for multicollinearity and save the model output.

```
model03 <- lm(formula = Rating ~ Fiber + Potass +
Sugars, data = cereals)
```

Finally, we use the **vif()** command on the model.

```
vif(model03)
```

The sole required input to the **vif()** command is the name we saved our model as. The output, shown in Figure 12.4, is the VIF for each predictor variable.

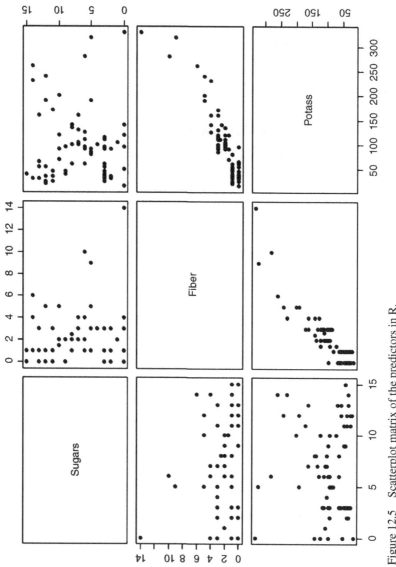

Figure 12.5　Scatterplot matrix of the predictors in R.

12.4 PRINCIPAL COMPONENTS ANALYSIS

So, now that we have identified the multicollinearity among our predictors, what do we do now?

One solution is to apply *principal components analysis*. Principal components analysis (PCA) seeks to account for the correlation structure of a set of predictor variables, using a smaller set of uncorrelated linear combinations of these variables, called *components*. The total variability produced by the complete set of m predictors can often be mostly accounted for by a smaller set of $k < m$ components. This means that there is almost as much information in the k components as there is in the original m variables. In addition, the k components are uncorrelated with each other, unlike the original correlated predictors. If desired, the analyst can then replace the original m variables with the $k < m$ components, so that the working data set now consists of n records on k components, rather than n records on m predictors. This is dimension reduction!

The analyst should note that PCA acts solely on the predictor variables and ignores the target variable. Also, the predictors should be either standardized or normalized. Mathematically, the principal components are uncorrelated linear combinations Y_i of predictors, with the following characteristics:

- The first principal component is usually the most important. It accounts for greater variability among the predictors than any other component.

- The second principal component accounts for the second-most variability and is uncorrelated with the first.

- The third principal component accounts for the third-most variability and is uncorrelated with the first two, and so on.

12.5 AN APPLICATION OF PRINCIPAL COMPONENTS ANALYSIS

To illustrate the application of PCA, we turn to the *clothing_store_PCA_training* and *clothing_store_PCA_test* data sets. We are interested in estimating the response *Sales per Visit* using the predictors *Purchase Visits, Days on File, Days between Purchases, Different Items Purchased*, and *Days since Purchase*. However, Figure 12.6 shows that there is substantial correlation among the predictors. In addition, Figure 12.7, showing the regression of *Sales per Visit* versus the predictors, indicates some moderately inflated VIF metrics.

We therefore perform PCA on these predictors, using *varimax rotation* on the training data set.

Rotating the PCA solution helps in the interpretability of the components. Examining the rotated components in Figure 12.8, we find that, if we extract only the first principal component, we will account for only 31.3% of the variance among the predictors. If we extract two components, we account for about 52.2% (see *Cumulative Var* in Figure 12.8), and so on. So, the question arises, how many components should we extract?

	Days.since.Purchase.Z	Purchase.Visits.Z	Days.on.File.Z
Days.since.Purchase.Z	1.000	-0.440	-0.159
Purchase.Visits.Z	-0.440	1.000	0.364
Days.on.File.Z	-0.159	0.364	1.000
Days.between.Purchases.Z	0.573	-0.453	0.203
Diff.Items.Purchased.Z	-0.379	0.821	0.303

	Days.between.Purchases.Z	Diff.Items.Purchased.Z
Days.since.Purchase.Z	0.573	-0.379
Purchase.Visits.Z	-0.453	0.821
Days.on.File.Z	0.203	0.303
Days.between.Purchases.Z	1.000	-0.371
Diff.Items.Purchased.Z	-0.371	1.000

Figure 12.6   Correlation matrix from R shows substantial correlation among the predictors.

Days.since.Purchase.Z	Purchase.Visits.Z	Days.on.File.Z
1.701947	3.793173	1.536395
Days.between.Purchases.Z	Diff.Items.Purchased.Z	
2.145807	3.076706	

Figure 12.7   Regression from R shows some tending toward moderately large VIFs.

Loadings:

	RC1	RC2	RC3	RC4	RC5
Days.since.Purchase.Z			0.935		
Purchase.Visits.Z	0.725				0.573
Days.on.File.Z		0.971			
Days.between.Purchases.Z				0.910	
Diff.Items.Purchased.Z	0.965				

	RC1	RC2	RC3	RC4	RC5
SS loadings	1.566	1.045	1.035	1.006	0.348
Proportion Var	0.313	0.209	0.207	0.201	0.070
Cumulative Var	0.313	0.522	0.729	0.930	1.000

Figure 12.8   Excerpt from PCA results from R.

12.6   HOW MANY COMPONENTS SHOULD WE EXTRACT?

Recall that one of the motivations for PCA was to reduce the dimensionality. The question arises, "How do we determine how many components to extract?" For example, should we retain only the first two principal components, since they explain over half (52% Cumulative Var) of the total variability? Or should we retain all five components, since they explain 100% of the variability? Well, clearly, retaining all five components does not help us to reduce the dimensionality. As usual, the answer lies somewhere between these two extremes.

12.6.1   The Eigenvalue Criterion

In Figure 12.8, the eigenvalues are labeled as "SS loadings." An eigenvalue of 1.0 would mean that the component would explain about "one predictor's worth" of the total variability. The rationale for using the eigenvalue criterion is that each

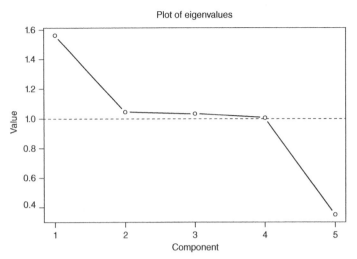

Figure 12.9   Plot of eigenvalues from R, with dotted line at eigenvalue of 1.

component should explain at least one predictor's worth of the variability, and therefore, the eigenvalue criterion states that only components with eigenvalues greater than one should be retained. Note that, if there are fewer than 20 predictors, the eigenvalue criterion tends to recommend extracting too few components, while, if there are more than 50 variables, this criterion may recommend extracting too many.

From Figure 12.9, we see that four of the rotated components have eigenvalues greater than 1, and are therefore retained. Component 5 has a rotated eigenvalue much below 1.0, so we do not include Component 5. The eigenvalue criterion therefore suggests that we extract $k = 4$ principal components.

12.6.2   The Proportion of Variance Explained Criterion

For the proportion of variance explained criterion, the client or analyst first specifies what proportion of the total variability that he or she would like the principal components to account for. Then, the analyst simply selects the components one by one until the desired proportion of variability explained is attained. For example, suppose we would like our components to explain about 70% of the variability in the predictors. Then, from Figure 12.8, we would choose components 1–3, which together explain 72.9% of the variability. On the other hand, if we wanted our components to explain 90% of the variability, then we would need to include component 4 as well, which together with the first three components would explain 93% of the variability. Without further input from the client, we might just say that the proportion of variance explained criterion suggests we go with either $k = 3$ or $k = 4$ components.

Since the eigenvalue criterion suggested $k = 4$ components, and the proportion of variance explained criterion is fine with either $k = 3$ or $k = 4$ components, we therefore by consensus settle on extracting $k = 4$ components.

12.7 PERFORMING PCA WITH $K = 4$

Figure 12.10 shows the resulting (i) unrotated and (ii) rotated component matrices for extracting three components. Let us examine the *rotated* matrix first in Figure 12.10b. Note that the component weights less than 0.5 have been suppressed, to enhance interpretability. The first principal component (*RC1* for Rotated Component 1) is a combination of *Different Items Purchased* and *Purchase Visits*, which are positively correlated with each other, since their component weights have the same sign. Components can contain combinations of predictors that are either positively or negatively correlated with each other. Had exactly one of the component weights been negative, then that would have been an indication that *Different Items Purchased* and *Purchase Visits* were negatively correlated. The remaining principal components are "singletons," containing only a single predictor each.

Now, suppose we had not rotated the component matrix, ending up with the unrotated component matrix in Figure 12.10a. Note that the interpretations of the principal components are less clear. Component 1 is huge, containing four of the five predictors, with both positive and negative correlations mixed in. Much cleaner is the interpretation of the rotated component matrix.

12.8 VALIDATION OF THE PRINCIPAL COMPONENTS

As with any other data science method, the results of the PCA should be validated, using the test data set. Figure 12.11 shows the proportions of variance explained by all five components, with percentages not much different from the training set

```
Loadings:
                       PC1     PC2     PC3     PC4
Days.since.Purchase    -0.718          0.569
Purchase.Visits         0.898
Days.on.File                    0.825
Days.between.Purchases -0.662   0.647
Diff.Items.Purchased    0.849
```

```
Loadings:
                       RC1     RC2     RC3     RC4
Days.since.Purchase                    0.933
Purchase.Visits         0.862
Days.on.File                    0.965
Days.between.Purchases                         0.898
Diff.Items.Purchased    0.948
```

figure 12.10   (a) component weights with no rotation, from r. (b) component weights with varimax rotation, from r.

```
                RC1    RC2    RC3    RC4    RC5
SS loadings    1.805  1.035  1.033  0.993  0.134
Proportion Var 0.361  0.207  0.207  0.199  0.027
Cumulative Var 0.361  0.568  0.775  0.973  1.000
```

Figure 12.11   Proportions of variance explained from R for the test data set.

```
Loadings:
                        RC1     RC2     RC3     RC4
Days.since.Purchase                     0.932
Purchase.Visits         0.891
Days.on.File                    0.965
Days.between.Purchases                          0.901
Diff.Items.Purchased    0.944
```

Figure 12.12   Component weights from R for the test data set.

```
> round(cor(pca02_rot$scores),2)
    RC1 RC2 RC3 RC4
RC1   1   0   0   0
RC2   0   1   0   0
RC3   0   0   1   0
RC4   0   0   0   1
```

Figure 12.13   R output showing the principal components are uncorrelated.

```
> vif(model.pca)
PC1 PC2 PC3 PC4
  1   1   1   1
```

Figure 12.14   R output showing that regression using the principal components eliminates multicollinearity.

results in Figure 12.8. The four rotated components for the test set, shown in Figure 12.12, are similar to those for the training set from Figure 12.10b.

So, did PCA alleviate our multicollinearity problem? We can check by examining

1. The correlations among the four components.
2. The predictor VIF for the regression of the response on the components.

The correlation matrix for the principal components is shown in Figure 12.13. All correlations are zero, meaning that the components are uncorrelated. Finally, we obtain the VIFs for the regression of *Sales per Visit* on the four extracted principal components substituted for the original predictors. These VIFs results shown in Figure 12.14 indicate that all VIFs equal 1, the minimum.

12.9   HOW TO PERFORM PRINCIPAL COMPONENTS ANALYSIS USING PYTHON

Load the required packages.

```
import pandas as pd
import numpy as np
from sklearn.preprocessing import StandardScaler
from sklearn.decomposition import PCA
```

	Days since Purchase	Purchase Visits	Days on File
Days since Purchase	1.000000	-0.439821	-0.158718
Purchase Visits	-0.439821	1.000000	0.363729
Days on File	-0.158718	0.363729	1.000000
Days between Purchases	0.573090	-0.453024	0.202890
Diff Items Purchased	-0.378658	0.821257	0.302624

	Days between Purchases	Diff Items Purchased
Days since Purchase	0.573090	-0.378658
Purchase Visits	-0.453024	0.821257
Days on File	0.202890	0.302624
Days between Purchases	1.000000	-0.371018
Diff Items Purchased	-0.371018	1.000000

Figure 12.15   Correlation matrix from Python.

Read in the two data sets, *clothing_store_PCA_training* and *clothing_store_PCA_test*, as *clothes_train* and *clothes_test*.

```
clothes_train = pd.read_csv("C:/.../clothing_store_PCA_training")
clothes_test = pd.read_csv("C:/.../clothing_store_PCA_test")
```

Separate the predictor variables from the rest of the training data set using the **drop()** command. Note that we drop the target variable *Sales per Visit*, so we are left with only the predictor variables. This approach is best suited for when the target variable and predictor variables of interest are the only variables in your data. Save the variables as **X**.

```
X = clothes_train.drop('Sales per Visit', 1)
```

Obtain the correlation matrix of the X variables by using the **corr()** command.

```
X.corr()
```

The output from the **corr()** command is shown in Figure 12.15.

Now, we will run PCA with five components. First we will specify the number of components using **n_components** in the **PCA()** command, then fit the PCA to the data using **fit_transform()** with **X** as the input.

```
pca01 = PCA(n_components=5)
principComp = pca01.fit_transform(X)
```

Once PCA is run, our next task is to look at the amount of variability explained by each component and the corresponding cumulative variability explained. Use the **pca01** object and **explained_variance_ratio_** to obtain the variability explained by each component.

```
pca01.explained_variance_ratio_
```

Obtain the cumulative variability explained by running the **cumsum()** command on **pca01.explained_variance_ratio_**.

```
np.cumsum(pca01.explained_variance_ratio_)
```

Our results in this section are for the original, unrotated components. As of this writing, Python's *sklearn* package does not have an "out of the box" command to perform varimax rotation on the components.

12.10   HOW TO PERFORM PRINCIPAL COMPONENTS ANALYSIS USING R

Import the *clothing_store_PCA_training* and *clothing_store_PCA_test* data sets as *clothes_train* and *clothes_test*, respectively. To simplify code that comes later, we will separate the training and test data into X and y variables.

```
y <- clothes_train$Sales.per.Visit
X <- clothes_train[, c(1:5)]
X_test <- clothes_test[, c(1:5)]
```

Remember to standardize the predictor variables.

```
X_z <- as.data.frame(scale(X))
colnames(X_z) <- c("Days.since.Purchase.Z", "Purchase.
Visits.Z", "Days.on.File.Z",
     "Days.between.Purchases.Z", "Diff.Items.Purchased.Z")
```

To obtain the correlation matrix, we use the **cor()** command.

```
round(cor(X_z), 3)
```

The **cor()** command, with the predictor variables **X_z** as input, is placed inside the **round()** command. The second input of the **round()** command is the number of significant digits the answers will be rounded to. In our case, we have specified three significant digits. The output from the **round()** command is shown in Figure 12.6.

To obtain the VIF values, we need to run the regression model first, then use the **vif()** command from the *car* package as detailed in the previous R section.

```
model01 <- lm(formula = y ~ Days.since.Purchase.Z +
Purchase.Visits.Z + Days.on.File.Z +
     Days.between.Purchases.Z + Diff.Items.Purchased.Z,
     data = X_z)
vif(model01)
```

The output of the **vif()** command is shown in Figure 12.7.

To run PCA, we must first install and open the *psych* package.

```
install.packages("psych"); library(psych)
```

Once the package is open, we use the **principal()** command to perform PCA.

```
pca01 <- principal(r = X_z, rotate = "varimax", nfactors = 5)
```

We are using the **principal()** command with three input values. The input **r = X_z** specifies the variables we want to analyze. The **rotate = "varimax"** input tells R to perform varimax rotation on the components before presenting the results. Finally, the **nfactors = 5** input states that we want five components. We save the PCA output as **pca01**.

We are interested in the **loadings** of the **pca01** results.

```
print(pca01$loadings, cutoff = 0.49)
```

We use cutoff = 0.49 to suppress small PCA weights. The output generated by the code above is shown in Figure 12.8.

To create a plot of the eigenvalues, we need the eigenvalues of the rotated components. These are located under "SS Loadings" in Figure 12.8. Once you save these values as their own vector, plot them using the **plot()** command.

```
ss.load <- c(1.566, 1.045, 1.035, 1.006, 0.348)
plot(ss.load, type = "b", main = "Plot of Eigenvalues",
ylab = "Value",
          xlab = "Component"); abline(h = 1, lty =2)
```

The input **type = "b"** plots the eigenvalues using both points and connecting lines. The **main**, **xlab**, and **ylab** input customize the title and axes labels. The **abline()** command adds a line to the plot. The input value **h = 1** adds the line with horizontal location 1 and the input **lty = 2** specifies a dashed line. The result is shown in Figure 12.9.

To compare the results of no rotation versus varimax rotation, run the **principal()** command using **rotate = "none"** for no rotation and **rotate = "varimax"** for the varimax rotation.

```
pca02_norot <- principal(r = X, rotate = "none",
nfactors = 4)
print(pca02_norot$loadings, cutoff = 0.5)
pca02_rot <- principal(r = X, rotate = "varimax",
nfactors = 4)
print(pca02_rot$loadings, cutoff = 0.5)
```

An excerpt from the **print()** output of **pca02_norot$loadings** is shown in Figure 12.10a, while an excerpt from the **print()** output of **pca02_rot$loadings** is shown in Figure 12.10b. Note that both commands use **cutoff = 0.5** to suppress weights below 0.5.

To validate the PCA results, run the algorithm on the test data. First, standardize the data.

```
X_test_z <- scale(X_test)
```

Then, confirm that four components are recommended.

```
pca02_test <- principal(r = X_test_z, rotate =
"varimax", nfactors = 5)
pca02_test$loadings
```

An excerpt of the output is shown in Figure 12.11. After confirming that four components are recommended, examine the component weights.

```
pca02_test <- principal(r = X_test_z, rotate =
"varimax", nfactors = 4)
print(pca02_test$loadings, cutoff = 0.5)
```

An excerpt of the output is shown in Figure 12.12.

To obtain the correlation of the components in the training data set, run the **round(cor())** command on the scores from **pca02_rot**.

```
round(cor(pca02_rot$scores),2)
```

In this case, we round to two significant digits. The result is shown in Figure 12.13.

To regress the target variable on the components, you may want to save each component as its own variable. This is shown below.

```
PC1 <- pca02_rot$scores[,1]; PC2 <- pca02_rot$scores[,2]
PC3 <- pca02_rot$scores[,3]; PC4 <- pca02_rot$scores[,4]
```

Now you can run the regression model and obtain the VIFs. The code is shown below.

```
model.pca <- lm(y ~ PC1 + PC2 + PC3 + PC4); vif(model.pca)
```

The output from the **vif()** command is shown in Figure 12.14.

12.11 WHEN IS MULTICOLLINEARITY NOT A PROBLEM?

Now, depending on the task confronting the analyst, multicollinearity may not in fact present a fatal defect. Weiss[1] notes that multicollinearity "does not adversely affect the ability of the sample regression equation to predict the response variable." He adds that multicollinearity does not significantly affect point estimates of the target variable, confidence intervals for the mean response value, or prediction

[1] Weiss, *Introductory Statistics*, Ninth Edition, Pearson, London, 2010.

intervals for a randomly selected response value. However, the data scientist must therefore strictly limit the use of a multicollinear model to estimation and prediction of the target variable. Interpretation of the model would *not* be appropriate, since the individual coefficients may not make sense, in the presence of multicollinearity. To summarize, *models not accounting for multicollinearity may be used for estimation, but not for description or interpretation.*

REFERENCES

The name of the *car* package sands for Companion to Applied Regression, and the details can be found here: John Fox and Sanford Weisberg, *An {R} Companion to Applied Regression*, Second Edition, Sage, Thousand Oaks, CA, 2011.

The psych package, which let us to PCA with varimax rotation, is documented here: W. Revelle, *Psych: Procedures for Personality and Psychological Research*, Northwestern University, Evanston, IL, 2018.

EXERCISES

CLARIFYING THE CONCEPTS

1. What do we mean by high dimensionality in data science?

2. Why do we need dimension reduction methods?

3. What does principal components replace the original set of *m* predictors with?

4. Which principal component accounts for the most variability?

5. Which of the other principal components is correlated with the first principal component?

6. Why do we use rotation?

7. Explain the eigenvalue criterion?

8. What is the proportion of variance explained criterion?

9. True or false: It is not necessary to perform validation of the principal components.

10. When we use the principal components as predictors in a regression model, what value do the VIFs take? What does this indicate?

WORKING WITH THE DATA

For the following exercises, work with the *clothing_store_PCA_training* and *clothing_store_PCA_test* data sets. Use either Python or R to solve each problem.

11. Standardize or normalize the predictors.

12. Construct the correlation matrix for the predictor variables Purchase Visits, Days on File, Days between Purchases, Different Items Purchased, and Days since Purchase. Which variables are highly correlated?

13. Calculate the VIFs for each of the predictor variables. Which predictor variable VIFs indicate the multicollinearity is a problem?

14. Run PCA using varimax rotation and five components. What percent of the variability is explained by one component? By two components? By all five components?

15. Make a plot of the eigenvalues. Using the eigenvalue criterion, how many components would you retain?

16. Say we want to explain at least 80% of the variability. How many components would you retain?

17. Run PCA using varimax rotation and four components. What percent of the variability do the four components explain?

18. What variable or variables are contained in each of the components?

19. Use the four components as the predictor variables in a regression model to estimate Sales per Visit. What are the regression coefficients of the four components?

20. What are the VIFs of the four components in the regression model?

HANDS-ON ANALYSIS

For the following exercises, work with the *cereals* data set. Use either Python or R to solve each problem.

21. Standardize or normalize the predictors Sugars, Fiber, and Potass.

22. Construct the correlation matrix for Sugars, Fiber, and Potass. Which variables are highly correlated?

23. Build a regression model to estimate Rating based on Sugars, Fiber, and Potass. Obtain the VIFs from the model. Which VIFs indicate that multicollinearity is a problem?

24. Run PCA using varimax rotation and three components. What percent of the variability is explained by one component? By two components? By all three components?

25. Make a plot of the eigenvalues of the three components. Using the eigenvalue criterion, how many components would you retain?

26. Say we want to explain at least 70% of the variability. How many components would you retain?

27. Run PCA using varimax rotation and two components. What percent of the variability do the two components explain?

28. What variable or variables are contained in Component 1? What variable or variables are contained in Component 2?

29. Use the two components as the predictor variables in a regression model to estimate Rating. What are the regression coefficients of the two components?

30. What are the VIFs of the two components in the regression model?

For the following exercises, work with the *red_wine_PCA_training* and *red_wine_PCA_test* data sets. Use either Python or R to solve each problem. The target variable is the wine *quality*. The predictors are *alcohol, residual sugar, pH, density*, and *fixed acidity*.

31. Standardize or normalize the predictors.

32. Construct the correlation matrix for the predictors. Between which predictors do you find the highest correlations?

33. Build a regression model to estimate *quality* based on the predictors. Obtain the VIFs from the model. Which VIFs indicate that multicollinearity is a problem? Compare the variables with high VIF to the correlated variables from the previous exercise.

34. Perform PCA using varimax rotation. Show the rotated proportions of variance explained for extracting up to five components. What percent of the variability is explained by one component? By two components? By three components? By four components? By all five components?

35. Say we want to explain at least 90% of the variability. How many components does the proportion of variance explained criterion suggest we extract?

36. Make a plot of the eigenvalues of the five components. According to the eigenvalue criterion, how many components should we extract?

37. Combine the recommendations from the two criteria to reach a consensus as to how many components we should extract.

38. Profile each of your components, stating which variables are included, and noting their within-component correlation (positive or negative). For simplicity, consider components weights greater than 0.5 only.

39. Produce the correlation matrix for the components. What do these values mean?

40. Next, use only the components you extracted to estimate wine quality using a regression model. Do not include the original predictors.

    a. Compare the values of s and R^2_{adj} between the PCA regression and the original regression model.

    b. Explain why the original model slightly outperformed the PCA model.

    c. Explain how the PCA model may be considered superior, even though slightly outperformed?

41. In your regression from the previous exercise, what are the VIFs of the two components in the regression model? What do these values mean?

CHAPTER 13

GENERALIZED LINEAR MODELS

13.1 AN OVERVIEW OF GENERAL LINEAR MODELS

In Chapter 11, the linear regression models we examined each had a continuous response variable. However, what happens if we want to build a regression model for a binary response instead? Or for a numeric discrete response? Luckily, there is a family of linear models that includes all three cases – continuous, numeric discrete, and binary – of regression response variables: *General Linear Models* (GLMs).

To explain how regression for three different kinds of responses can be related, we will briefly take another look at the parametric regression equations for each case. Once we establish how they are related, we will then use their descriptive versions, just as we did in Chapter 11.

Recall the parametric model for multiple regression, given here.

$$y = \beta_0 + \beta_1 x_1 + \beta_2 x_2 + \cdots + \beta_p x_p + \varepsilon$$

The sum $\beta_0 + \beta_1 x_1 + \beta_2 x_2 + \cdots + \beta_p x_p$ is called the *linear predictor*. For brevity, we will write the linear predictor as $X\beta$. The formula that connects the linear predictor to the mean μ of the y variable at a set of given values of predictor variables is called the *link function*, $g(\mu)$.

Different link functions entail different regression models, with each link function associated with a particular response type. For each different response type we discuss, we will specify a particular $g(\mu)$ so that $X\beta = g(\mu)$, and solve for μ to obtain the final form of the model.

We begin by demonstrating how GLMs work by showing how linear regression can be expressed as a GLM. We then demonstrate two new regression models as GLMs: logistic regression and Poisson regression.

Data Science Using Python and R, First Edition. Chantal D. Larose and Daniel T. Larose.
© 2019 John Wiley & Sons, Inc. Published 2019 by John Wiley & Sons, Inc.

13.2 LINEAR REGRESSION AS A GENERAL LINEAR MODEL

When the response variable has a Normal distribution at each set of given predictor variable values, then we are back in the realm of linear regression. In this realm, the link function is simply the identity function, where

$$g(\mu) = \mu$$

Setting $X\beta$ equal to $g(\mu)$ using this identity link gives us $X\beta = g(\mu) = \mu$.

Once we have a functional relationship between $X\beta$ and μ, we can work backwards to obtain the final form of the regression model by expanding our abbreviated notation. Doing so gives us the population equation for linear regression:

$$y = \beta_0 + \beta_1 x_1 + \beta_2 x_2 + \cdots + \beta_p x_p + \varepsilon$$

from which we can obtain the descriptive form

$$\hat{y} = b_0 + b_1 x_1 + b_2 x_2 + \cdots + b_p x_p$$

which we worked with in Chapter 11.

13.3 LOGISTIC REGRESSION AS A GENERAL LINEAR MODEL

Next, suppose we are trying to predict a binary response, such as whether or not a customer has a store credit card. In this case, the distribution of our response variable will be binary: 1 or 0, indicating a Yes or No.

The link function for a binary response variable is $g(\mu) = \ln\left(\dfrac{\mu}{1-\mu}\right)$. We set this function equal to our linear predictor $X\beta$ to obtain

$$X\beta = \ln\left(\frac{\mu}{1-\mu}\right)$$

To isolate μ, we use the fact that $e^{\ln(x)} = x$, and obtain

$$\mu = \frac{e^{X\beta}}{1 + e^{X\beta}}$$

The above formula ensures the mean value of the response variable, μ, will always be between zero and one. In other words, the value the regression model may be used to estimate the *probability* that $y = 1$.

To clarify that our predicted values from logistic regression are probabilities, instead of binary values, let us write the regression model as predicting $p(y)$, the probability that $y = 1$. If we work backwards from our abbreviated notation, we get the parametric form of the model

$$p(y) = \frac{\exp\left(\beta_0 + \beta_1 x_1 + \beta_2 x_2 + \cdots + \beta_p x_p\right)}{1 + \exp\left(\beta_0 + \beta_1 x_1 + \beta_2 x_2 + \cdots + \beta_p x_p\right)} + \varepsilon$$

and can write the descriptive form as

$$\hat{p}(y) = \frac{\exp\left(b_0 + b_1 x_1 + b_2 x_2 + \cdots + b_p x_p\right)}{1 + \exp\left(b_0 + b_1 x_1 + b_2 x_2 + \cdots + b_p x_p\right)}$$

13.4   AN APPLICATION OF LOGISTIC REGRESSION MODELING

Let us revisit the *clothing_sales_training* and *clothing_sales_test* data sets. This time, our goal is to determine whether or not customers have a store credit card, so our marketing team can send out advertisements to non-holders, enticing them to sign up for a card. Our response variable in this case is binary: Yes, the customer has a card; or No, the customer does not. Since the response variable is binary, we will use logistic regression.

Our provisional logistic regression model will be

$$\hat{p}(credit\,card) = \frac{\exp\left(b_0 + b_1\left(Days\,between\,Purchases\right) + b_2\left(Web\,Account\right)\right)}{1 + \exp\left(b_0 + b_1\left(Days\,between\,Purchases\right) + b_2\left(Web\,Account\right)\right)}$$

The results of the regression of Credit Card on the two predictor variables are shown in Figure 13.1. The *p*-values shown in the output tell us that both variables belong in the model. When we cross-validate the results with the test data set, we obtain the results shown in Figure 13.2.

The test model confirms that both variables belong in the model. Using the coefficients from the training data set, we obtain our final logistic regression model:

$$\hat{p}(credit\,card) = \frac{\exp\left(0.496 - 0.004\left(Days\,between\,Purchases\right) + 1.254\left(Web\,Account\right)\right)}{1 + \exp\left(0.496 - 0.004\left(Days\,between\,Purchases\right) + 1.254\left(Web\,Account\right)\right)}$$

```
-----------------------------------------------------------------
        Coef.    Std.Err.      z      P>|z|    [0.025    0.975]
-----------------------------------------------------------------
const   0.4962   0.0887    5.5968    0.0000    0.3224    0.6699
Days   -0.0037   0.0004   -8.4491    0.0000   -0.0046   -0.0028
Web     1.2537   0.3307    3.7914    0.0001    0.6056    1.9018
=================================================================
```

Figure 13.1   Python logistic regression results for the training data set.

	Coef.	Std.Err.	z	P>|z|	[0.025	0.975]
const	0.4634	0.0873	5.3105	0.0000	0.2924	0.6345
Days	-0.0035	0.0004	-8.2261	0.0000	-0.0043	-0.0026
Web	1.0973	0.2830	3.8780	0.0001	0.5427	1.6519

Figure 13.2   Python logistic regression results for the test data set.

So, how do we interpret the logistic regression coefficients? Each regression coefficient describes the estimated change in the log-odds of the response variable when the coefficient's predictor variable increases by one. To illustrate, consider the binary predictor variable *Web Account*. The regression coefficient for *Web Account* is 1.254. By calculating $e^{1.254} = 3.504$, we find that a customer is about 3.5 times as likely to have a store credit card if they have a web account compared to if they do not have a web account.

We can perform a similar operation for the coefficient of *Days between Purchases*. By calculating $e^{-0.004} = 0.996$, we find that for every additional day between purchases, the customer is 0.4% less likely to have a store credit card. Since counting the individual days might be too narrow of a measurement, we can multiply the coefficient by 30 to obtain $e^{30 \times -0.004} = 0.89$, and discover that, for every 30 days without a purchase, the customer is another 11% less likely to have a store credit card.[1]

13.4.1 How to Perform Logistic Regression Using Python

Load the required packages, and import the *clothing_sales_training* and *clothing_sales_test* data sets as *sales_train* and *sales_test*, respectively.

```
import pandas as pd
import numpy as np
import statsmodels.api as sm
from scipy import stats
sales_train = pd.read_csv("C:/.../clothing_sales_
training.csv")
sales_test = pd.read_csv("C:/.../clothing_sales_test.
csv")
```

For simplicity, we separate the variables into predictor variables **X** and response variable **y**. Add a constant to the **X** data frame in order to include a constant term in our regression model.

```
X = pd.DataFrame(sales_train[['Days', 'Web']])
X = sm.add_constant(X)
y = pd.DataFrame(sales_train[['CC']])
```

[1]For more on logistic regression, see *Data Mining and Predictive Analytics*.

To perform logistic regression, use the **Logit()** and **fit()** commands. Save the model output and run the **summary2()** command on the saved model output to view the model results.

```
logreg01 = sm.Logit(y, X).fit()
logreg01.summary2()
```

An excerpt of the results is shown in Figure 13.1.

To validate the model, perform the same steps on the test data set. The code is given below.

```
X_test = pd.DataFrame(sales_test[['Days', 'Web']])
X_test = sm.add_constant(X_test)
y_test = pd.DataFrame(sales_test[['CC']])
logreg01_test = sm.Logit(y_test, X_test).fit()
logreg01_test.summary2()
```

An excerpt of the results is shown in Figure 13.2.

13.4.2   How to Perform Logistic Regression Using R

Import the *clothing_sales_training* and *clothing_sales_test* data sets as *sales_train* and *sales_test*, respectively.

To run the logistic regression model, we will use the **glm()** command.

```
logreg01 <- glm(formula = CC ~ Days + Web, data = sales_
train, family = binomial)
```

Much of the code is similar to that in Chapter 11; the **formula** input lists the response and predictor variables, and the **data = sales_train** input specifies the data set. The only changes are the **glm()** command and adding the **family = binomial** input. The **glm()** command will run GLM analysis, and **family = binomial** specifies a logistic regression model. Save the model output as **logreg01**.

To view the summary of the model, run the **summary()** command with the name of the saved model as the sole input. An excerpt from the output is shown in Figure 13.3.

```
summary(logreg01)
```

```
Coefficients:
             Estimate Std. Error z value Pr(>|z|)
(Intercept)  0.4961706  0.0886529   5.597 2.18e-08 ***
Days        -0.0037016  0.0004381  -8.449  < 2e-16 ***
Web          1.2536955  0.3306672   3.791  0.00015 ***
---
Signif. codes:  0 '***' 0.001 '**' 0.01 '*' 0.05 '.' 0.1 ' ' 1
```

Figure 13.3   Logistic regression results from R for the training data set.

```
Coefficients:
             Estimate Std. Error z value Pr(>|z|)
(Intercept)  0.4634478  0.0872706   5.310 1.09e-07 ***
Days        -0.0034721  0.0004221  -8.226  < 2e-16 ***
Web          1.0972994  0.2829570   3.878 0.000105 ***
---
Signif. codes:  0 '***' 0.001 '**' 0.01 '*' 0.05 '.' 0.1 ' ' 1
```

Figure 13.4   Logistic regression results from R for the test data set.

To validate the model, run the same model on the test data and obtain the summary of the model (Figure 13.4). The code is given below.

```
logreg01_test <- glm(formula = CC ~ Days + Web, data =
sales_test, family = binomial)
summary(logreg01_test)
```

13.5   POISSON REGRESSION

There are many other kinds of regression models that fall under the umbrella of GLM. We will examine one other: Poisson regression. Poisson regression is used when you want to predict a count of events, such as how many times a customer will contact customer service. The distribution of the response variable will be a count of occurrences, with a minimum value of zero.

The link function for a count response variable is $g(\mu) = \ln(\mu)$. We set the link function equal to our linear predictor to obtain

$$X\beta = \ln(\mu)$$

After isolating μ, we have

$$\mu = e^{X\beta}$$

Working backwards from our abbreviated notation, we find the parametric version of the Poisson regression equation

$$y = e^{\beta_0 + \beta_1 x_1 + \beta_2 x_2 + \cdots + \beta_p x_p} + \varepsilon$$

from which we can write the descriptive form

$$\hat{y} = e^{b_0 + b_1 x_1 + b_2 x_2 + \cdots + b_p x_p}$$

13.6   AN APPLICATION OF POISSON REGRESSION MODELING

We will use the *churn* data set to build a model that estimates the number of customer service calls based on whether a customer churned. Our response variable is an integer-valued variable, which is why we use Poisson regression instead of linear regression for this estimation.

	coef	std err	z	P>|z|	[0.025	0.975]
const	0.3714	0.016	23.877	0.000	0.341	0.402
Churn = True	0.4305	0.034	12.582	0.000	0.363	0.498

Figure 13.5   Python Poisson regression results for predicting number of customer service calls.

The structure of our Poisson regression model will be

$$CustServ\ Calls = \exp\big(b_0 + b_1\big(Churn\big)\big)$$

The result of the regression analysis is given in Figure 13.5. Using the coefficients given above, we can build the Poisson regression model

$$CustServ\ Calls = \exp\big(0.3714 + 0.4305\big(Churn = True\big)\big)$$

Now, how do we interpret the Poisson regression coefficients? When used as the exponent of e, the regression coefficient describes the estimated multiplicative change in the response variable when the coefficient's predictor variable increases by one. In our case, the regression coefficient is 0.4305, which gives us $e^{0.4305} = 1.538$. The coefficient's predictor, *Churn*, is zero if the customer does not churn and one if they do. Therefore, the movement from a non-churning to churning customer increases the predicted number of customer service calls that customer makes by 1.538 times, or 53.8%.

13.6.1   How to Perform Poisson Regression Using Python

Naturally, in order to validate our modeling results, you would first split the data into training and test data sets. As cross-validation has been shown in other chapters as well as for logistic regression, we restrict this section to illustrating how to build the Poisson regression model.

Load the required packages.

```
import pandas as pd
import numpy as np
import statsmodels.api as sm
import statsmodels.tools.tools as stattools
```

Read in the *churn* data set into Python as *churn*.

```
churn = pd.read_csv("C:/.../churn")
```

Our predictor variable is *Churn*, which is categorical. Similar to previous modeling tasks, we need to change the categorical values of *Churn* into dummy variables. For this exercise we will use one dummy variable, which equals one if a customer has churned.

```
churn_ind = pd.get_dummies(churn['Churn'], drop_first =
True)
```

The **get_dummies()** command creates two indicator variables, one for each categorical value in *Churn*. The **drop_first = True** input will drop the first dummy variable, which corresponds to *Churn = False* in our case, and retain the remaining dummy variable, which corresponds to *Churn = True*.

The remaining commands save the new dummy variable as a data frame, add a constant term so our regression model will have a constant, and renames the columns so the output will be easier to read.

```
X = pd.DataFrame(churn_ind)
X = sm.add_constant(X)
X.columns = ['const', 'Churn = True']
```

We also prepare the response variable.

```
y = pd.DataFrame(churn[['CustServ Calls']])
```

Finally, we run Poisson regression using the **GLM()** command.

```
poisreg01 = sm.GLM(y, X, family = sm.families.
Poisson()).fit()
```

Notice the three input values of the **GLM()** command. The first two, **y** and **X**, specify the response variable and predictor variables, respectively. The third, **family = sm.families.Poisson()**, specifies that Poisson regression should be used. The **fit()** command will fit the model to our data. We save the result as **poisreg01**.

Use the **summary()** command to view the results of the model.

```
poisreg01.summary()
```

An excerpt from the output of **summary()** is shown in Figure 13.5.

13.6.2   How to Perform Poisson Regression Using R

As with our Python example, we restrict this section to illustrating how to build the Poisson regression model. We return to the **glm()** command, which we used previously to build a logistic regression model, to now build a Poisson regression model.

```
poisreg01 <- glm(formula = CustServ.Calls ~ Churn, data =
churn, family = poisson)
```

```
Coefficients:
            Estimate Std. Error z value Pr(>|z|)
(Intercept)  0.37377    0.01638   22.82   <2e-16 ***
ChurnTrue    0.42795    0.03602   11.88   <2e-16 ***
---
Signif. codes:  0 '***' 0.001 '**' 0.01 '*' 0.05 '.' 0.1 ' ' 1
```

Figure 13.6   Poisson regression results from R.

The **formula** input now specifies *CustServ Calls* as the response variable and *Churn* as the predictor variable. The input **family = poisson** specifies that Poisson regression should be applied to the data. Save the regression output as **poisreg01**.

Use the **summary()** command to view details about the model.

```
summary(poisreg01)
```

An excerpt from the **summary()** command is shown here in Figure 13.6.

REFERENCE

For a full text on exploring the world of GLM: P. McCullagh and J. A. Nelder, *Generalized Linear Models*, Second Edition, Chapman & Hall, London, 1992.

EXERCISES

CLARIFYING THE CONCEPTS

1. What are the three cases of regression response variables discussed in this chapter?

2. What category of regression models includes all three cases of response variables?

3. What do we call the linear predictor? How to we write it in its abbreviated form?

4. The link function connects what two things? How do we write it in its abbreviated form?

5. What is the link function for linear regression?

6. What kind of regression should we use when trying to predict a binary response variable?

7. What is the link function for logistic regression?

8. Are the predicted values from logistic regression probabilities or binary values?

9. What is the descriptive form of the logistic regression model?

10. What kind of regression should we use when trying to predict a count response variable?

11. What is the link function for Poisson regression?

12. What is the descriptive form of the Poisson regression model?

WORKING WITH THE DATA

For the following exercises, work with the *clothing_sales_training* and *clothing_sales_test* data sets. Use either Python or R to solve each problem.

13. Create a logistic regression model to predict whether or not a customer has a store credit card, based on whether they have a web account and the days between purchases. Obtain the summary of the model.

14. Are there any variables that should be removed from the model? If so, remove them and rerun the model.

15. Write the descriptive form of the logistic regression model using the coefficients obtained from Question 1.

16. Validate the model using the test data set.

17. Obtain the predicted values of the response variable for each record in the data set.

For the following exercises, work with the *churn* data set. Use either Python or R to solve each problem.

18. Create a Poisson regression model to predict the number of customer service calls a person makes, based on whether or not that customer churned. Obtain a summary of the model.

19. Write the descriptive form of the Poisson regression model from the previous exercise.

HANDS-ON ANALYSIS

For the following exercises, work with the *adult* data set. Use either Python or R to solve each problem.

20. Build a logistic regression model to predict the income of a person based on their age, education (as a number, with variable *education.num*), and the hours worked per week. Obtain the summary of the model.

21. Are there any variables that should be removed from the model from the previous exercise? If so, remove the variables and rerun the model.

22. Write the descriptive form of the final logistic regression model from the previous exercise.

23. Interpret the coefficient of the *age* variable.

24. Find the impact on the probability of having high income for every 10 years a person is older.

25. Interpret the coefficient of the *education.num* variable.

26. Find the impact on the probability of having high income for every four more years of education a person has.

27. Interpret the coefficient of the *hours.per.week* variable.

28. Find the impact on the probability of having high income for every five more hours per week a person works.

29. Obtain the predicted values using the model from the previous exercise. Compare the predicted values to the actual values.

30. Build a Poisson regression model to predict the years of education a person has (using the variable *education.num*) based on a person's age and the hours they work per week. Obtain the summary of the model.

31. Are there any variables that should be removed from the model from the previous exercise? If so, remove the variables and rerun the model.

32. Write the descriptive form of the final Poisson regression model from the previous exercise.

33. Obtain the predicted values using the model from the previous exercise. Compare the predicted values to the actual values.

CHAPTER 14

ASSOCIATION RULES

14.1 INTRODUCTION TO ASSOCIATION RULES

Association rules seek to uncover associations among the variables and take the form "If *antecedent*, then *consequent*," along with a measure of the support and confidence associated with the rule. For example, a particular supermarket may find that of the 1000 customers shopping on a Thursday night, 200 bought diapers, and of the 200 who bought diapers, 50 bought beer. Thus, the association rule would be: "If buy diapers, then buy beer," with a *support* of 50/1000 = 5% and a *confidence* of 50/200 = 25%.

The daunting problem that awaits any such algorithm is the *curse of dimensionality*: The number of possible association rules grows exponentially in the number of attributes. Specifically, if there are k attributes, we limit ourselves to binary attributes, we account only for the positive cases (e.g. *buy diapers = yes*), there are on the order of $k \cdot 2^{k-1}$ possible association rules.[1] Consider that a typical application for association rules is market basket analysis and that there may be *thousands* of binary attributes (*buy beer? buy popcorn? buy milk? buy bread?* etc.), the search problem appears at first glance to be utterly hopeless. For example, suppose that a tiny convenience store has only 100 different items and a customer could either buy or not buy any combination of those 100 items. Then, there are $2^{100} \cong 1.27 \times 10^{30}$ possible association rules that await your intrepid search algorithm. Thankfully, however, the a priori *algorithm* for mining association rules takes advantage of structure within the rules themselves to reduce the search problem to a more manageable size.[2]

---

[1] David J. Hand, Heikki Mannila, and Padhraic Smyth, *Principles of Data Mining*, MIT Press, Cambridge, 2001.

[2] For details on how the a priori algorithm works, see *Data Mining and Predictive Analytics*.

Data Science Using Python and R, First Edition. Chantal D. Larose and Daniel T. Larose.
© 2019 John Wiley & Sons, Inc. Published 2019 by John Wiley & Sons, Inc.

14.2 A SIMPLE EXAMPLE OF ASSOCIATION RULE MINING

We begin with a simple example. Suppose that a local farmer has set up a roadside vegetable stand and is offering the following items for sale: {asparagus, beans, broccoli, corn, green peppers, squash, and tomatoes}. Denote this set of items as *I*.

One by one, customers pull over, pick up a basket, and purchase various combinations of these items, subsets of *I*.

Let *D* be the set of transactions represented in Table 14.1, where each transaction *T* in *D* represents a set of items contained in *I*.

Suppose that we have a particular set of items *A* (e.g. beans and squash) and another set of items *B* (e.g. asparagus). Then, define an *association rule* as follows:

An *association rule* takes the form:

$$\textit{if A then B}\,(\text{i.e. } A \Rightarrow B),$$

where the *antecedent A* and the *consequent B* are proper subsets of *I*, and *A* and *B* are mutually exclusive.

This definition would exclude trivial rules such as *if beans and squash, then beans*.

TABLE 14.1   Transactions made at the roadside vegetable stand

Transaction	Items Purchased
1	Broccoli, green peppers, corn
2	Asparagus, squash, corn
3	Corn, tomatoes, beans, squash
4	Green peppers, corn, tomatoes, beans
5	Beans, asparagus, broccoli
6	Squash, asparagus, beans, tomatoes
7	Tomatoes, corn
8	Broccoli, tomatoes, green peppers
9	Squash, asparagus, beans
10	Beans, corn
11	Green peppers, broccoli, beans, squash
12	Asparagus, beans, squash
13	Squash, corn, asparagus, beans
14	Corn, green peppers, tomatoes, beans, broccoli

14.3 SUPPORT, CONFIDENCE, AND LIFT

Measures of goodness of an association rule include *support*, *confidence*, and *lift*. The *support* for a particular association rule $A \Rightarrow B$ is the proportion of transactions in *D* that **contain both *A* and *B***. That is,

$$support = P(A \cap B) = \frac{\textbf{number of transactions containing both A and B}}{\textbf{total number of transactions}}$$

The *confidence* of the association rule $A \Rightarrow B$ is a measure of the accuracy of the rule, as determined by the percentage of transactions in D **containing A that also contain B.** In other words,

$$confidence = P(B \mid A) = \frac{P(A \cap B)}{P(A)}$$
$$= \frac{\textbf{number of transactions containing both A and B}}{\textbf{number of transactions containing A}}$$

In the language of probability, confidence represents the conditional probability of B, given A.

For example, consider the association rule, "If buy squash, then buy beans," where A represents squash and B represents beans. From Table 14.1, we have the following **seven** transactions where squash was bought (Table 14.2). The **six** transactions where beans were also bought are shown in bold.

Thus:

$$support = P(A \cap B) = \frac{\textbf{transactions containing both A and B}}{\textbf{total transactions}} = \frac{6}{14} = 42.9\%$$

$$confidence = P(B \mid A) = \frac{\textbf{transactions containing both A and B}}{\textbf{transactions containing A}} = \frac{6}{7} = 85.7\%$$

Another measure for quantifying the usefulness of an association rule is *lift*. Lift compares the confidence in using our association rule to the probability of just choosing the consequent at random without recourse to association rules. We define lift as follows:

$$Lift = \frac{\textit{Rule confidence}}{\textit{Prior proportion of the consequent}}$$

TABLE 14.2   Transactions where squash was bought

Transaction	Items Purchased
2	Asparagus, squash, corn
3	**Corn, tomatoes, beans, squash**
6	**Squash, asparagus, beans, tomatoes**
9	**Squash, asparagus, beans**
11	**Green peppers, broccoli, beans, squash**
12	**Asparagus, beans, squash**
13	**Squash, corn, asparagus, beans**

Recall the supermarket example where, of 1000 customers, 200 bought diapers, and of these 200 customers who bought diapers, 50 also bought beer.

Suppose 100 of the 1000 customers bought beer. The prior proportion of those who bought beer is thus $100/1000 = 10\%$. The rule confidence is $50/200 = 25\%$. Therefore, the lift for the association rule, "If buy diapers, then buy beer," is

$$Lift = \frac{Rule\ confidence}{Prior\ proportion\ of\ the\ consequent} = \frac{0.25}{0.10} = 2.5$$

This may be interpreted as, "Customers who buy diapers are 2.5 times as likely to buy beer as customers from the entire data set." Clearly, this association rule would be useful to a store manager wishing to sell more beer.

For the association rule, "If buy squash (A) then buy beans (B)," we have:

$$Lift = \frac{Rule\ confidence}{Prior\ proportion\ of\ the\ consequent} = \frac{6/7}{9/14} = 1.33$$

Customers who buy squash are 33% more likely to buy beans than the general population of customers.

14.4 MINING ASSOCIATION RULES

So, let us get our hands dirty mining for association rules using the *Churn_Training_File* data set. Prepare by doing the following:

- Subset the following variables into their own data frame: *VMail Plan, Intl Plan, CustServ Calls*, and *Churn*.
- Set *CustServ Calls* to be an ordinal factor.

Let us begin by finding the "baseline" proportions for the various variables, so that we may later check the confidence levels of our association rules against these baseline levels. These proportions may be found in Figures 14.1 and 14.2. For example, the proportion of customers who churn is 14.53%.

Now, let us generate some association rules, using the following settings:

- Specify the type of association to obtain as "rules"
- Minimum support equals 0.01 (1%)
- Minimum confidence equals 0.4 (40%)
- Maximum number of antecedents 1

Once the rules are generated, you may have to delete rules that contain Churn in the antecedent. The resulting rules after doing so are shown in Figure 14.3, sorted by lift.

```
> t11
                 Intl.Plan = no  Intl.Plan = yes
Count                2705.0000          295.0000
Proportion              0.9017            0.0983
> t22
                 VMail.Plan = no  VMail.Plan = yes
Count                2170.0000          830.0000
Proportion              0.7233            0.2767
> t33
                 Churn = False  Churn = True
Count                2564.0000      436.0000
Proportion              0.8547        0.1453
```

Figure 14.1   Proportions for International Plan, Voicemail Plan, and Churn from R.

```
> t44
                 CSC = 0    CSC = 1   CSC = 2    CSC = 3    CSC = 4
Count          626.00000 1068.000 679.00000 383.00000 149.00000
Proportion       0.20867    0.356   0.22633   0.12767   0.04967
                 CSC = 5    CSC = 6 CSC = 7 CSC = 8 CSC = 9
Count           61.00000 22.00000 8.00000 2.00000 2.00000
Proportion       0.02033  0.00733 0.00267 0.00067 0.00067
```

Figure 14.2   Proportions for Customer Service Calls from R.

```
      lhs                        rhs                  support    confidence lift        count
[1]   {CustServ.Calls=5} => {Churn=True}     0.01200000 0.5901639 4.0607610   36
[2]   {CustServ.Calls=4} => {Churn=True}     0.02266667 0.4563758 3.1402007   68
[3]   {Intl.Plan=yes}    => {Churn=True}     0.04233333 0.4305085 2.9622143  127
[4]   {CustServ.Calls=3} => {VMail.Plan=no}  0.09933333 0.7780679 1.0756699  298
[5]   {VMail.Plan=yes}   => {Churn=False}    0.25200000 0.9108434 1.0657294  756
[6]   {CustServ.Calls=1} => {Churn=False}    0.32000000 0.8988764 1.0517275  960
[7]   {CustServ.Calls=3} => {Churn=False}    0.11433333 0.8955614 1.0478487  343
[8]   {CustServ.Calls=4} => {VMail.Plan=no}  0.03733333 0.7516779 1.0391860  112
[9]   {CustServ.Calls=2} => {Churn=False}    0.20066667 0.8865979 1.0373611  602
[10]  {Intl.Plan=no}     => {Churn=False}    0.79866667 0.8857671 1.0363890 2396
```

Figure 14.3   The first 10 association rules uncovered by R, sorted by lift.

The association rule with the greatest lift is the first one, with Rule ID [1]:

If customer service calls = 5 then Churn = True

The lift for Rule ID [1] is about 4.06.

14.4.1   How to Mine Association Rules Using R

Read in the *Churn_Training_File* data set and name it *churn*. The first step is to subset from the data set only the columns we want association rules for.

```
min.churn <-
  subset(churn, select = c("Intl.Plan", "VMail.Plan",
"CustServ.Calls",
        "Churn"))
```

As we have seen before, the **subset()** command takes a data set and extracts the specified rows or columns from it. Since we want four columns, we put their names in a vector under the input **select**. We name our new data frame **min. churn**.

To change Customer Service Calls to a factor, we use the **ordered()** command.

```
min.churn$CustServ.Calls <- ordered(as.factor(min.
churn$CustServ.Calls))
```

We work with two nested commands here. First, **as.factor()** takes the **CustServ.Calls** variable and makes a factor of the different values. However, the variable will be treated as nominal, not ordinal. To set the levels are ordinal, we include the **as.factor()** command inside the **ordered()** command. The order of the levels in the factor **CustServ.Calls** will now be set to be in ascending order.

To obtain the baseline distributions of the four variables, we use tables. The code for the first table is shown below. The remaining three tables are left as an exercise.

```
t1 <- table(min.churn$Intl.Plan)
t11 <- rbind(t1, round(prop.table(t1), 4))
```

The **table()**, **prop.table()**, and **round()** commands have been discussed in previous chapters. The table **t1** contains a count of how many customers have and do not have the International Plan, while the **prop.table()** command returns a table with the proportions for those same categories. The **rbind()** command creates a matrix with the counts and proportions together. Save the matrix as **t11**.

To make the table more readable, we add column and row names.

```
colnames(t11) <- c("Intl.Plan = no", "Intl.Plan = yes")
rownames(t11) <- c("Count", "Proportion")
t11
```

To know what order to put the **colnames()** values, take a look at **t1**. The first column has the "no" values. We use this information to inform the order of the **colnames()** values. Namely, the "Intl.Plan = no" value comes first, followed by "Intl.Plan = yes." The result, **t11**, is shown as the first table in Figure 14.1.

Once we are done setting up the data and obtaining baseline distribution information, install and load the package for association rules: the *arules* package.

```
install.packages("arules"); library(arules)
```

To obtain the association rules, run the **apriori()** command from the **arules** package.

```
all.rules <- apriori(data = min.churn, parameter =
list(supp = 0.01, target = "rules",
        conf = 0.4, minlen = 2, maxlen = 2))
```

```
        lhs                      rhs            support     confidence lift      count
[1]    {CustServ.Calls=5} => {Churn=True}    0.01200120 0.6060606  4.182195   40
[2]    {CustServ.Calls=4} => {Churn=True}    0.02280228 0.4578313  3.159321   76
[3]    {Intl.Plan=yes}    => {Churn=True}    0.04110411 0.4241486  2.926889  137
[4]    {Churn=True}       => {VMail.Plan=no} 0.12091209 0.8343685  1.153443  403
[5]    {VMail.Plan=yes}   => {Churn=False}   0.25262526 0.9132321  1.068001  842
[6]    {CustServ.Calls=3} => {VMail.Plan=no} 0.09930993 0.7715618  1.066618  331
[7]    {CustServ.Calls=3} => {Churn=False}   0.11551155 0.8974359  1.049528  385
[8]    {CustServ.Calls=1} => {Churn=False}   0.31773177 0.8966977  1.048664 1059
[9]    {CustServ.Calls=2} => {Churn=False}   0.20162016 0.8853755  1.035423  672
[10]   {Churn=False}      => {Intl.Plan=no}  0.79927993 0.9347368  1.035042 2664
```

Figure 14.4   The top 10 rules from all. rules from R, sorted by lift value.

While the only required input is **data = min.churn**, we need to specify the parameter settings outlined previously. First, **supp = 0.01** will set the minimum support to 1%. The **target = "rules"** input specifies that we want association rules. The **minlen = 2** and **maxlen = 2** input values specify that we want antecedents with exactly one item, since a rule with an empty antecedent is considered to have a length of one. Finally, **conf = 0.4** will set the minimum support to 40%. Save the result of this algorithm as **all.rules**.

To look at the top 10 rules we have obtained, sorted by their lift values, use the commands **inspect()** and **head()**.

```
inspect(head(all.rules, by = "lift", n = 10))
```

The **by** and **n** values specify the criterion to sort by, and the maximum number of rules to return. The result is shown in Figure 14.4.

Notice that Figure 14.4 contains some rules that have Churn in the antecedent ("lhs," or "left-hand side"). We do not want these rules. This means our next step is to subset from **all.rules** only the rules which do not contain Churn in the antecedent.

To begin, we need to identify which rules have Churn in the antecedent, **lhs**. To work with **lhs**, we need our rules to be formatted as a data frame. However, the **apriori()** algorithm does not return output formatted as a data frame. To convert the format of **lhs** to a data frame, we use two **as()** commands.

```
all.rules.ant.df <- as(as(attr(all.rules, "lhs"),
"transactions"), "data.frame")
```

The core code, **attr(all.rules, "lhs")**, specifies that we are working with the antecedents (**lhs**) of the rules contained in **all.rules**. The first **as()** command, which takes the **attr()** code as input and adds the additional input **"transactions"**, changes the antecedents into a format specific to the **arules()** package called **transactions**. This step is required, since an object of type **transactions** can then be transformed to a **data.frame** frame format using a second **as()** command, this time using the second input value **"data.frame"**. We save the result as **all.rules. ant.df** to signify that the antecedent ("ant") of the **all.rules** object has been turned into a data frame ("**df**").

Now that we have isolated the antecedents in a form we can work with, we examine them to see which contain either *Churn = True* or *Churn = False*.

```
t1 <- rules.dataframe$items == "{Churn=True}"
t2 <- rules.dataframe$items == "{Churn=False}"
non.churn.ant <- abs(t1+t2-1)
```

The vectors **t1** and **t2** are a series of zeros and ones, where zero means the antecedent did not meet the condition and one means that it did. When we take the absolute value of **t1+t2-1** using the **abs()** command, the result is a single vector of zeros and ones, where the ones indicate antecedents that do not contain *Churn*. We save this binary vector as **non.churn.ant**.

Finally, we subset from **all.rules** only those rules that have **non.churn.ant** equal to one. In other words, we subset only those rules that do not have *Churn* in the antecedent.

```
good.rules <- all.rules[non.churn.ant == 1]
```

Save the resulting rules as **good.rules**.

We can look at **good.rules** sorted by descending lift values by using the commands **inspect()** and **head()** once more.

```
inspect(head(good.rules, by = "lift", n = 28))
```

The first 10 rows of output from this command are shown in Figure 14.3.

To make the contingency table of Churn and Customer Service Calls, which will be utilized below, run the following code:

```
t.csc.churn <- table(min.churn$Churn, min.churn$CustServ.
Calls)
colnames(t.csc.churn) <- c("CSC = 0", "CSC = 1", "CSC =
2", "CSC = 3", "CSC = 4",
        "CSC = 5", "CSC = 6", "CSC = 7", "CSC = 8", "CSC = 9")
rownames(t.csc.churn) <- c("Churn = False", "Churn = True")
addmargins(A = t.csc.churn, FUN = list(Total = sum),
quiet = TRUE)
```

The result is provided in Figure 14.5.

	CSC = 0	CSC = 1	CSC = 2	CSC = 3	CSC = 4
Churn = False	540	960	602	343	81
Churn = True	86	108	77	40	68
Total	626	1068	679	383	149

	CSC = 5	CSC = 6	CSC = 7	CSC = 8	CSC = 9	Total
Churn = False	25	8	4	1	0	2564
Churn = True	36	14	4	1	2	436
Total	61	22	8	2	2	3000

Figure 14.5   Contingency table of Churn and Customer Service Calls from R.

14.5 CONFIRMING OUR METRICS

We will call Rule ID [1] "Rule 1." Next, let us confirm the following values for Rule 1, using what we have learned so far:

1. Support,
2. Confidence,
3. Lift.

1. Support.

$$s = support = P(CSC = 5\,and\ Churn = True)$$
$$= \frac{\text{transactions with both}\,CSC = 5\,\text{and Churn} = \text{True}}{\text{total number of transactions}} = \frac{36}{3000} = 1.2\%$$

How did we get the 36? Support requires the intersection of two events, which can be found by generating the contingency table of customer service calls vs churn, shown in Figure 14.5. Note that the cell for $CSC = 5$ and $Churn = True$ contains $Count = 36$, represented 1.2% of the total number of records.

2. Confidence. Use the contingency table to confirm that this equals the conditional probability $P(B\,|\,A)$.

$$confidence = P(Churn = True\,|\,CSC = 5) = \frac{P(Churn = True\,and\,CSC = 5)}{P(CSC = 5)}$$
$$= \frac{\text{number of transactions containing both}\,CSC = 5\,\text{and Churn} = \text{True}}{\text{number of transactions containing}\,CSC = 5}$$

Both of these quantities are found in Figure 14.5. Thus,

$$confidence = P(Churn = True\,|\,CSC = 5) = \frac{36}{61} = 59.016\%$$

3. Lift. Interpret this value.

$$Lift = \frac{Rule\ confidence\ for\ Rule\,1}{Prior\ proportion\ of\ Churn = True}$$

From (2) we have confidence = 59.016%. From Figure 14.1, we have the prior percentage of $Churn = True$ to be 14.53%. Therefore,

$$Lift = \frac{Rule\ confidence\ for\ Rule\,ID\,2}{Prior\ proportion\ of\ Churn = True} = \frac{0.59016}{0.1453} = 4.061$$

In other words, customers who have made five calls to customer service are 4.061 times as likely to churn than our general population of customers.

14.6 THE CONFIDENCE DIFFERENCE CRITERION

The association rules above were generated using the minimum confidence criterion. However, other criteria exist for generating association rules. Next, we consider the *confidence difference criterion*. The confidence difference evaluation measure gives the *absolute difference* between the **prior probability of the consequent** (here, churn status) and the **confidence of the rule**. So, rules would be included in this case only if:

$$|Prior\ probability\ of\ consequent - Rule\ confidence| \geq 0.40$$

Figure 14.6 shows the only association rule generated using a confidence difference lower bound of 40 (along with minimum antecedent support of 1%, minimum rule confidence of 5%, and maximum antecedents of 1).

This association rule has Rule confidence 0.59016 and prior probability of *Churn = True* of 0.14533, giving us:

$$|Prior\ prob\ of\ consequent - Rule\ confidence|$$

$$= |0.14533 - 0.59016| = 0.44483 \geq 0.40$$

The **diff** statistic from Figure 14.6 equals this absolute difference, 0.44483.

The rules that have confidence similar to the prior probability of the consequent may not be interesting. For example, by randomly selecting a transaction from the data, the probability of obtaining a churning customer is 0.14533. If the rule generated gives a confidence measure that is not far from 0.14533, random selection might as well be used. Therefore, the confidence difference can indicate rules which deviate from random selection. In the case here, it can be seen that customers who have made five customer service calls have churn rates that appear quite different from random customers selected from the data. The confidence difference measure helps to weed out obvious rules, such as "If pregnant, then female." It also accounts for skewed or uneven distributions.

14.6.1 How to Apply the Confidence Difference Criterion Using R

To include the confidence different criterion in our association rule settings, we return to the **apriori()** command and add additional input values.

```
      lhs                    rhs            support confidence diff      lift      count
[1] {CustServ.Calls=5} => {Churn=True} 0.012    0.5901639  0.4448306 4.060761 36
```

Figure 14.6 Association rule found using confidence difference lower bound = 40.

```
rules.confdiff <- apriori(data = min.churn, parameter =
list(arem = "diff", aval = TRUE,
        minval = 0.4, supp = 0.01, target = "rules", conf
        = 0.05, minlen = 2, maxlen = 2))
```

Note the three new input settings under **parameter = list()**. The first one, **arem = "diff"**, specifies that the confidence difference criterion should be used. The second, **aval = TRUE**, states that the value of the criterion should be reported when the results are shown. The third, **minval = 0.4**, sets the lower bound of the confidence difference at 40. Save the output as **rules.confdiff**.

To view the new rules,[3] use the **inspect()** and **head()** commands, this time using **rules.confdiff** as the primary input.

```
inspect(head(rules.confdiff, by = "lift", n = 10))
```

14.7   THE CONFIDENCE QUOTIENT CRITERION

To demonstrate the *confidence quotient criterion*, we generate rules using a lower bound of 40 (along with minimum antecedent support of 1%, minimum rule confidence of 5%, and maximum antecedents of 1). After removing any rules with *Churn* in the antecedent, we obtain the three association rules shown in Figure 14.7.

The confidence quotient evaluation measure gives the *absolute ratio* between the **prior probability of the consequent** (*Churn = True*) and the **confidence of the rule.** So, rules would be included in this case only if:

$$
\begin{cases}
1 - \dfrac{Rule\ confidence}{Prior\ proportion\ of consequent} \geq 0.40 \\
\\
or \\
\\
1 - \dfrac{Prior\ proportion\ of\ consequent}{Rule\ confidence} \geq 0.40
\end{cases}
$$

whichever is not negative.

```
   lhs                    rhs              support    confidence quot      lift      count
[1] {CustServ.Calls=5} => {Churn=True} 0.01200000 0.5901639  0.7537407 4.060761   36
[2] {CustServ.Calls=4} => {Churn=True} 0.02266667 0.4563758  0.6815490 3.140201   68
[3] {Intl.Plan=yes}    => {Churn=True} 0.04233333 0.4305085  0.6624147 2.962214  127
```

Figure 14.7   Association rules in R found using confidence quotient lower bound = 40.

---

[3] The output will have rules that have Churn in the antecedent. After subsetting only those rules without Churn in the antecedent, as demonstrated in the previous R section, the output will match that shown in Figure 14.6.

Let us confirm the calculations for Rule [3] from Figure 14.5. This rule has confidence 0.43051. From Figure 14.1, the prior proportion of the consequent (Churn = True) equals 0.14533. Thus,

$$1 - \frac{Prior\ proportion\ of\ consequent}{Rule\ confidence} = 1 - \frac{0.14533}{0.43051} = 0.66242 \geq 0.40$$

Allowing for rounding error, the **quot** statistic from Figure 14.7 equals the value we obtained above, 0.66242.

Like Confidence Difference, this method takes uneven distributions into account. It is especially good at finding rules that predict rare events. Of course, like any other data science task using cross-validation, association rule mining needs to be validated. We show how to do this in the exercises.

14.7.1 How to Apply the Confidence Quotient Criterion Using R

To include the confidence different criterion in our association rule settings, we return to the **apriori()** command and change the input values.

```
rules.confquot <- apriori(data = min.churn, parameter =
list(arem = "quot", aval = TRUE,
        minval = 0.4, supp = 0.01, target = "rules", conf =
0.05, minlen = 2, maxlen = 2))
inspect(head(rules.confquot, by = "lift", n = 10))
```

The output of the above code, which is not shown, includes rules with *Churn* in the antecedent.

Our next step is to subset from the rules we have obtained only those which do not have *Churn* in the antecedent. We follow the same general steps as in Section 14.4.1.

```
rules.confquot.ant.df <- as(as(attr(rules.confquot,
"lhs"), "transactions"), "data.frame")
t1 <- rules.confquot.ant.df$items == "{Churn=True}"
t2 <- rules.confquot.ant.df$items == "{Churn=False}"
non.churn.ant <- abs(t1+t2-1)
good.rules.confquot <- rules.confquot[non.churn.ant == 1]
inspect(good.rules.confquot)
```

The result is shown in Figure 14.7.

VALEDICTION

The authors would like to thank you for joining us as we learned about *Data Science Using Python and R*. You should take a moment to savor your accomplishment! Look how much you have learned! We wish you all the best as you continue your journey through life, and through data science.

Chantal Larose
Daniel Larose

REFERENCES

Our work with association rules has leaned heavily on the arules package, whose citations follow: Michael Hahsler, Christian Buchta, Bettina Gruen, and Kurt Hornik, arules: Mining Association Rules and Frequent Itemsets. R package version 1.6-1, 2018. https:// CRAN.R-project.org/package=arules

Michael Hahsler, Bettina Gruen, and Kurt Hornik, arules – A Computational Environment for Mining Association Rules and Frequent Item Sets, *Journal of Statistical Software*, 14(15), 2005. doi:https://doi.org/10.18637/jss.v014.i15.

Michael Hahsler, Sudheer Chelluboina, Kurt Hornik, and Christian Buchta, The arules R-package ecosystem: analyzing interesting patterns from large transaction datasets, *Journal of Machine Learning Research*, 12, 1977–1981, 2011.

EXERCISES

CLARIFYING THE CONCEPTS

1. How does the curse of dimensionality make it a challenge to uncover association rules?

2. What form do association rules take?

3. In your own words, explain what we mean by the support for an association rule.

4. The confidence of a rule is equivalent to what probability?

5. Explain what is meant by lift.

6. What is the confidence difference criterion, and why is it used?

7. Describe the confidence ratio criterion.

    Use Table 14.1 to answer the following questions.

8. Calculate the support for the rule, "If corn, then tomatoes."

9. Find the confidence for the rule, "If corn, then tomatoes."

10. Calculate the lift for the rule, "If corn, then tomatoes."

WORKING WITH THE DATA

For the following exercises, work with the *Churn_Training_File data* set. Use R to solve each problem.

11. Subset the variables *VMail Plan, Int'l Plan, CustServ Calls*, and *Churn* into their own data frame. Change *CustServ Calls* into an ordered factor.

12. Create tables for each of the four variables. Include both counts and proportions in each table. Use the tables to discuss the "baseline" distribution of each variable.

13. Obtain the association rules using the settings outlined in Section 14.4.

14. Subset the rules from the previous exercise so none of the antecedents contain the Churn variable. Display the rules, sorted by descending lift value.

15. Obtain association rules using the confidence difference criterion outlined in Section 14.6.

16. Confirm by hand that the value of the confidence different criterion for the first rule in the previous exercise is correct.

17. Obtain association rules using the confidence quotient criterion outlined in Section 14.7. Subset only those rules without Churn in the antecedent.

18. Confirm by hand that the value of the confidence quotient criterion for the first rule in the previous exercise is correct.

HANDS-ON ANALYSIS

For the following, work with the *Adult* data set. Use R to solve each problem.

19. Subset the variables *education*, *marital.status*, and *income* into their own data frame.

20. Create tables for each of the variables. Include both counts and proportions in each table. These tables will be used to obtain the prior proportions of various values.

21. Obtain the association rules using minimum support of 2%, minimum confidence of 50%, and maximum antecedents of 1.

22. Subset the rules from the previous exercise so none of the antecedents contain the *income* variable. Display the rules, sorted by descending lift value.

23. Obtain association rules using the confidence difference criterion, with a confidence difference lower bound of 30, minimum antecedent support of 2%, minimum rule confidence of 50%, and maximum antecedents of 1.

24. Subset the rules from the previous exercise so none of the antecedents contain the *income* variable. Display the rules, sorted by descending lift value.

25. Confirm by hand that the value of the confidence different criterion for the first rule in the previous exercise is correct.

26. Obtain association rules using the confidence quotient criterion, with a confidence quotient lower bound of 30, minimum antecedent support of 2%, minimum rule confidence of 50%, and maximum antecedents of 1.

27. Subset the rules from the previous exercise so none of the antecedents contain the *income* variable. Display the rules, sorted by descending lift value.

28. Confirm by hand that the value of the confidence quotient criterion for the first rule in the previous exercise is correct.

For the following exercises, use the *AR_Training* and *AR_Test* data sets. *Response* is the target variable, so only consider rules where it is the only possible consequent. The other variables are the predictors, so only consider rules where the predictors are the antecedents. Use the training set until notified otherwise.

29. Create tables for each of the variables. Include both counts and proportions in each table. These tables will be used to obtain the prior proportions of various values.

30. Generate association rules using minimum support of 5%, minimum confidence of 5%, and maximum antecedents of 1. Display the rules, sorted by descending lift value.

31. Select the rule from the previous exercise with the greatest lift. Interpret this lift value for someone unfamiliar with data science.

32. Continue with the association rule from the previous exercise. Find any prior proportions and build any contingency tables you need to confirm by hand the values you obtained for the following quantities:

    a. Support

    b. Confidence

    c. Lift

33. Generate association rules using minimum support of 5%, minimum confidence of 5%, and maximum antecedents of 2. Display the rules, sorted by descending lift value.

34. Select the rule from the previous exercise with the greatest lift. Compare this rule with the highest lift rule for antecedents = 1.

    a. Which rule has the better lift?

    b. Which rule has the greater support?

    c. If you were a marketing manager, and could fund only one of these rules, which would it be, and why?

35. Obtain association rules using the confidence difference criterion, with a confidence difference lower bound of 30, minimum support of 5%, minimum confidence of 5%, and maximum antecedents of 1. Display the rules, sorted by descending lift value.

36. Select the rule from the previous exercise with the greatest lift. Confirm by hand the value for the confidence difference.

37. Obtain association rules using the confidence difference criterion, with a confidence difference lower bound of 10, minimum support of 5%, minimum confidence of 5%, and maximum antecedents of 2. Display the rules, sorted by descending lift value.

38. Select the rule from the previous exercise with the second greatest lift. Compare this rule with the highest lift rule for antecedents = 1.

    a. Which rule has the better lift?

    b. Which rule has the greater support?

    c. If you were a marketing manager, and could fund only one of these rules, which would it be, and why?

39. Obtain association rules using the confidence quotient criterion, with a confidence quotient lower bound of 30, minimum antecedent support of 5%, minimum rule confidence of 5%, and maximum antecedents of 3. Display the rules, sorted by descending lift value.

40. Select the rule from the previous exercise with the greatest lift. Confirm by hand the value for the confidence quotient.

For the next set of Exercises, we will be validating the association rules we found earlier. Use the *AR_Test* data set.

41. Create tables for each of the variables. Include both counts and proportions in each table. These tables will be used to obtain the prior proportions of various values.

42. Generate association rules using minimum support of 5%, minimum confidence of 5%, and maximum antecedents of 1. Display the rules, sorted by descending lift value.

43. Compare the rules you obtained in the previous exercise with the rules you obtained using the same criteria from the training data set. Would you say that our association rules have been validated?

DATA SUMMARIZATION
AND VISUALIZATION

Here we present a very brief review of methods for summarizing and visualizing data. For deeper coverage, please see *Discovering Statistics* by Daniel T. Larose (W.H. Freeman, second edition, 2013).

PART 1: SUMMARIZATION 1: BUILDING BLOCKS
OF DATA ANALYSIS

- **Descriptive statistics** refers to methods for summarizing and organizing the information in a data set.

  Consider Table A.1, which we will use to illustrate some statistical concepts.

- The entities for which information is collected are called the **elements**. In Table A.1, the elements are the 10 applicants. Elements are also called **cases** or **subjects**.

- A **variable** is a characteristic of an element, which takes on different values for different elements. The variables in Table A.1 are *marital status, mortgage, income, rank, year*, and *risk*. Variables are also called **attributes**.

- The set of variable values for a particular element is an **observation**. Observations are also called **records**. The observation for Applicant 2 is:

Applicant	Marital Status	Mortgage	Income ($)	Income Rank	Year	Risk
2	Married	Yes	32,000	7	2010	Good

- Variables can be either *qualitative* or *quantitative*.
  - A **qualitative variable** enables the elements to be classified or categorized according to some characteristic. The qualitative variables in Table A.1 are *marital status, mortgage, rank*, and *risk*. Qualitative variables are also called **categorical variables**.

Data Science Using Python and R, First Edition. Chantal D. Larose and Daniel T. Larose.
© 2019 John Wiley & Sons, Inc. Published 2019 by John Wiley & Sons, Inc.

TABLE A.1   Characteristics of 10 loan applicants

Applicant	Marital Status	Mortgage	Income ($)	Income Rank	Year	Risk
1	Single	Yes	38,000	2	2009	Good
2	Married	Yes	32,000	7	2010	Good
3	Other	No	25,000	9	2011	Good
4	Other	No	36,000	3	2009	Good
5	Other	Yes	33,000	4	2010	Good
6	Other	No	24,000	10	2008	Bad
7	Married	Yes	25,100	8	2010	Good
8	Married	Yes	48,000	1	2007	Good
9	Married	Yes	32,100	6	2009	Bad
10	Married	Yes	32,200	5	2010	Good

- ○ A **quantitative variable** takes numeric values and allows arithmetic to be meaningfully performed on it. The quantitative variables in Table A.1 are *income* and *year*. Quantitative variables are also called **numerical variables**.
- Data may be classified according to four *levels of measurement*: *nominal, ordinal, interval*, and *ratio*. Nominal and ordinal data are categorical; interval and ratio data are numerical.
  - ○ **Nominal data** refer to names, labels, or categories. There is no natural ordering, nor may arithmetic be carried out on nominal data. The nominal variables in Table A.1 are *marital status, mortgage*, and *risk*.
  - ○ **Ordinal data** can be rendered into a particular order. However, arithmetic cannot be meaningfully carried out on ordinal data. The ordinal variable in Table A.1 is *income rank*.
  - ○ **Interval data** consist of quantitative data defined on an interval without a natural zero. Addition and subtraction may be performed on interval data. The interval variable in Table A.1 is *year*. (Note that there is no "year zero." The calendar goes from 1 BCE to 1 CE)
  - ○ **Ratio data** are quantitative data for which addition, subtraction, multiplication, and division may be performed. A natural zero exists for ratio data. The interval variable in Table A.1 is *income*.
- A numerical variable that can take either a finite or a countable number of values is a **discrete** variable, for which each value can be graphed as a separate point, with space between each point. The discrete variable in Table A.1 is *year*.
- A numerical variable that can take infinitely many values is a **continuous variable**, whose possible values form an interval on the number line, with no space between the points. The continuous variable in Table A.1 is *income*.

- A **population** is the set of all elements of interest for a particular problem. A **parameter** is a characteristic of a population. For example, the population is the set of all American voters, and the parameter is the proportion of the population who supports a $1 per ton tax on carbon.

  ○ The value of a parameter is usually unknown, but it is a constant.

- A **sample** consists of a subset of the population. A characteristic of a sample is called a **statistic**. For example, the sample is the set of American voters in your classroom, and the statistic is the proportion of the sample who supports a $1 per ton tax on carbon.

  ○ The value of a statistic is usually known, but it changes from sample to sample.

- A **census** is the collection of information from every element in the population. For example, the census here would be to find from every American voter whether they support a $1 per ton tax on carbon. Such a census is impractical, so we turn to statistical inference.

- **Statistical inference** refers to methods for estimating or drawing conclusions about population characteristics based on the characteristics of a sample of that population. For example, suppose 50% of the voters in your classroom support the tax; using statistical inference we would *infer* that 50% of all American voters support the tax. Obviously, there are problems with this. The sample is neither random nor representative. The estimate does not have a confidence level, and so on.

- When we take a sample for which each element has an equal chance of being selected, we have a **random sample**.

- A **predictor variable** is a variable whose value is used to help predict the value of the *response variable*. The predictor variables in Table A.1 are all the variables except *risk*.

- A **response variable** is a variable of interest whose value is presumably determined at least in part by the set of predictor variables. The response variable in Table A.1 is *risk*.

PART 2: VISUALIZATION: GRAPHS AND TABLES FOR SUMMARIZING AND ORGANIZING DATA

A.1 Categorical Variables

- The **frequency** (or **count**) of a category is the number of data values in each category. The **relative frequency** of a particular category for a categorical variable equals its frequency divided by the number of cases.

- A (**relative**) **frequency distribution** for a categorical variable consists of all the categories that the variable assumes, together with the (relative) frequencies for each value. The frequencies sum to the number of cases; the relative frequencies sum to 1.

TABLE A.2 **Frequency distribution and relative frequency distribution**

Category of *Marital Status*	Frequency	Relative Frequency
Married	5	0.5
Other	4	0.4
Single	1	0.1
Total	**10**	**1.0**

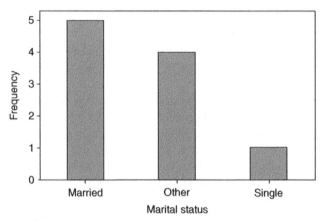

Figure A.1   Bar chart for *marital status*.

- For example, Table A.2 contains the frequency distribution and relative frequency distribution for the variable *marital status* for the data from Table A.1.
- A **bar chart** is a graph used to represent the frequencies or relative frequencies for a categorical variable. Note that the bars do not touch.
  - A **Pareto chart** is a bar chart where the bars are arranged in decreasing order. Figure A.1 is an example of a Pareto chart.
- A **pie chart** is a circle divided into slices, with the size of each slice proportional to the relative frequency of the category associated with that slice. Figure A.2 shows a pie chart of *marital status*.

A.2   Quantitative Variables

- Quantitative data are grouped into **classes**. The **lower (upper) class limit** of a class equals the smallest (largest) value within that class. The **class width** is the difference between successive lower class limits.
- For quantitative data, a **(relative) frequency distribution** divides the data into nonoverlapping classes of equal class width. Table A.3 shows the

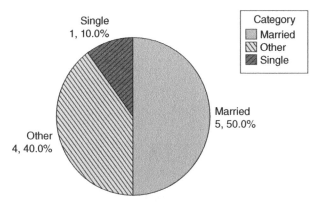

Figure A.2   Pie chart of *marital status*.

TABLE A.3   Frequency distribution and relative frequency distribution of *income*

Class of *Income* ($)	Frequency	Relative Frequency
24,000–29,999	3	0.3
30,000–35,999	4	0.4
36,000–41,999	2	0.2
42,000–48,999	1	0.1
Total	**10**	**1.0**

TABLE A.4   Cumulative frequency distribution and cumulative relative frequency distribution of *income*

Class of *Income* ($)	Cumulative Frequency	Cumulative Relative Frequency
24,000–29,999	3	0.3
30,000–35,999	7	0.7
36,000–41,999	9	0.9
42,000–48,999	10	1.0

frequency distribution and relative frequency distribution of the continuous variable *income* from Table A.1.

- A **cumulative (relative) frequency distribution** shows the total number (relative frequency) of data values less than or equal to the upper class limit (Table A.4).

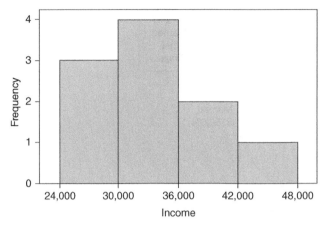

Figure A.3   Histogram of *income*.

- A **distribution** of a variable is a graph, table, or formula that specifies the values and frequencies of the variable for all elements in the data set. For example, Table A.3 represents the distribution of the variable *income*.

- A **histogram** is a graphical representation of a (relative) frequency distribution for a quantitative variable (Figure A.3). Note that histograms represent a simple version of *data smoothing* and can thus vary in shape depending on the number and width of the classes. Therefore, histograms should be interpreted with caution. See *Discovering Statistics* by Daniel T. Larose (W.H. Freeman) Section 2.4 for an example of a data set presented as *both* symmetric and right-skewed by altering the number and width of the histogram classes.

- A **stem-and-leaf display** shows the shape of the data distribution while retaining the original data values in the display, either exactly or approximately. The leaf units are defined to equal a power of 10, and the stem units are 10 times the leaf units. Then, each leaf represents a data value, through a stem-and-leaf combination. For example, in Figure A.4, the leaf units (right-hand column) are 1000s and the stem units (left-hand column) are 10,000s. So, "2 4" represents $2 \times 10,000 + 4 \times 1000 = \$24,000$, while "2 55" represents two equal incomes of $25,000 (one of which is exact, the other approximate – $25,100). Note that Figure A.4, turned 90° to the left, presents the shape of the data distribution.

- In a **dotplot** each dot represents one or more data values, set above the number line (Figure A.5).

- A distribution is **symmetric** if there exists an axis of symmetry (a line) that splits the distribution into two halves that are approximately mirror images of each other (Figure A.6a).

```
Stem-and-leaf of Income
Leaf Unit = 1000

        2   4
        2   55
        3   2223
        3   68
        4
        4   8
```

Figure A.4   Stem-and-leaf display of *income*.

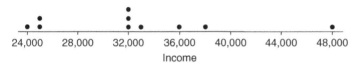

Figure A.5   Dotplot of *income*.

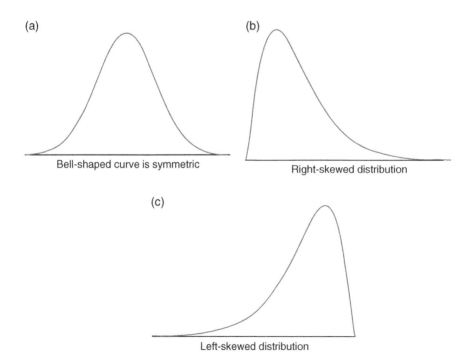

Figure A.6   (a) Bell-shaped curve is symmetric. (b) Right-skewed distribution. (c) Left-skewed distribution.

- **Right-skewed** data have a longer tail on the right than the left (Figure A.6b). **Left-skewed** data have a longer tail on the left than the right (Figure A.6c).

PART 3: SUMMARIZATION 2: MEASURES OF CENTER, VARIABILITY, AND POSITION

- The *summation notation* Σx means to add up all the data values x. The sample size is n and the population size is N.
- **Measures of center** indicate where on the number line the central part of the data is located. The measures of center we will learn are the *mean*, the *median*, the *mode*, and the *midrange*.
  - ○ The **mean** is the *arithmetic average* of a data set. To calculate the mean, add up the values and divide by the number of values. The mean income from Table A.1 is:

$$\frac{38,000+32,000+\ldots+32,200}{10}=\frac{325,400}{10}=\$32,540$$

  - ○ The **sample mean** is the arithmetic average of a sample and is denoted $\bar{x}$ ("*x-bar*").
  - ○ The **population mean** is the arithmetic average of a population and is denoted μ ("*myu*," the Greek letter for *m*).
  - ○ The **median** is the middle data value, when there is an odd number of data values and the data have been sorted into ascending order. If there is an even number, the median is the mean of the two middle data values. When the income data are sorted into ascending order, the two middle values are \$32,100 and \$32,200, the mean of which is the median income, \$32,150.
  - ○ The **mode** is the data value that occurs with the greatest frequency. Both quantitative and categorical variables can have modes, but only quantitative variables can have means or medians. Each income value occurs only once, so there is no mode. The mode for *year* is 2010, with a frequency of 4.
  - ○ The **midrange** is the average of the maximum and minimum values in a data set. The midrange income is

$$midrange\left(income\right)=\frac{\left(\max\left(income\right)+\min\left(income\right)\right)}{2}=\frac{48,000+24,000}{2}=\$36,000$$

- **Skewness and measures of center.** The following are tendencies, and not strict rules.

- ○ For symmetric data, the mean and the median are approximately equal.
- ○ For right-skewed data, the mean is greater than the median.
- ○ For left-skewed data, the median is greater than the mean.
- **Measures of variability** quantify the amount of *variation, spread,* or *dispersion* present in the data. The measures of variability we will learn are the *range,* the *variance,* the *standard deviation,* and, later, the *interquartile range* (IQR).
  - ○ The **range** of a variable equals the difference between the maximum and minimum values. The range of *income* is: range = max(*income*) − min(*income*) = 48,000 − 24,000 = $24,000.
  - ○ A **deviation** is the signed difference between a data value and the mean value. For Applicant 1, the deviation in *income* equals $x - \bar{x} = 38,000 - 32,540 = 5460$. For any conceivable data set, the *mean deviation* always equals zero, because the sum of the deviations equals zero.
  - ○ The **population variance** is the mean of the squared deviations, denoted as σ^2 (*"sigma-squared"*):

$$\sigma^2 = \frac{\sum (x - \mu)^2}{N}$$

  - ○ The **population standard deviation** is the square root of the population variance: $\sigma = \sqrt{\sigma^2}$.
  - ○ The **sample variance** is approximately the mean of the squared deviations, with n replaced by $n - 1$ in the denominator in order to make it an *unbiased estimator* of σ^2. (An **unbiased estimator** is a statistic whose expected value equals its target parameter.)

$$s^2 = \frac{\sum (x - \bar{x})^2}{n - 1}$$

  - ○ The **sample standard deviation** is the square root of the sample variance: $s = \sqrt{s^2}$.
  - ○ The variance is expressed in *units squared,* an interpretation that may be opaque to nonspecialists. For this reason, the standard deviation, which is expressed in the original units, is preferred when reporting results. For example, the sample variance of *income* is $s^2 = 51,860,444$ *dollars squared,* the meaning of which may be unclear to clients. Better to report the sample standard deviation $s = \$7201$.
  - ○ The sample standard deviation s is interpreted as the size of the *typical deviation,* that is, the size of the typical difference between data values and

the mean data value. For example, incomes typically deviate from their mean by $7201.

- **Measures of position** indicate the relative position of a particular data value in the data distribution. The measures of position we cover here are the *percentile*, the *percentile rank*, the *Z-score*, and the *quartiles*.

  ○ The **pth percentile** of a data set is the data value such that *p* percent of the values in the data set are at or below this value. The 50th percentile is the median. For example, the median *income* is $32,150 and 50% of the data values lie at or below this value.

  ○ The **percentile rank** of a data value equals the percentage of values in the data set that are at or below that value. For example, the percentile rank of Applicant 1's income of $38,000 is 90%, since that is the percentage of incomes equal to or less than $38,000.

  ○ The **Z-score** for a particular data value represents how many standard deviations the data value lies above or below the mean. For a sample, the Z-score is:

$$Z\text{-score} = \frac{x - \bar{x}}{s}$$

For Applicant 6, the Z-score is

$$\frac{24,000 - 32,540}{7201} \approx -1.2$$

The income of Applicant 6 lies 1.2 standard deviations below the mean.

  ○ We may also find data values, given a Z-score. Suppose no loans will be given to those with incomes more than 2 standard deviations below the mean. Here, Z-score = −2 and the corresponding minimum income is:

$$income = Z\text{-}score \cdot s + \bar{x} = (-2)(7201) + 32\ 540 = \$18,138$$

No loans will be provided to applicants with incomes below $18,138.

  ○ If the data distribution is normal, then the **Empirical Rule** states:

    - About 68% of the data lies within one standard deviation of the mean.

    - About 95% of the data lies within two standard deviations of the mean.

    - About 99.7% of the data lies within three standard deviations of the mean.

  ○ The **first quartile (Q1)** is the 25th percentile of a data set; the **second quartile (Q2)** is the 50th percentile (median); and the **third quartile (Q3)** is the 75th percentile.

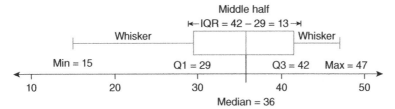

Figure A.7   Boxplot of left-skewed data.

- ○ The **IQR** is a measure of variability that is not sensitive to the presence of outliers. $IQR = Q3 - Q1$.
- ○ In the **IQR method for detecting outliers**, a data value x is an outlier if either
  - • $x \leq Q1 - 1.5(IQR)$, or
  - • $x \geq Q3 + 1.5(IQR)$.
- • The **five-number summary** of a data set consists of the *minimum, Q1*, the *median, Q3*, and the *maximum*.
- • The **boxplot** is a graph based on the five-number summary, useful for recognizing symmetry and skewness. Suppose for a particular data set (not from Table A.1) we have *Min* = 15, *Q1* = 29, *Median* = 36, *Q3* = 42, and *Max* = 47. Then the boxplot is shown in Figure A.7.
  - ○ The box covers the "middle half" of the data from Q1 to Q3.
  - ○ The left whisker extends down to the minimum value that is not an outlier.
  - ○ The right whisker extends up to the maximum value that is not an outlier.
  - ○ When the left whisker is longer than the right whisker, then the distribution is left skewed, and vice versa.
  - ○ When the whiskers are about equal in length, the distribution is symmetric. The distribution in Figure A.7 shows evidence of being left-skewed.

PART 4: SUMMARIZATION AND VISUALIZATION OF BIVARIATE RELATIONSHIPS

- • A **bivariate relationship** is the relationship between two variables.
- • The relationship between two categorical variables is summarized using a **contingency table**, which is a crosstabulation of the two variables, and contains a cell for every combination of variable values (that is, for every

contingency). Table A.5 is the contingency table for the variables *mortgage* and *risk*. The total column contains the **marginal distribution** for *risk*, that is, the frequency distribution for this variable alone. Similarly, the total row represents the marginal distribution for *mortgage*.

- Much can be learned from a contingency table. The *baseline proportion* of *bad risk* is 2/10 = 20%. However, the proportion of *bad risk* for applicants without a mortgage is 1/3 = 33%, which is higher than the baseline; and the proportion of *bad risk* for applicants with a mortgage is only 1/7 = 1%, which is lower than the baseline. Thus, whether or not the applicant has a mortgage is useful for predicting risk.

- A **clustered bar chart** is a graphical representation of a contingency table. Figure A.8 shows the clustered bar chart for *risk*, clustered by *mortgage*. Note that the disparity between the two groups is immediately obvious.

- To summarize the relationship between a quantitative variable and a categorical variable, we calculate summary statistics for the quantitative variable for each level of the categorical variable. For example, Minitab provided

TABLE A.5 Contingency table for *Mortgage* versus *Risk*

		Mortgage		
		Yes	**No**	**Total**
Risk	**Good**	6	2	**8**
	Bad	1	1	**2**
	Total	**7**	**3**	**10**

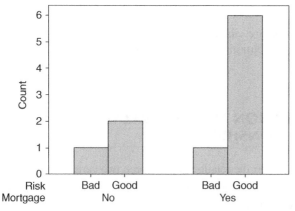

Figure A.8   Clustered bar chart for *risk*, clustered by *mortgage*.

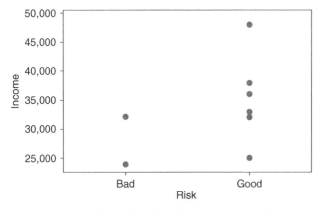

Figure A.9   Individual value plot of *income* versus *risk*.

the following summary statistics for *income*, for records with *bad risk* and for records with *good risk*. All summary measures are larger for *good risk*. Is the difference significant? We need to perform a hypothesis test to find out (Chapter 4).

Descriptive Statistics: Income

	Risk	Mean	Std Dev	Minimum	Median	Maximum
Variable	Bad	28,050	5728	24,000	28,050	32,100
Income	Good	33,663	7402	25,000	32,600	48,000

- To visualize the relationship between a quantitative variable and a categorical variable, we may use an **individual value plot**, which is essentially a set of vertical dotplots, one for each category in the categorical variable. Figure A.9 shows the individual value plot for *income* versus *risk*, showing that incomes for *good risk* tend to be larger.

- A **scatter plot** is used to visualize the relationship between two quantitative variables, *x* and *y*. Each (*x*, *y*) point is graphed on a Cartesian plane, with the *x* axis on the horizontal and the *y* axis on the vertical. Figure A.10 shows eight scatter plots, showing some possible types of relationships between the variables, along with the value of the *correlation coefficient r*.

- The **correlation coefficient** *r* quantifies the strength and direction of the linear relationship between two quantitative variables. The correlation coefficient is defined as

$$r = \frac{\sum (x - \bar{x})(y - \bar{y})}{(n-1)s_x s_y}$$

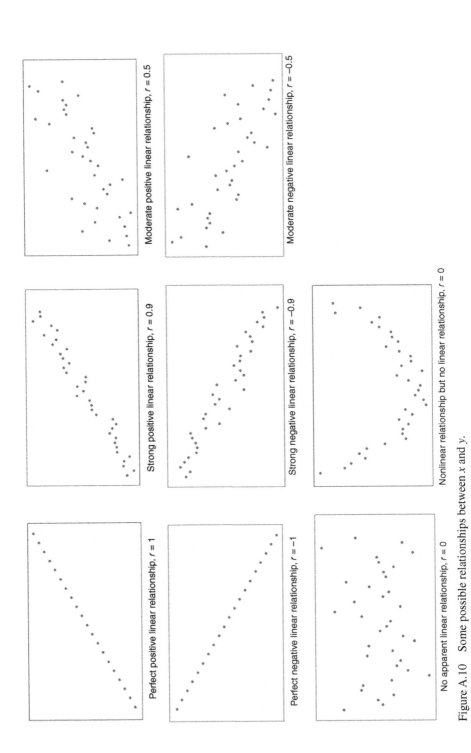

Figure A.10   Some possible relationships between x and y.

where s_x and s_y represent the standard deviation of the x-variable and the y-variable, respectively. $-1 \leq r \leq 1$.

○ In data mining, where there are a large number of records (over 1000), even small values of r, such as $-0.1 \leq r \leq 0.1$ may be statistically significant.

○ If r is positive and significant, we say that x and y are *positively correlated*. An increase in x is associated with an increase in y.

○ If r is negative and significant, we say that x and y are *negatively correlated*. An increase in x is associated with a decrease in y.

INDEX

Data Science Using Python and R, First Edition. Chantal D. Larose and Daniel T. Larose.
© 2019 John Wiley & Sons, Inc. Published 2019 by John Wiley & Sons, Inc.

Printed and bound by CPI Group (UK) Ltd, Croydon, CR0 4YY

27/10/2024

14580472-0001